S0-AEV-695

CROSSING THE THINNEST LINE

HOW EMBRACING DIVERSITY—FROM THE OFFICE TO THE OSCARS—MAKES AMERICA STRONGER

LAUREN LEADER-CHIVÉE

CENTER
STREET

New York   Nashville

Center Street
Hachette Book Group
1290 Avenue of the Americas
New York, NY 10104
centerstreet.com
twitter.com/centerstreet

Originally published in hardcover and ebook by Center Street in September 2016.
First Trade Paperback Edition: December 2017

Center Street is a division of Hachette Book Group, Inc.
The Center Street name and logo are trademarks of Hachette Book Group, Inc.

The publisher is not responsible for websites (or their content) that are not owned by the publisher.

Library of Congress Cataloging-in-Publication Data

Names: Leader-Chivee, Lauren, author.
Title: Crossing the thinnest line : how embracing diversity—from the office to the Oscars—makes America stronger / Lauren Leader-Chivee.
Description: New York : Center Street, 2016. | Includes bibliographical references and index.
Identifiers: LCCN 2016015455 | ISBN 9781455539055 (hardback) | ISBN 9781478912668 (audio download) | ISBN 9781455539062 (ebook)
Subjects: LCSH: United States—Social conditions—21st century. | Cultural pluralism—United States. | Culture conflict—United States. | Social values—United States. | Social conflict—United States. | Polititcal culture—United States. | United States—Race relations. | United States—Ethnic relations. | BISAC: POLITICAL SCIENCE / Political Freedom & Security / Civil Rights. | POLITICAL SCIENCE / Political Freedom & Security / Human Rights. | POLITICAL SCIENCE / Political Freedom & Security / Law Enforcement. | SOCIAL SCIENCE / Discrimination & Race Relations.
Classification: LCC HN59.2 .L43 2016 | DDC 306.0973—dc23 LC record available at https://lccn.loc.gov/2016015455

ISBN: 978-1-4555-3905-5 (hardcover), 978-1-4555-3904-8 (trade paperback), 978-1-4555-3906-2 (ebook)

Printed in the United States of America

LSC-C

10 9 8 7 6 5 4 3 2 1

For my girls, in honor of my teachers

Contents

Introduction

*#blacklivesmatter, #alllivesmatter, #notthere, #legalizelove,
#closethegap, #heforshe, #lovetrumpshate, #OscarsSoWhite*

America is polarized. Every survey of public opinion and cable news show proves that to be true. It's evident in every election, every post on social media, and through the twenty-four-hour cable news cycle. We are constantly assaulted with a barrage of stories underlining these divisions, from racially charged police killings, to sexist tropes in the media or from public figures, to fights for gay rights, to anti-Semitic vandalism, anti-immigration rhetoric, and a seemingly endless assault on the question of what it means to be American. Every day it seems another screaming inequity comes to light on the front page of the *New York Times*. It seems as if a war is being waged—on the streets and in the courts, in Washington, and in town hall meetings. It's also quietly being waged in living rooms, boardrooms, classrooms, and dorm rooms all over our country.

At the heart of the conflict are fundamental questions about our values and identity as a nation. What does it mean to be American? Is the playing field really level for everyone? Are women fully equal? Should gays and lesbians have equal rights? Does racism still exist? What should we do about immigration? How can citizens of one of the most diverse nations on earth live together peacefully and productively? Can we find a way to make our multifaceted diversity an asset, economically and socially, or will it continue to be our deepest and most painful source of conflict?

I've been thinking about, living with, and working through these questions my entire life, both personally and professionally. I may not look like the typical activist, yet I have been on some of the front lines in this debate, working with both corporate and political leaders and advocating for a more inclusive nation that ensures full contributions from and equal opportunities for all.

Throughout my life, I have worked to connect people across the visible and invisible lines that divide us—lines of race, gender, class, political party, nationality, and religion. It's never easy or simple, but the experience has led to the greatest joys and deepest rewards of my life. From meeting and falling in love with my French, Roman Catholic husband (becoming the first person in my immediate family to intermarry culturally and religiously) to adopting my beautiful biracial/African American daughters to devoting my career to advancing women and minorities in the workplace and in the political realm, nothing has been closer to my heart and soul.

On a small, personal scale, I have grappled with the very questions we're stumbling through as a nation, and I have something to say about how we must address them. I cannot pretend to fully understand the experience of being a visible minority in this country. I have faced very few of the challenges that many minorities in our country face. I have had all the privileges and advantages of my white female identity—great schools, financial security, open doors. Yet I feel compelled to write what hasn't yet been written, because I have felt the sting of exclusion and I have a deep sense of empathy for the challenges many in our country face.

And I believe we can do better. This book seeks to tell a story of possibility and promise for our nation without overlooking the very real, complex, and profound challenges we face. I believe that it *is* possible to bridge our divides. It *is* possible to turn our differences into a source of ingenuity, innovation, prosperity, and peace. It *is* possible to talk about difference so that everyone becomes part of the solution, and it *is* possible to make big changes if we decide we want to.

Crossing the Thinnest Line argues for the possibility, power, purpose, and payoff of embracing difference, with both hard facts and deeply personal stories of commitment, understanding, and purpose. I hope I will speak to the heart and the mind so we can have a richer, more nuanced national conversation about the promise of a stronger, more united, yet wildly diverse nation. Are we really ready to do that? I'm not sure—but I really hope so.

Clearly questions of race, gender, and identity are already a regular part of the national dialogue. The election of Barack Obama, the campaigns of Donald Trump and Hillary Clinton, the ongoing conflicts between police and minority citizens, the advent of marriage equality, the fight for equal pay, even the celebrity of Caitlyn Jenner, have all contributed to the modern conversation on diversity. The idea of America as a nation of nations, drawing strength from the world's many cultures, is familiar to everyone. And yet I don't believe we have ever collectively really decided that our differences are an asset and made a commitment to embracing that truth. Instead, we mostly have struggled with those differences, treating them as a highly charged set of political issues to fight about.

We are urgently in need of a better, more solution-focused conversation about diversity, and this book strives to spur that. The subject at hand is so vast that every chapter could be a book unto itself. But my hope is that recognizing the many facets of the diversity opportunity for the nation will inspire us to work harder to do better. The economic and social stakes are high and getting higher. The world economy is global and interconnected, and already the vast majority of the world's educated population is either female or multicultural. In less than a generation, the United States will become a "minority-majority" nation. Embracing diversity has never been more essential. Yet the share of women in the US workforce is declining; Americans believe race relations are getting worse, not better; immigration reform has ground to a halt; and the political climate has become intensely divided, partisan, and polarized. These are ingredients for disaster. *Crossing the Thinnest Line* will, I hope, inspire Americans to rise to the challenge and do better.

This book stands on two important ideas. First, that being in close contact with people from different backgrounds from our own confers economic, intellectual, social, spiritual, personal, and competitive benefits that are measurable and profound.

Second, for diversity to add value rather than create conflict, we must learn how to cross the lines that divide us and find our common humanity. If we do, the possibilities are endless. If we don't, we're doomed to repeat the long, painful history of struggle and division that has dogged our nation since its founding.

In support of the first concept, I will demonstrate the compelling economic, social, and personal benefits that diversity brings to society. I'll use research and data, but also unforgettable stories from the Civil War to the Internet boom that prove how greatly our society and economy have advanced and prospered because of diversity. I'll use cautionary tales that show what's at stake. And I'll share the personal stories of individuals from presidents to average citizens whose lives were profoundly enriched through diversity.

But what distinguishes this book in a way that I hope will elevate our national consciousness and change people's lives is my argument that every American, no matter what they look like or where they come from, can play a critical role in ensuring that our differences become our strength.

Most books on diversity posit that having more diversity of any kind in every situation automatically makes things better. It's simply not true. It's become unequivocally clear to me, and clear to many Americans given the polarization in the country, that putting diverse groups together and hoping for a good outcome just through the collision of cultures and ideas rarely works on its own. It takes more than just throwing people together to enjoy benefits from diversity. It takes an entire system of openness, leadership, personal responsibility, accountability, and celebrations of progress. In short, it takes work.

For our highly diverse nation to function and prosper, everyone must find shared human experiences and common understanding and build real, meaningful relationships—not by ignoring differences in an effort to become generic, identity-free Americans but by learning to respect and embrace the alchemy and magic of unity in diversity. From the streets to the boardroom, this kind of authentic, meaningful connection and understanding between profoundly different people is critical to our future. And it will be especially critical that Americans currently in the majority of leadership positions, namely white men, take a leading role in pushing for change. In many ways, large and small, it's in their and our interest to do so.

Americans who actively embrace diversity have enormous advantages over those who ignore or actively reject it. They lead richer and more meaningful lives, make smarter business decisions, work more effectively with people of every kind, have empathy and understanding for others, and navigate the complexities of today's business and social terrain more nimbly. I will show how and why this is true.

In bringing these ideas to life, I will share interviews and stories of leaders, academics, policy makers, and extraordinary citizens on the front lines of today's biggest diversity challenges. I'll call out examples from every sector where diversity has had a real, transformational, and inspirational effect.

Crossing the Thinnest Line strives to frame a tangible path forward, not through dry policy or corporate strategy but through unforgettable stories and concrete examples. I'll introduce some of the archetypal leaders for today—people with the sensitivity and insight required to reach across national, ethnic, racial, religious, and gender lines to live and work effectively with people of all kinds. These models include well-known political leaders like Rand Paul and Cory Booker; figures from academia like Katherine Phillips at Columbia Business School, a powerful advocate for cultural literacy as a core competency among business leaders; and media figures such as Soledad O'Brien, a broadcast journalist inspired by her own diverse background to devote her talent to addressing tough issues about race that all too often go undiscussed. I'll describe organizations, companies, and institutions that are demonstrating the power of diversity by creating communities of unparalleled openness, dynamism, creativity, and innovation.

I deeply believe that we are capable of transforming a never-ending source of conflict into an economic, social, and societal asset if we embrace the challenge in the right way. When we begin to appreciate individually and collectively how to cross the lines that divide us, we can move forward in new and profound ways. Crossing both the thinnest and thickest lines will bring us closer to our humanity, to each other, to lasting prosperity, and to the soul of America.

1. From Passion to Purpose

If civilization is to survive, we must cultivate the science of human relationships—the ability of all peoples, of all kinds, to live together and work together, in the same world, at peace.
—Franklin D. Roosevelt

As Americans, each of us has some experience that ties us to the complex quilt of cultures, identities, and backgrounds that define our patchwork nation. Most of us are American because an ancestor left somewhere else to move here. Each of those ancestors was once a stranger in a strange land. We come to our American identity in this way—not as inheritors of a shared lineage or culture but as people who forged our own identity from a chaotic, unblended combination of differences. We've all known, or our ancestors have known, what it is to be an outsider. Even the only real nonimmigrants among us, Native Americans, have had to adapt and adjust to fit (or not) this spicy, complex mix of flavors that make us who we are.

This uniquely American identity should mean that as a nation we are better able to embrace the power and possibility that our diversity confers. It should mean that we live and work together better than people anywhere else. It should mean that everyone can relate on a personal, emotional level to the challenges faced by today's minorities. It should uniquely position us to be the most creative, collaborative, peaceful nation on earth.

But, as we know, it doesn't. We are instead a nation of perpetual contradictions—one with an appalling, shameful history of institutional discrimination, but also one where anything is possible. One that has been late to ensure the full rights and privileges of all our citizens, but also one where those who were once held back are able to rise to unimaginable heights.

On a macro and micro level, I have been trying to parse these contradictions most of my life. At every turn, I have felt compelled to dive deeply into them and to understand them personally, emotionally, academically, intellectually, and passionately. I guess it's a bit odd. On the surface there isn't much about my privileged white persona that would point to someone relentlessly and obsessively focused on understanding the challenges of diversity. But here I am.

My deepest passions are rooted in my childhood, and my upbringing, family, and early social and educational experiences inform the shape of my life and work.

Washington, DC, was a strange and alluring place to live in the 1970s and '80s—gritty and chaotic, full of contradictions and contrasts. My parents moved there in 1974 from Ithaca, New York, where they had been political science professors. Looking for enriching professional experiences, they came to DC to start a new life—my father at a think tank and my mother at the Justice Department in the civil rights division. After a long search for a home they could afford, in 1975 they settled in a modest but comfortable house in a middle-class, liberal, mostly white neighborhood of DC's Upper Northwest, with a good public school, a community center, and a collection of small shops. Our neighbors were former Peace Corps volunteers, aging hippies, elderly couples whose children had attended the local Catholic school, and more than a few lawyers and public servants.

My mother was a passionate feminist and had established with my father a coequal partnership. He cooked and did dishes and laundry, but so did all the other dads on our block. There was never any question as to whether my mother would work, and I can't remember a single stay-at-home mother among our family friends or neighbors. Our world on McKinley Street was pretty idyllic. Everyone knew each other; we felt safe and at ease in a community of people who were very much like us. It was a bubble of bucolic life in a city in severe decline.

Washington, DC, has a uniquely complex, contradictory, and fascinating history. It was founded as a strongly Southern city completely dependent on the work of African Americans—overwhelmingly slaves—who hewed it from the marshy swamps. But unlike the rest of the South, the District of Columbia was ruled directly by the US Congress, as mandated in the Constitution. So in 1862, when Congress passed the District of Columbia Emancipation Act, the slaves in the District were freed nine months before Lincoln's Emancipation Proclamation ended slavery throughout the South. In 1867, the Reconstruction Act gave black men in Washington the right to vote three years before the passage of the Fifteenth Amendment to the Constitution did the same for black males throughout the country. Under congressional rule during the latter decades of the nineteenth century, the District was largely free of the Jim Crow legal codes that imposed odious racial distinctions elsewhere in the South. For example, schoolteachers in Washington, who were federal employees, were paid the same regardless of race.

Partly as a result of opportunities like this, the District's black population swelled year by year, and by 1900, Washington had the highest percentage of African Americans of any major US city. Black culture also flourished. Howard University, the nation's most illustrious black college, was founded there in 1867. Prominent black leaders like the abolitionist writer and orator Frederick Douglass made their homes in the city, along with hundreds of black business owners, artists, writers, musicians, and social activists.

But the capital city wasn't immune to the racism that infected the entire nation, and in fact it was deeply segregated in social and geographic terms. In 1913, President Woodrow Wilson, a Southern Democrat, imposed segregation in federal departments for the first time in fifty years, exacerbating tensions between whites and blacks. (As the 2015 controversy over Wilson's legacy at Princeton University suggests, his bigoted act, like so much else in our nation's checkered racial history, continues to spark debate.) In July 1919, during the so-called Red Summer of racial violence around the country, white mobs attacked blacks at random in the streets of Washington. When the police refused to intervene, groups of armed blacks fought back. Fifteen were killed and hundreds injured.

Under President Franklin D. Roosevelt, segregation policies in the federal government began to be lifted. Blacks in Washington, DC, were among the early participants in the nascent civil rights movement, helping to organize economic and political actions like the "Don't Buy Where You Can't Work" campaign of the 1930s. In 1939, when the famed contralto Marian Anderson was prevented from singing at Washington's Constitution Hall because she was black, Eleanor Roosevelt helped arrange her appearance on the steps of the Lincoln Memorial, where she performed a concert before an audience of seventy-five thousand people. Twenty-four years later, when Martin Luther King Jr. organized the famous March on Washington, he chose the same steps to deliver his "I Have a Dream" speech.

By 1975, the year I was born, Washington was 70 percent black and suffering from the same urban troubles that many cities across the nation were experiencing. The Washington neighborhoods that had burned in the riots following King's assassination in 1968 had barely recovered. Huge swaths of largely poor, black neighborhoods in the Southeast and Anacostia regions were decimated by poverty, crime, drug use, and the flight of middle-class whites and blacks to the suburbs.

Of course, there was a special irony in the fact that the nation's capital was in such decline. Just blocks from the pristine White House, entire neighborhoods were blighted. Marion Barry, who served as the city's mayor from 1979 to 1991 and again from 1995 to 1999, was controversial even before his infamous 1990 arrest for smoking crack cocaine on camera. By the early 1990s, Washington had the dubious distinction of being the murder capital of the nation.

For many of us who lived in the District during those troubled years, it seemed as if the city was broken. My mother was always on the phone with a city agency, trying to get the garbage collected or some basic service restored. A drive within a few blocks of the city's stately memorials took us past prostitutes and drug dealers openly soliciting on Fourteenth Street.

But while many of Washington's inner-city blacks were poor, living in the grimmest of circumstances, the city was also home to a large, very wealthy African American community living in expensive, elegant enclaves along the Sixteenth Street corridor, as physically and psychologically distant from places like Anacostia as my own home. They sent their children to the same elite private schools and summer camps I attended. They were part of refined Jack and Jill social clubs and were deeply connected and influential in Washington society. These were the black families I knew.

On September 20, 1984, *The Cosby Show* made its premiere on my ninth birthday. The affluent, professional black family the show portrayed was a novelty to most Americans but not to me— I knew lots of families like theirs.

The black community wasn't the only source of diversity in Washington. Embassies representing nearly every nation on earth are established there, each staffed by citizens who live in and around the District with their families. In my preschool, the children came from every corner of the world; Iran, Turkey, Ghana, Nigeria, and Mexico were all represented. One of my earliest memories is learning to say "Good morning!" in a different language each day. Birthday parties were often exotic affairs. I still remember trying baklava for the first time at the sixth birthday celebration of a Turkish boy in my class.

So while my immediate neighborhood was almost entirely white, the diversity of the larger city permeated every experience. At Lafayette Elementary School, where I spent several blissful years, the principal and all my most cherished, loving teachers were black. In every class, at least a third of the students were black, immigrant, or minority. Of my best friends in early childhood, Alison was white and Roman Catholic; Annie was black and adopted into a white Jewish family, along with three siblings; Alex and Jenny were African American twin children of diplomats who by the sixth grade had already lived in Cameroon and Egypt and would soon be heading to Israel. Racial and ethnic diversity was such a normal, constant part of my life that I barely noticed it. Those early friendships across lines of race and religion became a kind of template for my life. Maybe it's not a coincidence that my husband is Catholic and my children are black.

The Sting of Exclusion...The Joy of Community

In the seventh grade, my parents opted not to send me on to Alice Deal Middle School, the public junior high serving our neighborhood. It was excellent but huge, and they rightly concluded I was not self-motivated enough to succeed there. I was accepted by the prestigious Holton-Arms School in Bethesda, Maryland, one of the most respected girls' schools in the country. I wasn't thrilled at the prospect of leaving the neighborhood environment where I'd experienced so much happiness, but off I went.

My teachers were brilliant, and I thrived academically, but I struggled socially. Bethesda was less than thirty minutes from our house, but it could have been another country as far as I was concerned. The demographics of the wealthy Maryland suburb at the time could not have been more different from those of our neighborhood in the District. We were a liberal, Jewish, Democratic family, and my mother worked, while most of my classmates were wealthy, conservative, Protestant, Republicans, with mothers who stayed home. I took the bus or was driven to school in a '70s Ford with many, many miles on it, while everyone else pulled up in a shiny new Mercedes or BMW chauffeured by their beautifully dressed and coiffed mothers. I understood immediately that my family and I did not fit in.

I was totally unprepared for the exclusive, rarefied world at Holton-Arms. From day one, I knew I had left the easy acceptance of my Washington, DC, community behind. It all came to a head in the eighth grade on the day of my classmate Jennifer's birthday party, which was held at the Chevy Chase Club. Every girl in the class was invited—except me. I can still hear the barely controlled rage in my mother's voice as she explained why: Jews were not welcome at the club. The Chevy Chase Club, just blocks from our home on the DC/Maryland border, was founded in the 1890s by US senator Francis G. Newlands of Nevada, who helped to develop the town of Chevy Chase, Maryland, with the avowed intention of keeping it both white and Christian. By the time of Jennifer's birthday party in the late eighties, the club's only Jewish member, at least according to my mother, was Henry Kissinger. (Today the club is less impenetrable but still exclusive. I know a number of prominent Jewish Washingtonians who are members, so things have most certainly changed.)

My mother seized the moment as an opportunity to bitterly remind me of the long, painful history of Jews in the United States and elsewhere. My own family, having fled brutal anti-Semitism in Eastern Europe at the turn of the century, couldn't escape prejudice here. My maternal grandfather legally changed his name from Goldberg to Gilbert because, as a traveling salesman with a Jewish last name, there were many places he couldn't get a hotel room in the 1950s.

For me as a thirteen-year-old, there was something shocking and soul-crushing about this kind of exclusion. It burned: I was angry and hurt, and there was nothing I could do about it. It was a feeling I will never forget. I left Holton after the eighth grade— I was just too different and had made few friends. Fortunately, a spot finally opened up for me at liberal Georgetown Day School, to which my family had applied repeatedly since I was in kinder-garten. It changed my life forever.

Georgetown Day School was founded in 1945 as Washington's first racially integrated school at a time of intense segregation, and it retains a commitment to diversity and liberal values to this day. (If I need shorthand to explain to anyone from Wash-ington, DC, the kind of person I am, I say I attended GDS, and they understand immediately.) The culture and values of GDS embodied everything I had learned growing up. It was open, liberal, creative, and welcoming of even the oddest of oddball characters. GDS saw qualities in people that no one else did. We had at least three openly gay teachers at a time when that was cer-tainly not true of most other schools. One of our English teachers had dreadlocks and played in a local reggae band.

By the ninth grade, I'd joined the ranks of the oddballs. My experience at Holton had triggered a major rebellion. I dyed my hair jet-black, streaked it with purple, and took to wearing combat boots and various other outward signs of teen angst. But at GDS there were plenty of other kids experimenting with rebellion and identity, and the school embraced us all.

The teachers and administration of Georgetown Day understood that sorting through the many complex facets of identity was as important to our education as passing AP exams and the SATs, and they had plenty of opportunities to prove their commitment. When I entered GDS in September 1989, race had become a heated and complicated issue at the school. A number of black juniors and seniors contended that cliquey white seniors treated them as second-class citizens. Angry exchanges erupted in the hallways. To their huge credit, the administration seized on the conflict as an opportunity to launch a school-wide discussion. Journalist Juan Williams, who had just published *Eyes on the Prize*, his extraordinary book about the American civil rights movement, was invited to address the students and facilitate dialogue at daylong assemblies. His wise, soothing presence was a perfect counterpoint to the high emotions we were all experiencing. For nearly a week, we talked about nothing but race. The more I listened to the pain expressed by my minority classmates, the more I felt I understood.

First of all, I loved them. My best friend at GDS, Caroline, was biracial and had been struggling with feeling like an outsider herself. I also worshipped from afar the group of black senior girls who had triggered the discussion. They seemed so powerful and strong. But there was also something familiar about the particular variety of exclusion and marginal status they expressed—after all, I had been excluded, too. By the end of the week, I didn't just understand them—I burned for them, I cried for them, I yearned for them, and I loved them even more. In my heart they were my sisters and brothers. I was never the same again.

Growing up, I never thought my life was especially exceptional or unique, but today I realize how unusual it was. The opportunity to explore issues of race and identity at such a formative time was extraordinary and rare. Not nearly enough people have opportunities like this. Too few of us live or work in environments where this kind of open learning and sharing is even possible. It's a shame, because if more Americans had the chance to contemplate and work through issues of difference in the way I did, we might be a different nation.

These early experiences made two things clear to me. First, being in close contact with people from different backgrounds, races, and cultures made my life more interesting, rewarding, enriching, and meaningful. Being surrounded by diversity had opened my heart, broadened my horizons, and helped me learn more, think more clearly, and understand the world more deeply.

Second, I'd discovered that, for diversity to add value rather than create conflict, we have to work incredibly hard to understand each other. We must be able to appreciate and embrace one another, and we must find the threads of common human experience that unite us. We have to find shared experience in order to fully appreciate the value that difference brings. We must find ways to cross the lines that divide us.

Hearing and Heeding the Call

The experiences of my youth and many since have persuaded me that we are missing an enormous opportunity as a nation. Why don't we Americans invest more effort in seriously pursuing ways to embrace difference? Why are we so resigned to conflict? Why do we seem to repeat the same mistakes over and over again?

Now, with the wisdom of my forty years, I see that I was destined to devote my life to seeking the answers to these questions. But it was far from immediately obvious. When I was young, I never imagined I'd be doing what I do today.

I meandered in early adulthood. For a while, I wanted to be an actress, then an opera singer. In 1994, I moved to New York to be close to a voice teacher I was devoted to. I eventually wound up at Barnard College, which I loved, and did temp jobs at Wall Street firms, answering phones to pay for my expensive singing lessons. Eventually I landed a steady part-time job, and three days a week I made the trek after classes from 116th Street to Water Street to work at a small but prestigious investment firm called Weiss, Peck & Greer. I made fifteen dollars an hour—a fortune for me then—and I was surprised to find that I enjoyed the work. I rose from receptionist to human resources assistant to recruiter. By the time I graduated from Barnard in 1998, I'd built a decent résumé of credible jobs in HR.

I puttered along at corporate jobs for several years, still convinced my real calling was music. But when I met my husband, I realized I wanted a different kind of life and began to pursue a business career more seriously. After much soul-searching, I let go of my musical aspirations and dived into several HR roles at start-up companies.

I met Philippe at a wedding in a tiny town not far from Lyon, France. In high school I had studied French and participated in an exchange program with a French family. I became close friends with Flore, my host family's daughter, and when she was married in 2002, my mother and I flew to France for the wedding. Philippe was the best man, and I was seated next to him for the reception. There was a lot of wine served at dinner, and it wasn't until many bottles were emptied that we noticed each other. But when we did, our attraction was instantaneous.

That said, there was absolutely nothing about the situation that would have made a relationship, let alone a marriage lasting more than a decade, even occur to us. First of all, we lived in two separate countries. There was also a distinct language barrier. My French was far from perfect, and his English wasn't much better. And yet, as they say, we spoke the language of love.

The long story short is that Philippe had total conviction that we were meant for each other and that we could overcome any obstacles. At first, I wasn't convinced. Most of my life I had believed that it was my obligation and moral duty to marry within the Jewish faith. My parents were both secular and certainly never pressured me to make traditionally Jewish choices, but my grandparents, the rabbis I grew up with, and everyone around me insisted that marrying outside the faith was a kind of betrayal. The dwindling number of Americans strongly identifying with their Jewish faith had been a worrisome reality for years.

For all these reasons, I struggled with my love for Philippe. I tried more than once to end our relationship. But Philippe was undeterred. As we built our relationship in trips back and forth between France and New York, Philippe kept insisting that if the point of religion and of a connection with God was love, how could loving someone be a betrayal of faith?

It took real self-examination for me finally to acknowledge that he was right. Nothing matters more than love. We were married in New York on January 11, 2004, in a Jewish ceremony with friends and family from France and the United States in a circle around us.

I by no means want to gloss over the challenges inherent in intermarriage, nor do I want to diminish the validity of marrying within one's own faith. There were certainly trying moments and complicated discussions with our families on both sides. For me, though, it was unquestionably the right decision, and I'm grateful to Philippe that he held up a mirror to my bias and helped me break through that limitation.

Through my early thirties, my professional career started to come together. I found myself in a decision-making leadership role at a growing outsourcing firm. As head of HR, I was responsible for advising the young, brash, mostly male leadership team on a range of people-related issues from benefits to compensation. It wasn't easy. A huge fight broke out over the maternity leave policy. The leadership team wanted to grant the senior women ten weeks' paid leave but the secretaries much less. I was appalled—after all, the secretary needs the support as much as, if not more than, the woman making five times her salary. In my next job I found myself fighting the same battle again, this time as the only woman on the leadership team. I was fed up.

The fact that the United States was the only industrialized nation with no legal mandate for *any* paid maternity leave made me crazy. All the social justice and feminism of my upbringing kicked in. I vowed to do something about it.

I remembered Judith Lichtman, the mother of my classmate Julia from Georgetown Day School. Judy was a pioneer in the women's movement. In 1991, during my sophomore year of high school, she had been part of the team working with Anita Hill when Hill testified against Clarence Thomas's nomination to the Supreme Court. She founded the National Partnership for Women and Families in 1971, and she had been instrumental in passing the Family and Medical Leave Act of 1993, the only Federal legislation to this day that offers any kind of job protection for maternity leave. I e-mailed Julia for her mother's number, then picked up the phone and called her office.

To my surprise and delight, Judy invited me to Washington to meet with her lobbyists on Capitol Hill. Over the course of several months, I accompanied them to visits with members of Congress to press for expanded family leave. I was hooked. I realized that nothing could possibly be more important than fighting for women. I vowed to do more, having no idea what that would be, but I soon got my chance.

In July 2009, the economic skies were falling. The worst financial crisis since the Great Depression had hit Wall Street. Bear Stearns and Lehman Brothers had gone under; the markets were tumbling. The Harlem apartment we had bought at the top of the market in 2006 was now underwater, its value less than the amount we owed on its mortgage. At work, I had to fire nearly everyone at our firm. Then I was let go myself. The same month, my husband also lost his job. And in the middle of that crazy, scary summer, we learned we would be adopting a baby girl once she was born—the culmination of a grueling process we'd inaugurated months before when our career prospects seemed much brighter. We were thrilled at the news, but the timing was terrible. When we brought newborn Stella Rose home in early September, money was quickly running out.

I needed a job desperately. I had no idea what I would do next, but I knew it had to be connected in some way to advancing diversity.

In late September 2009, I met Sylvia Ann Hewlett, an economist and thought leader best known for a series of controversial books she had written in the 1990s about the needs of women and children, including *When the Bough Breaks* and *The War Against Parents* (coauthored with Cornel West). In 2004, she'd founded a think tank called the Center for Work-Life Policy, later renamed the Center for Talent Innovation. The center did critical research on the underlying challenges facing diverse employees of big companies and had set up the beginnings of a consulting firm dedicated to helping companies work through those challenges.

Miraculously, the center was surviving the financial crisis, and they had a job for me that seemed perfect. I started working there a few hours a week (Stella was just a newborn), writing short paragraphs for new reports and interviewing leaders from big companies about their programs. The pay was modest. But within a few months it was clear there could be a great opportunity to build the separate but associated for-profit consulting business, and Sylvia offered me a full-time job. With her enthusiastic support, by early 2010 the consulting practice began to grow. I dived into my work with all the love and passion I could muster.

I was completely committed to my work on corporate diversity at the Center for Talent Innovation and spent four wonderful years partnering with an amazing, enthusiastic team and passionate, dedicated clients who sincerely wanted to make a difference. I spoke at conferences and meetings around the world and wrote articles for well-known publications. It was an extraordinary time for me. Sylvia was hugely generous, adding my name to the company and regularly improving the terms of my compensation and partnership. I was doing work every day that felt like my true calling.

But it was not to last, and in retrospect it was never really meant to be. As our business became more successful and I became more independent, my relationship with Sylvia grew increasingly strained. Our clashes grew more contentious. Finally, in November 2013, just a few months after appointing me president of the center, ostensibly to be her successor, she fired me.

I was shocked and devastated. I had loved Sylvia and was devoted to her and the organization, and I had always thought we would work out our differences. She clearly disagreed, and we have never spoken since.

My split with Sylvia was traumatic. I had lost the work I loved and the team I built, and I couldn't imagine another job ever bringing me as much joy. It was a reflective and difficult time in my life, but now, looking back, I'm grateful for the opportunity it gave me to rethink my focus. I moved forward with the recognition that I was lucky to be able to make a career out of my passions and my values as a person.

For several weeks following my split from Sylvia, I was still in shock. Struggling to find my new direction, I reached out to all the mentors and advisors I most admired. One conversation stands out from the rest. Maynard Webb, former COO of eBay and chairman of the board of Yahoo, had become one of my dear mentors, and he was gracious enough to offer his wise counsel in my time of need. What he said will stick with me forever. "Lauren, there is really only one important question you need to ask yourself right now, and that is, what is the impact you want to have on the world? If you can answer that, everything else will become clear."

He was right. Moving past my self-absorbed personal drama and focusing on something greater than myself enabled me to see possibilities I hadn't seen before. I knew instantly what the answer was for me, and I have worked on it every day since.

I chose to devote myself, no matter what, to advancing equality, diversity, fairness, representation, and progress. And for me that has been as much about self-exploration as it has been about anything else. By addressing these issues, I've begun to see how much richer and more meaningful our lives become when we work to overcome the large and small divisions between us. I'll explain in later chapters how I founded All In Together, my nonprofit organization dedicated to advancing the interests and influence of women leaders, and my ongoing work to help corporations take full advantage of the opportunities diversity provides. But it all came from a simple call to make a difference in the world and to start the process by looking relentlessly at myself.

I know how fortunate I am to have the opportunity to explore important questions and to forge bonds with people different from myself. I also know that I'm lucky to have found a way to earn a living doing something I care passionately about. And as someone who works on the topics in this book every day, I recognize that I am focused on them more than the average person. But the reality is, no matter what our job or life story, no matter who you are, where you live, or where you come from, you can make a difference.

For us to make progress as a society on the big, difficult, seemingly intractable challenges posed by our ethnic, racial, religious, and cultural differences, we all need to do our part. What I hope my story and all the other stories in the book will make clear is that to capitalize fully on the promise of diversity, we need a nation of champions dedicated to the cause. Each of us must become an agent of change, willing to make a positive difference. In the chapters that follow, I'll describe the countless ways Americans are doing this every day, as well as the countless ways we could be doing more. I'm honored to play some small part.

2. The Diversity Dividend

He who is different from me does not impoverish me—he enriches me. Our unity is constituted in something higher than ourselves—in Man . . . For no man seeks to hear his own echo, or to find his reflection in the glass.

—*Antoine de Saint-Exupéry,* Flight to Arras

The annual Milken Global Conference, held every spring in Los Angeles, is one of the more rarefied forums where business leaders gather. Founded by former Wall Street tycoon Michael Milken, it brings together a who's who of global business and political leaders to think about big ideas and rub elbows with other power players.

In April 2015, I was invited to speak at one of the conference discussions on women in elected office and had the privilege of attending many of the sessions. The event on the second day was a lunch in the posh grand ballroom of the Beverly Hills Hotel featuring Sheryl Sandberg, the COO of Facebook and author of the best-selling 2013 book *Lean In: Women, Work, and the Will to Lead,* in conversation with three former secretaries of the US Treasury: Henry Paulson, Timothy Geithner, and Robert Rubin. Sandberg led an insightful, wide-ranging discussion about the global economy, and the three secretaries offered thoughtful, authoritative opinions on every issue.

But then Sandberg raised what seemed to me a fundamental issue about the future of the US economy. She quoted the legendary investor Warren Buffett as saying that one reason he had been so successful was that he was competing "with only half the population"—that is, only with men. She went on to cite data from the International Monetary Fund showing that closing the gender gap between the workforce participation of men and women in the United States would increase the nation's gross domestic product by 5 percent.

"That's a big number," Sandberg said. "What needs to get done? How do we get women to be full participants in our workforce and at leadership levels?"

All three secretaries shifted visibly and uncomfortably in their chairs. Secretary Rubin immediately deferred to Secretary Geithner, who replied, "Sheryl, we should be asking you this! You know a lot more about it than we do."

After she replied, "I'm asking you," an awkward laugh broke out in the room.

Geithner finally answered the question. American companies, he said, should "hire more women, advance more women, and pay them equally. It's not rocket science."

"And yet it's not easy to do," Sandberg replied.

"No, it's not," he conceded.

In his response, Secretary Paulson ruminated on his earlier career at Goldman Sachs, where he observed the tendency of men to surround themselves with people like them. He made the case for CEO and board pressure to insist on gender equality at work. "There are huge advantages you get from having diversity. There's huge advantages for driving this."

Last to reply, Robert Rubin referenced his own career in the rarefied worlds of Goldman Sachs, Harvard, and the Treasury, and spoke about the women he knew who had opted to stay home with their children. "But I'll tell you something, Sheryl. I know the politically correct responses to give, and I could say things that would make everyone here stand up and clap. But I think it's very complicated and very hard to do. I think there's immense advantage to having women in the workforce, but it's far more difficult than we're making it out to be."

I was frankly stunned by these responses. That three Treasury secretaries who have steered the nation through such unimaginable trials as the financial crisis of 2008–9 consider the gender labor gap a *really* hard problem speaks volumes about the diversity challenges and the opportunities we face. The simple answers and the narrowness of their replies indicated they had not given it much thought. It struck me then, as it does now, that *anything* estimated to add 5 percent to the nation's gross domestic product (GDP) might be worth deeper reflection.

As a nation, in elite circles like the Milken conference and at a basic level on the street, we are perpetually struggling to reconcile the complex set of issues, challenges, and opportunities that come from questions like Sheryl's. Diversity is fundamental to a range of social and economic benefits, yet we're only beginning to understand what it means and how to deal with it.

Though now a common buzzword, the term *diversity* means many things to many people. In chapter three, I will talk about a new, expanded definition tied to people's attitudes and perspectives. But generally speaking, Americans—and that includes business, political, educational, and media leaders with the power to help shape our local, regional, and national institutions—define diversity by visible traits like race, gender, national origin, religion, sexual orientation, and disability. These immutable traits make up our *inherent diversity* as a nation.

This definition focuses on unchangeable personal characteristics that differentiate someone visibly from the white male population. They are categories rooted in conflict and confrontation. Today they define protected classes of individuals under the landmark Civil Rights Act of 1964 as well as subsequent laws such as the Americans with Disabilities Act of 1990. And while these legal protections are not always comprehensive or effective, there is growing consensus that all Americans, regardless of differences, should enjoy the same rights and protections. After all, the Declaration of Independence enshrines the rights of "life, liberty, and the pursuit of happiness" as fundamental for all Americans. Many of us agree that making exceptions to this principle is simply—well, un-American.

The legal framework for protecting citizens' rights and freedoms is essential to our national life, not just because of the undeniable moral imperative to treat everyone as equal but also because of what those protections enable in terms of social, civil, and economic prosperity. There is now overwhelming evidence that as our nation has embraced the equal protection and opportunities of our diverse citizens, we have reaped huge economic and social benefits. Diversity of all kinds powers economic growth and prosperity more directly and dramatically than almost anything else.

There are many powerful examples of this, but certainly the impact that women have had on the US economy paints a most dramatic picture. Between 1979 and 2014, the percentage of working-age women with full-time jobs in the United States grew from 28.6 to 40.7. The increase among women with children has been even greater—from 27.3 percent to 44.1 percent. That increase has been responsible for $1.7 trillion in economic output—equivalent to 11 percent of the economy as a whole.[1] All this even as women continue to lag men in wages. Today women earn about eighty-one cents for every dollar made by men.[2] Just closing the wage gap so that men and women are paid equally could add 3 to 4 percent to the economy.[3] To put that in perspective, the massive $700 billion stimulus package passed by Congress in 2008 under the name of TARP added just 1.5 percent to the economy.

Unfortunately, the gender wage gap persists as one of the more complicated and difficult issues to tackle, one that even Treasury secretaries struggle to deal with. The current figures are based on an average calculated by dividing the sum of all wages by the number of people in the workforce. This means that the gender wage gap is partially connected to both the overall wages women earn and the number of women in the workforce. After years of progress, the overall labor-force participation of women has recently begun to decline and is projected to follow the same downward trend in the future. The US Department of Labor expects the female labor-force participation rate to go from 57 percent today to only 47 percent in 2022.[4]

Mixed into that reality is the fact that women, especially women of color—for whom the wage gap is even more dramatic— continue to hold a disproportionate share of low-wage jobs. Fully 62 percent of minimum-wage earners in the United States are women, only 38 percent men.[5] All of this feeds the overall gender wage gap.

There is no question that in many fields the wage gap is exacerbated by wage differentials between men and women who occupy the same job. But that's incredibly difficult for employees to prove, and employers have largely not taken a proactive stance in self-auditing the wages of their employees and rectifying the situation. In one hopeful sign, tech company Salesforce.com recently audited every position in the company and adjusted the pay of any woman—or man—who was not being paid in line with peers. CEO Marc Benioff launched the effort after several senior women raised the issue. By his own account, he never expected to find the kinds of differentials that were uncovered. But to his credit, he ensured that every person in the company was paid the same as others with the same job.[6] Facebook and Microsoft both conducted similar audits, and they have taken steps to close the gaps they found. It's an obvious solution that should be getting more attention. In my view, every company in the country should undertake the same type of effort, no matter how complicated or costly it may be.

To close the national gender pay gap, however, will take a massive effort to move more women out of minimum-wage occupations and ensure that they enter higher-paying fields in greater numbers. The effort would not be wasted. As we showed earlier, closing the gender wage gap would be an enormous boost to the entire economy.

It's not just as employees that women are helping to build our national economy but also as entrepreneurs and business owners. A 2009 study by the Center for Women's Business Research found that women-owned businesses had a cumulative impact of $2.8 trillion on the US economy—more than the GDP of the nations of Canada, India, and Vietnam *combined*. Women-owned businesses were responsible for creating and maintaining twenty-three million jobs, about 16 percent of the entire workforce.[7]

Other diverse groups also contribute hugely to our economic prosperity. Consider, for example, the contributions of immigrants. The Economic Policy Institute showed that from 2009–11, immigrants made up 16 percent of the US workforce and produced over $743 billion of economic output—about 14.7 percent of the total. So while only around 13 percent of the US population is composed of immigrants, their economic contribution is significantly larger than their numbers. It's often assumed that immigrants drain our economy by taking advantage of generous policies that support people who don't work, but the statistics show that immigrants are more likely to work than native-born Americans.

What's more, the stereotype that immigrants occupy mainly minimally productive, low-wage jobs is also a fallacy. Almost as many immigrants hold white-collar jobs (46 percent) as all other jobs combined. And while the average education level of immigrants is slightly lower than that of native-born Americans, a similar percentage—46 percent—have at least some college education.[8]

Thus, women and immigrants are two powerhouse forces playing a major role in driving America's economic growth. Despite political rhetoric to the contrary, in an era when business and political leaders are struggling to find ways of boosting the rate of GDP growth above the anemic 1 to 2 percent level we've sustained for years, it's clear that encouraging even more economic participation by diverse Americans could make such an impact.

But the economic value of diversity isn't limited to the sheer number of jobs held by women, immigrants, or minorities. There's significant evidence that incorporating diversity into business leadership enhances the creativity of companies and boosts their economic performance.

Numerous analyses of real-world business data bear out this conclusion. In 2012, three McKinsey consultants studied the financial results achieved by 180 publicly traded companies in the United States, the United Kingdom, Germany, and France over a two-year period (2008–10). They then examined the senior leadership teams of those companies to determine the number of women and foreign nationals included (as a reasonable way of measuring executive diversity). They found that both return on equity and margins on earnings were significantly higher for companies in the top quartile of the diversity scale than for those in the bottom quartile.

Digging deeper, they discovered specific links between the companies' diversity initiatives and their business results. For example, Adidas, one of the most diverse firms in the study, launched a program to implement greater diversity in its design centers in hopes of jump-starting some fresh thinking about innovation. It worked. Adidas subsequently won a number of awards for product creativity.[9]

Global investment banking firm Credit Suisse launched their own studies examining the impact of female leadership on company performance. The researchers developed a database that maps the board structure and senior management of more than three thousand companies around the world. When they tracked the growth in market capitalization (i.e., company value) attained by these firms, they found that large companies with at least one female board member outperformed their peers by 26 percent over a period of six years. Gender-diverse firms also enjoyed higher rates of return on equity and higher price-to-book share values (which imply stronger market expectations for future growth). The Credit Suisse study didn't attempt to reach any definitive conclusions about the cause-and-effect connection between diversity and company performance. But the researchers commented: "Does this mean that better companies hire more women, or that women chose to work for more successful companies, or that women themselves help improve companies' performance? The most likely answer is probably a combination of the three."[10]

Regardless of cause, the economic benefit associated with women and other diverse populations entering the workforce is compelling. As the evidence mounts, the correlation between diversity, economic growth, and financial performance is becoming widely accepted.

Different, Special, Valuable

But *why* do the participation, presence, and engagement of diverse individuals drive so much economic value? It's certainly not magic. In the simplest terms, being inherently different from the majority shapes the attitudes, values, behaviors, and abilities of people to such a degree that they are able to make even greater contributions. The outsider experience sparks creativity and an ability to see the world through a different lens, and often outsiders identify needs in inventive ways.

This helps explain why so many of the most important innovators who have built, grown, and transformed the US economy in the last two hundred years have been diverse. List just a few of their names, and you've quickly generated an honor roll of remarkable entrepreneurs, inventors, and company founders who brought their talents to our shores from around the world. They include E. I. du Pont, the French-born chemist who created one of the world's greatest industrial empires; the Scottish-born Andrew Carnegie, who founded U.S. Steel; the Croatian-born inventor Nikola Tesla, who shaped America's electrical supply system; Alexander Graham Bell, another Scotsman, who launched the telephone industry; Helena Rubenstein, the Polish-born founder of a cosmetics empire; and, in more recent decades, such luminaries as Andrew Grove, the Hungarian-born cofounder of Intel; the Russian-born Sergey Brin, cofounder of Google; and Vinod Khosla, the Indian-born high-tech entrepreneur who helped launch Sun Microsystems.

And it's not that diverse individuals all secretly innovate in their garages late at night. The power of their diverse perspective makes everyone else around measurably better at solving problems and creative thinking. In his best-selling book *The*

Wisdom of Crowds, James Surowiecki uses examples from many fields to illustrate the power of diverse perspectives to solve problems, improve decision-making, and foster creativity. Surowiecki introduces the theme with an anecdote from the life of the eminent nineteenth-century scientist Francis Galton, who observed a guessing game at a rural county fair. Galton was stunned to discover that when hundreds of passersby guessed the weight of an ox, their median guess was closer to the true weight than the guesses of experienced cattle experts.

Taking off from this example, Surowiecki examines numerous instances in which the combined knowledge of many people generates insights more accurate and valuable than those of one or a few experts. Based on his analysis, Surowiecki concludes that four elements are essential to marshal the wisdom of a crowd—of which the first and most crucial is "diversity of opinion." Conversely, when a group of people exhibits "homogeneity" in their thinking, then nothing is gained from their individual contributions, no matter how numerous they may be.[11] When people bring diverse perspectives, knowledge, and insights to a problem, their ability to solve it increases dramatically.

If we accept that there is real economic advantage to diversity, the United States has a tremendous and growing economic advantage that is driven by our increasing demographic diversity. Experts predict that the United States is likely to become a minority-majority country sometime between 2041 and 2046.[12] It's a trend that means more Americans now have the opportunity to live and work among people of diverse backgrounds than ever before. This poses huge opportunities and equally huge challenges.

For many Americans, the opportunity to live and work in diverse communities has great appeal. They have experienced, as I did in Washington, DC, that diverse communities are simply more *interesting* than groups that lack such diversity. Indeed, metropolises like New York, Los Angeles, Chicago, and Miami are among the fastest-growing cities in the nation. Smaller but highly diverse cities like San Francisco, Boston, New Orleans, and Austin are growing dramatically, and their surrounding suburbs and "satellite cities," from Cambridge, Massachusetts, to Roswell, Georgia, are also big draws. Not coincidentally, places like these are home to the majority of America's most successful businesses, vibrant social and cultural institutions, innovative research organizations, hotbeds of artistic and intellectual ferment, and creative individuals, from Nobel Prize winners and MacArthur "geniuses" to best-selling authors and groundbreaking artists.

The energy, excitement, and dynamism that are almost universally attributed to cities are largely a product of their diversity. And while surveys (like a 2014 poll conducted by the Pew Research Center) show that pluralities of Americans, especially those who describe themselves as conservatives, *claim* they'd prefer to live in small towns, this supposed yearning for the homogeneity of rural life is more theoretical than real.[13] Over 80 percent of Americans live in urban areas, and population growth in cities continues to outpace growth in rural areas.[14] Of course, there are various factors that contribute to this trend, including more economic opportunities in big cities, but it seems clear that the economic dynamism of cities is itself partly a by-product of urban diversity.

Whatever the exact mix of causes, the fact is that millions of Americans, including most of those who are very ambitious and creative, vote for diversity with their feet. As soon as they are able, they move to large cities or to their nearby suburbs, where they can mingle with and be stimulated by vast numbers of people whose diversity makes them interesting to be around.

But of course, it's not all roses. There are serious challenges to diverse people living together profitably. Major cities from Detroit to Baltimore to St. Louis have also faced profound challenges managing their diversity in areas from policing to educational opportunities. I'll explore each of these issues in more depth later.

Despite the migrations to cities over the last decades, given the long and painful history of American segregation and discrimination, there are still plenty of Americans who live in social circles that are highly *non*-diverse. In 2013, the Public Religion Research Institute conducted a survey in which they asked respondents to identify up to seven people with whom they had "discussed important matters" during the previous six months—a way of winnowing out slight acquaintances and zeroing in on an individual's circle of close friends. They then asked respondents to identify the gender, race, ethnicity, and religious affiliation of those friends, if known.

The results were fascinating—and distressing. White respondents said that at least 91 percent of their friends were white. (The exact percentage is unclear, since 3 percent were labeled "don't know" or were not racially identified by the respondent.) Fully 75 percent of white respondents said their networks of close friends included *no* nonwhite people.[15] One journalist writing about the study, who had grown up in a small town in Iowa that was 90 percent white and described herself as "a pale girl of German-Irish descent," commented that, as far as the white respondents to the survey were concerned, "We're all living in our own private Iowa."[16]

The homogeneity of social networks among minority-group members in the survey was less dramatic. Black respondents reported that 83 percent of their friends were black, and 8 percent were white; 65 percent of blacks reported having friend networks containing only black people. Hispanics said that 64 percent of their friends were fellow Hispanics, while 19 percent were white; 46 percent of Hispanics reported having friend networks made up exclusively of Hispanics. Thus, African Americans and Hispanics have circles of friendship that are more diverse than those of whites. These results probably relate to the fact that whites remain a majority of the US population in most localities; it's simply harder for a black person (for example) to avoid white people than the reverse.

Studies like this reveal an important truth about our society. Despite the lore that describes our country as a melting pot, many Americans live in enclaves where contact with those of a different racial or ethnic background is rare. Economic disparities play a part, but so do historic and persistent patterns of racial and ethnic discrimination in housing.[17] But perhaps above all else, many of us are simply more comfortable living and working with those most like us. Just as men in Henry Paulson's tony world of high finance are drawn to work with other men, the same principle applies to everyday Americans. We can hardly be blamed: Why would we suddenly change how we've lived and worked for so long?

Truth and Consequences

The problem is that acceptance of our polarized ways of living and working has far-reaching social and economic consequences.

For generations after the Civil War, political leaders in the American South resisted granting legal and social equality to nonwhites. A strict code of segregation in housing, employment, and education was reinforced by the social separation mandated by the notorious Jim Crow legal code. The entire edifice was further strengthened by legal and extralegal practices that effectually barred black men and women from voting, serving in public office, or otherwise exercising their political rights.

Throughout this period, the South lagged the rest of the nation in economic growth and performance. This is one of the reasons the antipoverty programs of the New Deal and the Great Society, such as the Tennessee Valley Authority and the Rural Electrification Administration, placed special emphasis on the problems of the rural South.

In the decades since the civil rights movement of the 1960s, the "New South" has improved its record on racial equality and diversity. At the same time, with a boost from technological advances in transportation and communications—not to mention the spread of air-conditioning—the states of the entire so-called Sunbelt have enjoyed a growth spurt in population and economic development.

And yet the South still trails the rest of the country in terms of both diversity and economic performance. It's especially true of the portions of the South that were built on slavery. In a fascinating 2013 study, a team of political scientists from the University of Rochester did a county-by-county analysis of census data and opinion polls of more than 39,000 Southern whites. They found that in the 1,344 counties in the area once known as the "Black Belt"—the region stretching from southern Virginia to eastern Texas where slave-dependent cotton plantations dominated the economy—negative racial attitudes toward blacks are still markedly more prevalent among whites than elsewhere in the United States.[18]

These same counties also exhibit dramatically poorer economic performance than their counterparts in regions of the United States that have more fully embraced racial equality and diversity. Countless studies support this conclusion, but one really stands out: the 2015 ranking by *Business Insider* magazine of all fifty states and the District of Columbia in terms of their economic strength. The rankings are meaningful because they combine no fewer than seven economic measures: unemployment rates, GDP per capita, average weekly wages, and recent growth rates for nonfarm payroll jobs, GDP, house prices, and wages.

The results? Of the eight states geographically dominated by the old Black Belt, all but one rank in the bottom half of the United States. (The sole exception is Georgia, which ranks eighteenth.) The lowest-ranked state, Mississippi, has one of the darkest and most entrenched histories of racial injustice and intolerance of them all. Four other Black Belt states are in the bottom twelve (Alabama, Arkansas, Virginia, and Louisiana). The average ranking of those states overall is thirty-eighth, in the bottom economic quarter of the country.[19]

Of course, the Deep South was also slower to industrialize than other parts of the country, and the lingering effects of this late transition surely play a role in the economic weakness of the region. But a growing number of political scientists and economists see a specific connection between resistance to diversity and economic failure. Overall, segregated communities have slower rates of income growth and property value appreciation—and not just in the neighborhoods where minority residents are segregated but throughout the region. In other words, even affluent white suburbs suffer economically when a city chooses to resist diversity.[20]

By contrast, cities and states that have welcomed diverse populations have tended to thrive economically. Despite worries by labor groups and workers who feel vulnerable in times of economic uncertainty, most studies show that immigrant diversity increases a city's economic growth and ultimately leads to overall higher wage levels. When a city experiences an increase in diversity measured at just one standard statistical deviation, wages can be expected to increase by close to 6 percent.[21]

Recognizing this pattern, city officials and business leaders from communities around the United States have started to view diversity as one key to economic revitalization. In the last five years, Southern cities like Atlanta, Memphis, Nashville, Charlotte, and Louisville have launched "immigrant-friendly" programs in an effort to attract the productivity power of newcomers to our shores. So have cities in other regions, from Tucson, Arizona, in the West to Dayton, Ohio, in the Midwestern rust belt.

Many localities are already reaping the benefits. By 2012, Dayton reported that foreign-born residents contributed $115 million to the local economy and paid $15 million in state and local taxes. After launching its "global city" program, Nashville was named the friendliest city in America by *Travel & Leisure* magazine and—not coincidentally—led the nation in job growth in 2012. In Iowa, towns like Ottumwa and Marshalltown are experiencing an economic revival thanks to the arrival of new waves of immigrants.[22]

This story of success and failure illustrates the contradictions of our collective ambivalence about diversity. On one hand, large swaths of society live and work in diverse environments in order to reap the benefits. On the other, we have increasing levels of polarization and isolation and many Americans who are just plain uncomfortable about the changing face of the nation. The implications of which side we choose are huge.

Facing Change

The 2016 presidential election, particularly during the primary process, brought into stark relief the full spectrum of attitudes and fears about diversity in our nation. The highly partisan nature of our primary system encourages candidates to "appeal to the base," leading them to double down on policies that appeal to the most loyal and partisan voters. Particular candidates have attempted to use the anger of many voters, especially working-class white men, to their advantage. Donald Trump insists that the answer to American decline is to deport millions of immigrants who are living in the United States without legal documents. Over and over he has declared that immigrants are dangerous drug dealers and rapists who are taking American jobs. That he has no factual evidence to support this claim— and that Trump's own grandfather immigrated to the United States from Germany in the 1880s—is irrelevant. His rhetoric has pushed other Republicans toward more extreme anti-immigrant positions, a trend that is likely to have long-lasting repercussions.

Fear of change is a powerful inhibitor. Embracing diversity and empowering new groups to participate fully in the American experience *inevitably* changes our society. There is no doubt that many Americans are nervous about the demographic and social changes happening around them...and consequently want to turn back the clock on the forward march of history. Indeed, there is evidence this anxiety drove many people who voted for Trump. The questions about President Obama's nationality made the case perfectly. For many people, a black president shook up a world order that may not be just or rational but is at least familiar. Many of us grew up in a world where people of color were relegated to the margins of society, where no language other than English was likely to be encountered in the media, where gays and lesbians were hidden and invisible, and where women—with a handful of exceptions—were expected to confine their creativity and leadership skills to a few carefully selected arenas like nursing, teaching, and, of course, homemaking.

As we're confronted with a new world of unpredictable, hard-to-understand challenges, from climate change and frightening pandemics to cyber warfare and global terrorism, it's easy to idealize our childhood past as "the good old days" when life was predictable and safe. From there, it's only a small step to regarding the unfamiliar outsiders who are demanding changes in the political and economic status quo as dangerous agitators bent on destroying the American way of life. (And when some in the media and in politics play up this scary vision to boost their ratings or poll numbers, our sense of anxiety heightens still further.)

The tensions surrounding these issues are real, not imaginary, and they affect everyone. We need to recognize them and address them, not pretend they don't exist. But let's not allow the challenges to prevent us, as individuals and as a society, from enjoying the benefits that diversity can bring us. After all, aren't most worthwhile things difficult? We have to work hard to learn to play a musical instrument or a sport, to master a profession, to build a successful marriage. And in many cases, achieving something that is inherently good requires a reevaluation of how we think and everything we do—from where we live, to how we work, to the candidates we elect. That certainly applies to the benefits of diversity.

To discover those benefits, we need to find shared human experiences and build real and meaningful relationships with one another. From the streets to the boardroom, this authentic connection and understanding between profoundly different people makes everything possible. For diversity to add value rather than create discord, we must learn how to recognize and honor our common humanity. When we do, the possibilities are endless. If we don't, we're doomed to repeat the long, painful history of misunderstanding, mistrust, and conflict that our nation has been struggling to transcend since its founding.

Learning how to cross the visible and invisible lines that divide us couldn't be more urgent or important. It may just be the most significant opportunity of our time.

3. Love Across the Lines

Your task is not to seek for love, but merely to seek and find all
the barriers within yourself that you have built against it.
—*Jalal ad-Din Rumi*

I was sitting in a Boston restaurant one wintry afternoon with
Brian Donovan and Sean Cunniff, two colleagues of mine,
when they suddenly paused in our conversation to greet a passerby. "I missed you last week," Brian called out. The three men
launched into an animated conversation I couldn't quite follow—
something about a team and a place. *Maybe they play sports together*,
I thought. Seeing my puzzled expression, they took a quick breath
to explain—"prison ministry"—and finished their hurried chat.

Later, Brian and Sean filled in the story. Both are classic Irish
Catholic "Boston guys" and Boston College graduates. They're
almost fifty, generally conservative, and live in the suburbs. Both
are married, Brian with four children, Sean with three.

What I learned is that the two men are involved in a Christian ministry with many other men and women, including their
wives, from Boston and surrounding areas. This ministry involves
retreats both in and outside of prisons and supports homeless
shelters, food banks, and the like. Through this experience, they
have met with people of every race, age, and circumstance: incarcerated, recently released, homeless, dealing with post-traumatic
stress disorder (PTSD), broken marriages, addiction, abuse, etc.

They listen to the people's stories and offer moral and spiritual support during weekend retreats. Brian was drawn to the ministry for many reasons, not the least of which is his older brother, who was stricken with schizophrenia. Brian told me:

> *There is not a day that goes by that I don't think about the thin line between my life and my brother's, being on the streets or in prison. We all tend to think that "x" could never happen to us, but the reality is every person, every family, is dealing with something we know nothing about. Mercy and kindness can make up for that ignorance, and that is what the men and women of this ministry have taught me.*[1]

The prison visit experience, Sean recalled, had been life changing:

> *The first time I went in, I was terrified. It was way outside of my comfort zone. I just prayed that I would get through it. What could I possibly have to say to these men? The guys at my table seemed to be nothing like me—their life experience could not have been more different. But what I learned was they were just like me—and I realized that a lot of us on the outside were one bad decision away from being on the inside.*

I was astonished and moved by the stories Brian and Sean told me. What happens to enable a person to see profound differences of race, class, and circumstance as just a thin line? For Brian and Sean it is faith, maybe for others it is a unique perspective picked up from upbringing. But what's striking about the thin line for Brian and Sean is that they are not just touched by it but they take action to help others overcome it. Brian and Sean are more than colleagues. They are leaders who have a more holistic and personal view of the importance of diversity, in all of its forms, both in and outside of work. Diversity is more than lip service to them. It is personal and it matters.

Their colleague Susan Esper, a Deloitte Audit partner based in Boston, explained it this way: "Brian's priority in helping *all* our colleagues and clients achieve success is to make valuable and meaningful connections for everyone he meets. He truly wants the entire business community to know and value one another's ability to make an impact, and he sees himself as a catalyst to make that happen by helping people build relationships. He just gets it."[2]

Francis Hyatt was the passerby that day. As senior vice president of Enterprise Talent and Human Resource Services at Liberty Mutual, one of Boston's and the nation's most established and respected insurance companies, championing diversity is a priority for him both in and out of the office. "It *is* a thin line," he told me recently when discussing his work with prison inmates. "I say that all the time. I look at the men behind the walls, and they are no different than my son Joe and my son Danny. The difference is that they were in the wrong place at the wrong time." Like Brian's, Francis's experience of the thin line informs his work and worldview in crucial ways:

I'm amazingly humbled by the stories, by the quality of the people I meet in prison, by their transparency, by their candor, and by their diversity. When I went behind the walls for the first time, the guys on the inside were assembled in the gymnasium and they were sitting by cohort. The African American guys were in one place, the white guys were in another, the Latinos and the Caribbean folks all separated themselves according to their comfort zones. And yet over the course of the weekend, that all changed as the group moved closer to the goal of knowing yourself, getting to your God and Jesus Christ, and then figuring out how to integrate your faith into the world in which you live—simply said, how will you add flavor to the world around you by being "salt and light"?

During the weekend, through that experience, you start to see the walls come down between the groups. The guys meld together, and by the end of the weekend they get up and share the powerful, life-changing experience they had. And the thing they all agree on is that they realize they can't do this alone. They need their newfound faith and one another to lean on and to help them stand tall behind the walls. It is powerful to see that shift.

And so if you think about that experience, and then what we're trying to accomplish in business, there are a lot of parallels. There are walls across the business world that we need to break down, and we can't do it alone. We must work together to be successful. Issues around unconscious bias, lack of knowledge and understanding of difference, and lack of understanding of the definition of diversity are all things we need to address. Both in prison and in business, we need to understand that diversity is about all of us and about creating an environment that allows us to be our authentic selves. But it doesn't stop there. It's about changing mind-sets and behaviors and creating an environment where we are standing together, supporting one another. In short, it's about our common humanity.[3]

In an America rapidly becoming minority-majority, in a globalized world, the openness and insight of people like Brian and Francis matter more than ever. The truth is, for our nation to fully profit from diversity, we need many, many more Americans—to be blunt, especially straight white men—to lead the charge. As members of the majority (at least for now), straight white American men wield power and influence. They are the majority of business leaders, political leaders, entrepreneurs, and power brokers. Given this reality, their leadership, commitment, and openness to change and diversity have disproportionate positive impact. Conversely, without people like them, we have little hope of making lasting progress.

But the responsibilities do not rest exclusively on the shoulders of the majority. Bridging divides has never been more urgent for all of us. Crossing lines—whether of race, age, gender, culture, religion, sexual orientation, or of any other kind—brings immense personal rewards. It also enables us to make more meaningful and important contributions to society, business, and culture and is the best hope we have for a more peaceful coexistence.

The ability to recognize that the lines dividing us are thin, permeable, and often artificial doesn't just happen. Learning to understand and respect differences, then turn them into bridges rather than barriers, takes sustained effort and commitment.

Inherently diverse individuals bring extraordinary value to business and society. But men like Brian and Francis (who on the surface seem part of the status quo yet work tirelessly to ensure everyone succeeds) often drive equally significant positive change. They don't check any of the boxes on an equal-opportunity report, but they bring a similar kind of differentiated outsider understanding. Their actions and attitudes are often rooted in a life-altering event. Through a variety of learning experiences, they have gained insights that make them different—as if they have *acquired diversity*.

The idea that someone can acquire diversity might seem odd, but it's more common than most of us realize. If you have acquired diversity, you better understand, empathize with, and learn from others. Unlike inherent diversity, of course, you can't instantly see it. It's not about *what* you are but *who* you are. Acquired diversity is a perspective, a worldview, and a way of thinking, interacting, and working with others that's more inclusive, open, and critical.

We coined the term *acquired diversity* at the Center for Talent Innovation because we were intrigued by the exponential impact specific kinds of leaders had on a team's ability to overcome conflict and drive innovation. We found that leaders with certain life experiences were more likely to foster a speak-up culture, to support and encourage others, to be open to feedback, and to ensure everyone would be heard. Those behaviors turned out to have a measurable effect on the success of teams, especially diverse teams. In companies where even a small number of leaders had this type of acquired diversity, growth of the business and expansion into new markets were dramatically greater.[4]

So how and why does one acquire diversity? It may be developed from visiting prisons, living abroad, speaking a foreign language, having a gay family member, becoming close to a person from a different racial or ethnic group, or through other family, educational, work, or life experiences. Many people with acquired diversity have felt like an outsider at least once, so they relate to other outsiders more meaningfully. But fundamentally it is based on having been touched personally. Almost always, it involves connecting with someone markedly different from yourself—and in the process developing love, compassion, empathy, and understanding.

The idea that our attitudes, beliefs, and behaviors can be altered by spending time with people from different backgrounds is not just a spiritual or idealistic Pollyanna vision for world peace. It is a highly regarded concept of social psychology, supported by a significant body of research evidence, called *contact theory*.

Interest in the effects of contact between people of different social groups was originally stimulated by the impact of World War II on the American military. Because of a shortage of combat troops in the then–racially segregated US Army, General Dwight D. Eisenhower permitted black soldiers stationed in Europe to volunteer for combat duty, which brought them into close contact with white soldiers. Sociologists studied the effects of this experiment. Initially, 62 percent of white soldiers said they would dislike having to serve with blacks. But after semi-integrated combat units were formed that included soldiers of both races, that number dropped, and only 7 percent of the white soldiers who fought alongside blacks were unhappy with the arrangement. It seemed that working in close proximity to people of a different background broke down some of the barriers that prejudice had erected.[5]

Psychologists and sociologists were intrigued by this apparent shift in attitudes, and they studied whether the effect could be generalized to other circumstances. Social psychologist Gordon W. Allport is generally credited with formulating what became known as the *contact hypothesis*; his findings were later supported by hundreds of other confirming studies. In a landmark 1954 study, Allport summed it up this way:

> *Prejudice (unless deeply rooted in the character structure of the individual) may be reduced by equal status contact between majority and minority groups in the pursuit of common goals. The effect is greatly enhanced if this contact is sanctioned by institutional supports (i.e., by law, custom or local atmosphere), and provided it is of a sort that leads to the perception of common interests and common humanity between members of the two groups.[6]*

Allport's provisos are important. He emphasized that contact will not usually cause a decline in prejudice or hostility *unless* the people coming into contact are equal in status, share a common goal, and are meeting under conditions in which custom and authority encourage such contacts. These caveats explain why whites and blacks in the Jim Crow South rarely became mutually empathetic and understanding despite their close physical proximity: The required conditions of equality, a common goal, and social sanction didn't exist.

However, contact hypothesis suggests that when whites and blacks serve together in the same military unit, study in the same class at college, or work together on a factory assembly line, the conditions are ripe for them to develop acquired diversity. And we can see this happening in growing segments of American society today.

The history of contact-driven social and emotional change through military experience goes back farther than World War II. African Americans have always served our nation's military, even before the founding of the nation itself. Crispus Attucks, a merchant seaman of mixed African and Native American heritage, was the first man killed in the Boston Massacre of 1770 and is rightly considered one of the heroes of the battle for independence. But for generations, black Americans who wanted to fight for their country were channeled into menial support work or organized into segregated units—as in the black regiments authorized by President Abraham Lincoln, which helped the Union win the Civil War.

Lincoln himself seems to have acquired diversity through his Civil War experience. Raised in the border state of Kentucky, he grew up with many of the racial prejudices common to white people of that place and time. Even as a political opponent of slavery during the long run-up to the Civil War in the 1840s and 1850s, Lincoln remained convinced of the inherent inferiority of African Americans and doubted they could ever be successfully integrated into US society. Many historians believe his views on race changed largely as a result of two factors: Lincoln's friendship with the great Negro writer and activist Frederick Douglass and his admiration for the bravery and heroism of black Union soldiers. By the end of the war, Lincoln had not only abolished slavery but was advocating votes for blacks, a once unheard-of proposition among white politicians.

Lincoln's philosophical and political evolution is a classic example of acquired diversity through close personal contact—his heart changed, and along with that change came a broadening and deepening of attitudes and choices.

Many racial attitudes were transformed by the performance of black soldiers during the Civil War. Presidential aide William O. Stoddard summed up the phenomenon in a dispatch published in the *New York Examiner*: "It is surprising to see how rapidly men are losing their silly prejudices against the use of black soldiers. I mean in the army. Of course, the demagogues of the North are almost as loud as ever, but among the men in the field, the prevailing sentiment is getting to be . . . 'why, let 'em fight—they're as good as rebels, any day.'"[7] Stoddard never heard of acquired diversity, but he observed it at work among the white soldiers in the Union army.

The US military was finally racially integrated in 1948, and in the years that followed, it attempted to develop a truly bias-free meritocracy. Although prejudice lingered among many individual soldiers, blacks in the military were gradually given opportunities to compete, learn, excel, and lead alongside whites. By 1954—six years after President Truman issued his integration order—a young black American named Colin Powell found that the Reserve Officers' Training Corps (ROTC) program at New York's City College offered him the most attractive opportunity available for personal growth and development. "And by the time I entered the Army in 1958," Powell recalls, "ten years after the order was signed, the only thing they cared about was could I perform: Not whether I was black, white, poor, rich, West Pointer or non–West Pointer."[8] As a result of military integration, during the 1950s, '60s, and '70s, millions of young Americans experienced their first interracial relationships in Army barracks, on Marine training grounds, or aboard Navy ships.

Like most large institutions, the US military continues to struggle with diversity, and not every soldier, of course, develops acquired diversity. Racial, ethnic, and gender prejudices that are common throughout American society certainly still exist in the armed forces. In a 2004 survey, 27 percent of black and Hispanic US Army officers reported experiencing discrimination within their own units. Members of other ethnic groups sometimes encounter virulent hostility from their fellow soldiers.

In October 2011, Army Private Danny Chen was found dead of a gunshot wound in a guard tower in Kandahar, Afghanistan. Chen apparently committed suicide after weeks of reported physical abuse and racial taunting that included slurs like "chink," "gook," and "dragon lady." (Several soldiers in Chen's unit were later court-martialed for crimes related to his hazing.) Other Asian Americans have reported similar problems, including Anu Baghwati, a US Marine officer of Indian descent who left the service after five years because of the discrimination she experienced.[9]

Probably the most serious diversity problems in the American military today relate to women and gays. Experts say the data may be incomplete, but some 15 percent of women veterans from Iraq and Afghanistan who visited Veterans Administration hospitals reported sexual trauma experienced in the service at the hands of fellow American soldiers. [10] A 2012 Pentagon survey concluded that around twenty-six thousand service members—mostly women—had been sexually assaulted, though just one victim in eight filed an official report.[11] And the military has been slow to recognize women as equals. Only in 2015 did the elite Ranger School allow women to compete side by side with men for the first time, and the full opening of all combat roles to women remains a work in progress.

As for LGBT soldiers, until 1993 they were officially banned from military service and thereafter were permitted to serve only secretly under the notorious "Don't ask, don't tell" policy. Not until September 2011 were gays and lesbians able to serve openly in the US armed forces. But in one sign of how far the military has come, in April 2016, Secretary of Defense Ash Carter lifted the ban on transgender individuals serving in the military. In announcing a six-month review of the issue, Secretary Carter said, "We must ensure that everyone who's able and willing to serve has the full and equal opportunity to do so, and we must treat all our people with the dignity and respect they deserve. Going forward, the Department of Defense must and will continue to improve how we do both. Our military's future strength depends on it."[12]

So while the American military doesn't have a spotless track record when it comes to diversity, nor does service guarantee soldiers will become more open-minded or tolerant, the fact remains that, on balance, it has been a leader in the national struggle to embrace diversity—and for millions of Americans, military service has provided an important personal opportunity to see difference as a thin line.

A life experience like military service is just one of the many ways people gain acquired diversity. The unpredictable vagaries of love exert a powerful unifying force that encourages acquired diversity. Biological and emotional attractions between people show no respect for lines of race, religion, nationality, or class, and therefore, over generations, they knit human groups together into broader, more mutually respectful and understanding networks that are able to live and work together.

There's no way to really measure how many Americans might qualify as having acquired diversity, but given the huge numbers of intermarried, multicultural American families, it's safe to say the numbers are likely growing. In 1967, the landmark Supreme Court Case *Loving v. Virginia* opened up the legal right of blacks and whites to marry. As recently as 1970, fewer than 1 percent of all US marriages were between people of different races, but in 2008–10 they accounted for more than 15 percent—a record share.[13] These relationships have invariably changed the couples and their extended families at the same time.

One CEO I recently met with described how having a biracial nephew had changed his worldview, beginning with the disturbing realization that someone he knew and loved might be subject to racial profiling by suspicious traffic cops:

> *Never in my life had I really thought about what it was like for young black men until my beloved nephew turned sixteen and got his driver's license. We realized he needed an entirely different kind of education about being behind the wheel as a young black man than I'd have ever thought to explain to my own boys. After that conversation, I had a totally new appreciation for the lives of my black colleagues at work. I suddenly understood better, I think, what they deal with every day. The experience made me that much more resolved to work harder to understand others and to foster understanding in our company.*

As tens of thousands of Americans have expanded their families to include diverse individuals, the effect has been broad and meaningful. These intimate relationships based on knowing and loving someone very different translate to changed minds and acquired diversity for generations to come. Indeed, close family relationships are likely the most personal way people develop acquired diversity.

Over the past fifty years, hundreds of thousands of largely white American families have adopted children of different racial or ethnic backgrounds from their own. Celebrities like Angelina Jolie and Brad Pitt, Madonna, Sandra Bullock, Charlize Theron, and Hugh Jackman have adopted children from around the world. As of 2001, there were 1.5 million adopted children in the United States—that's 2.5 percent of all the children in the country. One study found that 58 percent of all Americans have either adopted a child, given up a child for adoption, or know someone who was adopted.[14] Of children adopted from overseas, particularly in the last twenty-five years, the majority have been Chinese or Korean. Some two hundred fifty thousand children adopted from Asia were living in the United States by 2009.

Inevitably, as these nontraditional families have become more and more common, attitudes and perspectives have changed. Today, whether in big cities or rural towns, fewer Americans are surprised to see these nontraditional families at church, school, or Walmart. The television show *Modern Family* has made a gay couple with an adopted Asian daughter a no-big-deal part of the story line. While adoption across lines of race and culture is not without difficulty—and there are certainly critics who believe minority children raised by white adoptive parents struggle disproportionately with issues of identity—on balance, it has been positive for the families involved and for the country.

As an adoptive parent myself, I believe the trend is overwhelmingly positive. When Philippe and I started our own adoption process in 2009, we were full of complex emotions. Adoptive parents are forced to ask themselves unique questions; almost from the beginning of the process you must decide whether you are open to adopting a child of another race or want to focus on finding a child who looks like you. We initially considered international adoption from Russia, in part because of my Russian origins and in part because it would make it more likely we could adopt a Caucasian child. When Russian adoptions to the United

States effectively ended after a series of diplomatic disputes, we refocused on domestic adoption. By being open to any racial profile, we increased our chances of finding a healthy child.

For me, this was not a complicated question. I was comfortable with the idea that my children wouldn't look like me, and I was completely at ease with the idea of race being part of our long-term family dialogue. For Philippe, it was a more complex question and one he needed some time to come to grips with. And my mother recently admitted that she had worried about what it would be like to have grandchildren that bore no resemblance to her. But when Stella and Serena entered our lives, I, my mother, Philippe, and our entire families instantly fell in love with them. Love is love, period.

I appreciate that it may not always be so simple, and that for some children and adoptive families it's not all a walk in the park. But adoption is one powerful way in which traditional lines between races and cultures are being crossed to exceptionally positive effect.

When Ann Dunham was attending the University of Hawaii in 1960, she got to know a handsome young student from Kenya. The two fell in love, got married, and produced a beautiful mixed-race child who grew up to be the forty-fourth president of the United States—Barack Obama.

The marriage between Ann Dunham and her husband, also named Barack Obama, didn't last. But Dunham had acquired a lifelong openness to and sympathy with global perspectives that relatively few Americans of her era shared. She later remarried, and she and her new husband, a Javanese surveyor named Lolo Soetoro, lived for four years in Jakarta with young Barack, where they were joined by a new baby daughter, Maya. The whole family, including the future president, imbibed even more multicultural influences from their sojourn in Indonesia.

Later, Barack Obama spent most of his formative years in America's most ethnically and culturally diverse state—Hawaii. There he was influenced by his mother's parents, Stanley and Madelyn Dunham, a couple of "old-fashioned" Americans from Kansas who fell in love with their bright young grandson and developed a serious case of acquired diversity of their own.

The Obamas are an obvious example of how inherent diversity can give rise to acquired diversity in an entire family. And given the unpredictable nature of human affections, acquired diversity can impact any family, regardless of their cultural or political characteristics.

The Bush family, America's most well-known Republican political dynasty, was impacted when Jeb Bush, the second son of President George H. W. Bush and his wife, Barbara, fell in love with Columba Garnica Gallo, the daughter of a migrant worker born in León, Guanajuato, Mexico, while Jeb was teaching English there. Jeb and Columba were married in 1974, and in 1988 she became a naturalized US citizen—largely, she said, in order to be able to vote for her father-in-law for president.[15]

Over time, the entire Bush clan developed a powerful case of acquired diversity through their interactions with Columba. Her husband, Jeb, having become fluent in Spanish, used his acquired diversity skillfully to support his own political career. He captured 61 percent of the Hispanic vote in his successful 1998 bid to become governor of Florida, and he did almost as well when he was reelected in 2002. In his unsuccessful campaign for the 2016 presidential nomination, Bush's acquired diversity featured prominently, but it proved to be a two-edged sword in the highly charged anti-immigrant atmosphere of this election cycle. When Bush accidentally checked a box identifying himself as Hispanic on an official voter registration document, the press pounced.[16] Perhaps the error can be explained by the possibility that Bush felt so close to his wife's life experience that he believed it was his own!

The Rising Tide

The civil rights movement of the 1960s made it easier for acquired diversity to spread more broadly. As US society as a whole gradually followed the lead of the military and became more racially and ethnically integrated, millions of Americans experienced increasingly diverse communities, social organizations, and businesses. College and university students discovered what it was like to study, play musical instruments, and compete in sports alongside people of other races, religions, and ethnic backgrounds. They found that face-to-face encounters can do more to erode prejudice and foster empathy than any number of lectures on democracy and equality. As Republican congressman and former pro football star Jack Kemp famously remarked when asked about his unusual ability to identify with the concerns of minority-group members, "I can't help but care about the rights of people I used to shower with."[17]

In post–World War II America, businesses that once served only homogeneous markets started serving customers of different backgrounds and eventually hired employees from the same diverse groups, in part so they could serve those growing and diversifying customer groups more effectively. (Some companies were more farseeing and opportunistic than others about the profits to be made from diversity. For example, the Pepsi-Cola Company gained an edge in the ongoing "cola wars" when it recruited a cadre of black salespeople and empowered them to promote their beverage in communities of color.)[18]

As racial barriers slowly fell, managers and executives learned and changed through increasing contact with colleagues, clients, business partners, and customers from varied backgrounds. In some states and cities, neighborhoods became at least partially integrated; it was increasingly rare for an American to live a whole life without ever meeting a person of a different race or religion.

The Millennial Moment

One of the largest generations of the last hundred years is the seventy-five million Americans who make up Gen Y, or the Millennial generation. Born roughly between 1980 and 1997 (depending on definitions, which vary), Millennials tend to be more inclusive, open-minded, and empathetic than any previous age cohort. Why? They are diverse. They are the children of intermarried couples. They have attended diverse schools. And they're connected to one another through technology in unprecedented ways.

The absolute explosion of all forms of electronic media—from the proliferation of cable television networks to the virtually infinite connectivity of the Internet and social media—has been a fundamental part of the Millennial experience. Often referred to as "digital natives" (as contrasted with the "digital immigrants" of older generations), they grew up online, and many are intuitively comfortable communicating with and sharing their experiences and interests with people from around the world.

American Millennials are the most highly educated generation in history. They have attended college at record rates, which has often thrown them into proximity with people of varied backgrounds and cultures, and they have increasingly participated in overseas studies and sought out foreign travel, including not just travel tourism destinations like Western Europe but regions of the world once considered exotic or forbidding, from Southeast Asia and sub-Saharan Africa to Latin America.

The resulting mind-set is unlike any previously known. Baby boomers experienced other cultures only in small, prepackaged slices: an article in *National Geographic*, a TV news story, a trip to Europe. Gen Xers like me felt the impact of diversity in a more powerful, less constrained fashion. But Millennials witness it twenty-four hours a day in vibrant HD, stereo sound, instantaneous news coverage, and live tweets and streaming video from celebrities and ordinary people. They've grown up immersed in multicultural experiences from Ethiopian hybrid pop and "Gangnam Style" to the Orange Revolution and the Arab Spring. These digital connections to the outside world can't help but enhance the acquired diversity of today's younger generation.

The result: Millennials are more inclusive and open to difference in their thinking. The Center for American Progress's comprehensive 2009 report concluded:

> *One likely consequence of the Millennial generation's rise is an end to the so-called culture wars that have marked American politics for the last several decades. Acrimonious disputes about family and religious values, feminism, gay rights, and race have frequently crippled progressives' ability to make their case to the average American. Millennials support gay marriage, take race and gender equality as givens, are tolerant of religious and family diversity, have an open and positive attitude toward immigration, and generally display little interest in fighting over the divisive social issues of the past. Almost two-thirds agree that religious faith should focus more on promoting tolerance, social justice, and peace in society, and less on opposing abortion or gay rights.[19]*

Other studies directly relate Millennials' inclusive attitudes to their career expectations and desires. A 2014 survey by Deloitte found that more than three-quarters of Millennials are eager to work at organizations that foster innovative thinking—and that 39 percent identify lack of diversity as one of the biggest barriers to such thinking at their current workplace.[20]

Similarly, a 2012 study for the American Advertising Federation based on conversations with panels of Millennials from five US cities observed: "Millennials desire work environments and brands that authentically embrace diversity and inclusion in the same way they do within their friendship circles and other networks." In fact, the desire to experience and learn from diversity is so deeply ingrained in most Millennials that they take it for granted: "Across the board Millennial panelists state that they do not discuss diversity and multiculturalism with peers; instead they live it."[21]

Whatever the combination of factors that is responsible, it's apparent that the trend among today's youth is toward greater acquired diversity (as well as the increased inherent diversity that demographic forces are producing). This is a huge potential cultural, political, social, and economic blessing for the United States.

Love Is Love

Nowhere is the promise of acquired diversity more apparent than in the changing social and societal landscape for LGBT Americans. With more and more LGBT men and women coming out of the closet to family members, friends, and coworkers, millions of Americans have discovered a new willingness to accept them as fellow humans entitled to love, respect, and equality.

In many cases, it's the love of a gay friend or relative that has triggered the change. A 2013 study found that 65 percent of Americans now say they have a close friend or family member who is gay or lesbian, nearly triple the number (22 percent) reported in 1993. This increase closely tracks the shift in attitudes toward issues like same-sex marriage, which is now supported by a majority of Americans (53 percent), a dramatic turnaround from just a decade ago. In fact, the link is quite direct: The same study found that Americans with a gay or lesbian friend or relative approve of same-sex marriage 27 percentage points higher than those without such a relationship (63 percent versus 36 percent).[22]

My friend Todd Sears, a former investment banker and founder of Out Leadership (a consortium of firms from a wide range of industries that are dedicated to LGBT equality), has watched up close as attitudes toward gay rights changed, particularly in the once supermacho, homophobic, and exclusionary world of finance. "At our recent diversity conference," Sears told me in 2015, "we had three Wall Street CEOs whose gay sons appeared on a panel with them. All three said that their understanding of LGBT issues changed 180 degrees when their sons came out to them. None of them were proud of that fact, because it showed their lack of empathy *before* their sons came out."[23] The story underscores the unmatched power of personal connections in driving attitudinal change.

The example of Paul Singer, a politically conservative hedge fund magnate and billionaire, typifies this. Singer provides financial support to a range of conservative causes and candidates, including many in the Republican right who oppose gay rights. But the experience of loving a son who came out as gay changed his views so dramatically that he reconsidered his philanthropic agenda. Today Paul Singer is one of the most important financial backers of the marriage equality movement and one of the country's most influential Republican supporters of gay rights.

People like Singer are not alone. In the last twenty years, millions of American families have come to see the love shared by gay people as equal to their own. The American public has embraced a range of gay entertainers and sports figures from Ellen DeGeneres to Billie Jean King to Jason Collins in ways unimaginable not long ago. In the process, many are finding that love trumps even the most closely held ideological views. Attitudes toward gay marriage equality changed faster the more the movement and public relations efforts focused on the idea that love is love, no matter what. When the issue is cast in those terms, it becomes harder for many to justify the continued exclusion of gays from the institution of marriage.

One Step Forward, Two Steps Back

Acquired diversity, openness to crossing lines, and ideology can have a powerful impact on societal attitudes. But sometimes the refusal to shift attitudes even in the face of a lifetime's worth of experience can be shockingly stubborn.

Perhaps the most striking example of resistance to acquired diversity is the persistence of barriers for women in American business. From a purely logical standpoint, it would seem that acquired diversity should have long ago demolished any remaining prejudice against women. After all, every man has a mother, and most men have studied and worked with women; the majority date, fall in love with, and marry women; and millions of men help to raise daughters. If personal contact with women always sufficed to produce deep understanding, empathy, openness, and support of women's aspirations, sexism would be unknown—and maybe the divorce rate would be lower, too.

But of course, that's not the case—even in the twenty-first century, after generations of effort and progress, biases against women remain, in the workplace and elsewhere.

This is not to say that men can never acquire diversity from their relationships with the women around them. Many do. In fact, a 2014 study of federal appeals court judges found a significant correlation between the sex of a judge's children and the rulings that judge makes in cases related to women's rights. Having at least one daughter correlates with a 7 percent increase in the number of "feminist" rulings issued by a judge; and among judges with only one child, those with a daughter showed an increase of 16 percent as compared with those with a son. In the words of Maya Sen, a professor of political science who coauthored the study, "By having at least one daughter, judges learn about what it's like to be a woman, perhaps a young woman, who might have to deal with issues like equity in terms of pay, university admissions or taking care of children."

Professor Sen went on to relate "the daughter effect" to the entire range of forces that can produce acquired diversity: "Justices and judges aren't machines. They are human, just like you and me. And just like you and me, they have personal experiences that affect how they view the world. Having daughters is just one kind of personal experience, but there could be other things—for example, serving in the military, adopting a child or seeing a law clerk come out as gay. All of these things could affect a justice's worldview."[24]

So acquired diversity can have a major impact on the attitudes, values, and behaviors of people right up to the rank of federal judge. But as the persistence of sexist attitudes in US society makes all too clear, making America truly inclusive will require much more acquired diversity.

The Outsiders

For some, acquired diversity is produced by the shock of direct outsider experience:

> *The thing that really changed me the most was living in Asia and seeing the world through a different lens...There's nothing like it, to be one of two or three* gaijin *out of 25,000. You are the minority. Your customs, your culture, your behavior—everything is foreign to these folks. You really do understand how to rethink a problem or reanalyze a situation.*[25]

The speaker is Sam Palmisano, famous as the chairman of IBM who turned the corporation around between 2002 and 2012, transforming it from a staid computer hardware and software company into a nimble innovator in IT services, analytics, and cloud computing. Now, having retired from IBM, Palmisano is directing his efforts into the importance of learning to think anew about life and business. In 2013, he founded the Center for Global Enterprise, which helps CEOs and academics collaborate in creating tools to prepare young people for leading organizations in today's global economy—including tools to develop a deeper appreciation of the outsider experience and the acquired diversity it can foster.

So being an outsider or understanding the feeling of being one can be an enormously educational experience—one that teaches you a lot about yourself and about the fascinating cultural differences that shape our worlds.

This understanding is important not only for individual Americans but also for our organizations, institutions, and society as a whole. Huge economic value can be derived from both inherent and acquired diversity. But at the heart and soul of all things related to diversity is the richness of human experience that comes from loving across the lines. The closer we come to those who are different, the better we are individually and collectively. It's certainly not easy or simple, but if we succeed, the rewards are limitless.

From Ordinary to Extraordinary

As we've begun to see, embracing diversity can be challenging—for an individual and for a nation. It may require adopting a whole new mind-set, abandoning familiar assumptions, and learning to see the world through entirely new lenses. At first, this can be frightening. But over time, it usually becomes exhilarating...and incredibly rewarding.

The story of how Jackie Robinson became the first black ballplayer in the modern major leagues is a familiar tale of heroism in adversity—a hard-won triumph for the principle of inherent diversity. Far less familiar is the story of Bobby Bragan, a white man whose life and heart were transformed by his relationship with Jackie Robinson. It's a powerful narrative that illustrates how acquired diversity can help turn an ordinary person into a hero in his own right.[26]

As a young minor-league infielder in the 1930s, Bobby Bragan was nicknamed "Nig." Of course, Bragan was a white man—Robinson wouldn't break baseball's color line until years later—but his complexion was on the dark side, so his buddies came up with the moniker. It didn't bother Bragan. Having grown up in Alabama, he knew black people only as servants or workers at his dad's construction company, and it didn't even occur to him that the nickname might be offensive. Such was the "innocence" of those days when Jim Crow still dominated the American South.

Bragan worked hard at the craft of baseball, but he didn't have a huge amount of talent. After many years of bouncing around baseball and a couple of years serving in the military during World War II, he ended up joining the Brooklyn Dodgers. By 1947, Bragan was on the roster as a backup catcher when word came down that the Dodgers were about to make history by calling up Jackie Robinson from the minor leagues to play for the big team in Brooklyn.

The news sent baseball into an uproar. Many players, executives, and reporters were outraged by the idea of a black big leaguer; many predicted that the Dodgers' grand experiment in racial equality was doomed to fail. And a group of players on the Dodgers, led by a popular star outfielder from Georgia known as Dixie Walker, were rumored to be in open revolt, threatening to go on strike if Jackie Robinson joined the team.

Bobby Bragan had to choose sides. His upbringing in the Deep South made it clear to him that blacks were inferior to whites. He didn't see how he could accept having a Negro as a teammate. Bragan visited Branch Rickey, the general manager of the Dodgers and the mastermind of the Robinson signing, and asked to be traded to another team.

Rickey thought for a moment, then asked Bragan, "If we call Jackie Robinson up, will you change the way you play for me?"

Bragan suddenly was forced to decide whether or not he was willing to open himself up to the possibility of being a black man's teammate. It was a life-changing decision. "No sir," he finally said, "I'd still play my best."

Rickey kept Bragan on the team. And as the 1947 season unfolded—and as Jackie Robinson emerged as the best player on the Dodgers—Bragan found himself tolerating, then grudgingly respecting, and eventually admiring him. The two teammates started playing cards together on the long train rides between cities and sitting side by side in the dugout talking baseball during the games. And when Bragan heard family and friends making racist remarks about Robinson, he was surprised to hear himself defending his friend.

But the impact of Jackie Robinson on Bragan's life was just beginning.

After Bragan's brief big-league career was over, he bounced around the minor leagues as a manager. In 1958, in Spokane, Washington, he managed a roster that included a highly talented but very unhappy young black shortstop named Maury Wills. Wills had lightning speed and a quick bat, but he was considered moody, aggressive, and incommunicative. It appeared he would never have the self-discipline to make the most of his ability. "I had just about given up on myself," he later wrote.

Bragan took Wills under his wing. After analyzing Wills's swing, he realized that his unique batting talents would be best served by becoming a switch-hitter, and he worked with him daily to teach him how. Bragan urged the Dodgers—playing in Los Angeles by then—to make Wills their shortstop. He ended up becoming a star, winning the Most Valuable Player award in 1962 and setting records for stolen bases.

Baseball writer Joe Posnanski sums it up this way:

Thing is, Maury Wills knew in 1958 that Bragan was one of the men who at first refused to play with Jackie Robinson. He knew it, and his instincts would have been to not trust such a man. But by then—more than a decade later—Bobby Bragan was a different man. His generosity of spirit had been hard earned. His enthusiasm and newfound color blindness were irresistible. Maury Wills has credited much of his success in baseball and life to the friendship and mentorship of Bobby Bragan.[27]

When young Bobby Bragan decided to accept the idea of playing alongside a black teammate, he helped ease Jackie Robinson's groundbreaking achievement of success in the "white man's game." In the process, he also made possible a whole new career for himself.

When Bragan was an old man and was asked by a reporter to name his greatest achievement in baseball, he didn't talk about any of the games he'd played, the stars he'd known, or the young players like Wills he'd helped. Instead, he proudly cited the fact that when he left the Dodgers in 1948, his job was taken by the first black catcher in the major leagues—the great Roy Campanella.

Bobby Bragan made a long journey from Birmingham, Alabama, to the big leagues. But the greater journey was in his mind and his spirit—from being an unthinking racist, just as he'd been raised, to being a friend, an admirer, and a mentor of black colleagues whose talent was far greater than his own.

That's the kind of amazing journey that can happen when a person chooses to embrace diversity and the world of new possibilities it opens.

4. Past as Prologue

The bosom of America is open to receive not only the Opulent and respectable Stranger, but the oppressed and persecuted of all Nations and Religions; whom we shall welcome to a participation of all our rights and privileges, if by decency and propriety of conduct they appear to merit the enjoyment.

—*George Washington, 1783*

In 2007, a remarkable story of international cooperation and openness began. In that year, more than a hundred thousand exiles from Bhutan—most of them Hindus who'd been forced from their largely Buddhist homeland because of their religion—began to find new homes after more than two decades in UN-run refugee camps. Over time, the Bhutanese were accepted in various countries around the world, including Australia and Canada, but the biggest number, around seventy thousand, gained entrance to the United States. It was one of the largest refugee resettlement programs of recent years.

And by all objective measures, it has been an enormous success. With modest assistance from local governments, churches, and social service agencies, the Bhutanese have made the difficult adjustment to life in communities like Manchester, New Hampshire, the New England city best known for its ultraconservative newspaper the *Union Leader.* They've found jobs, enrolled in local schools, mastered English, launched small businesses, and applied to nearby colleges and technical schools. On Manchester's main business street, the Himalayas General Store now boosts the local economy by catering to a Bhutanese American clientele, and plans for a Bhutanese restaurant are in the works. After only a few years in the country, Bhutanese receive welfare at a lower rate than the overall Manchester population, and their children are graduating from high school at a higher rate.

But online, another picture emerges. On Yahoo News, readers responded to an article about the Bhutanese in New Hampshire with an outpouring of vitriol—more than six hundred comments denouncing the newcomers. One typical remark: "If YOU are a taxpaying PRODUCTIVE citizen of this nation then YOU are the ones getting fvcked [sic] by these bleeding heart leeches." (The facts of the case—that the Bhutanese immigrants are contributing far more to the local economy and government than they receive in benefits—didn't seem to matter.)[1]

For every moment of accepting immigration, we have equally revolted against it. Our history as "a nation of immigrants" and a haven for people of varied backgrounds is long, complicated, and divisive. It's a tale of repeated cultural collisions, political and social conflict, and gradual, sometimes grudging acceptance. This history continues to repeat itself—right up to the present day.

Most Americans know at least the outlines of our immigration story, because it mirrors their own; Native Americans are the exception, but otherwise, we are *all* immigrants. My family came to America, along with millions of others like them, via Ellis Island from tiny, oppressive shtetls in Russia and Poland, where their lives were harshly circumscribed by widespread anti-Semitism. My maternal great-grandmother, Libby, eloped from a small Russian town with her young love, Issac, and arrived in New York via Canada at age sixteen. With no formal education, she built a thriving business as a tobacconist; yellowed newspaper clippings from her day, describing her as the country's most successful female tobacconist, have been passed down in our family. And while her children struggled economically, they built strong, educated, secure families. My paternal great-grandmother, Sarah, traveled to Hamburg, Germany, by train and managed to secure a place on the May 1914 Atlantic crossing of a liner called the *Amerika*—its last embarkation before the outbreak of World War I.

My great-grandmother was the lucky one. My paternal great-grandfather was a communist who left his family to return to Russia in the 1920s. A few years later he was killed in the Nazi Holocaust, along with everyone else I might have been descended from and millions of others.

As a third-generation American, I find the struggles my ancestors faced almost unimaginable. But in just one generation they established productive, educated families and fully integrated into the American way of life, all the while keeping the Jewish traditions of their homeland ever present. My ancestors landed on these shores along with many others in the large wave of Jewish and Eastern European immigration in the late-nineteenth and early-twentieth centuries. They were preceded by Irish and Germans in the 1800s and followed later by Asians and Latin Americans, who have dominated the immigration landscape since the 1970s. Every ethnic group had their own unique reasons for coming, but the thread that binds them all is a simple one—the search for a better life and the American dream.

Every community of immigrants to our shores, from the founding of our nation until now, has taken full advantage of the freedoms provided in our "land of opportunity" to become part of the "gorgeous mosaic" that is America. We won't tackle a complete history of immigration and its impact on our national diversity in this book. But we can enrich our understanding of how we came to be the complicated polyglot, multiethnic, omni-cultural nation we are today and consider whether we want to repeat our past history. I believe we can do better.

No symbol of our nation is more iconic than the Statue of Liberty, whose light of freedom has greeted generations of newcomers to one of the greatest seaports on America's eastern coast. We regard Lady Liberty as a representation of the idea that the United States has always extended an open hand to immigrants and refugees fleeing tyranny and economic distress in their native lands, and we recite with pride the famous lines from Emma Lazarus's sonnet "The New Colossus," inscribed on a bronze plaque at the foot of the statue:

> *Give me your tired, your poor,*
> *Your huddled masses yearning to breathe free,*
> *The wretched refuse of your teeming shore.*
> *Send these, the homeless, tempest-tost to me,*
> *I lift my lamp beside the golden door!*

It's nice to imagine that the United States has consistently lived up to this ideal. But, in fact, that has rarely been the case. The current national debate about immigration is complex and emotional, and in many ways it mirrors the debate we have been having for centuries. With every wave of new immigrants to our country has come passionate backlash.

American immigration law and practice have varied wildly from generation to generation, and for much of the past two centuries they have been crafted to deliberately exclude specific groups unfavored by those in power or by native-born groups who are fearful of social upheaval. Throughout our history, hundreds of thousands of immigrants from a variety of backgrounds have managed to skirt or evade existing immigration rules, but the most intense debates about "illegal immigration" have always

focused on specific categories of undocumented newcomers—
namely, those from ethnic or racial groups that are viewed with
suspicion by the majority.

The first immigration law passed by the United States, the
Naturalization Act of 1790, established simple rules for prospective citizens—they had to live in this country for two years and
maintain the same residence for at least one year. But it also
limited the right of citizenship to "free white persons" of "good
moral character," the latter a purposefully vague criterion that
has been used ever since as a way to justify and sanction exclusion
of people deemed unsuitable. The Naturalization Act reflected
the same racial bias that marked the US Constitution itself, with
its notorious "three-fifths clause," giving white Southern gentry
an electoral bonus for their ownership of slaves while excluding
those slaves from the rights of citizenship.

Later in the 1790s, other immigration and naturalization rules
followed, mainly intended to facilitate the exclusion or deportation of French immigrants who might have been politically radi-
calized by the French Revolution of 1789. (To me it's pretty ironic
that the French were the first group seen as possibly dangerous
radicals. My French husband recently became a US citizen, and
the only thing radical about him is that he wants wine with every
meal.) But over the years, similar rules were invoked to prohibit
people from Ireland, Germany, Italy, Russia, Cuba, and, most
recently, Muslims from Arab countries of the Middle East. In
each case, fears of political extremism, violent ideologies, or terrorist leanings have helped to motivate the exclusionary rules.
But the rules have often been formulated in such a way as to cast
a wide net over people with particular racial or ethnic characteristics, regardless of their political beliefs or criminal tendencies.
The latest example is the 2015 call by then candidate Donald
Trump to exclude all Muslims (not just suspected terrorists)

from entering the United States—a proposal that has garnered wide support in a number of polls.[2] It seems our compulsion to bar potential enemies with the wrong backgrounds never fades—only the targets change.

As varying foreign groups arrived on our shores, those who feared un-American influence shifted their targets accordingly. During the 1830s and 1840s, white nativist groups like the Order of the Star Spangled Banner and the Know-Nothing Party campaigned against European immigration, especially of Roman Catholics. After tens of thousands of Asians immigrated to the United States during the California gold rush (beginning in 1849) to provide manual labor in the construction of the expanding railroad system, a wave of anti-immigrant hysteria triggered the passage of the Chinese Exclusion Act (1882)—the first law that explicitly locked America's doors against a particular national group. The act was initially limited to ten years, but subsequent laws extended it and increased its power, and it was not repealed until 1943. By then, thanks to World War II, the Chinese had become sympathetic victims of the Japanese, who were now considered the supreme embodiment of the "Yellow Peril" that supposedly threatened the survival of the white race.

In the decades that followed, a crazy quilt of other laws, generally driven by waves of social and political anxiety, created different restrictions on immigration to America. Fears that sickly and "feeble-minded" immigrants might weaken the genetic stock of Americans led to an 1882 law excluding those with infectious diseases and "lunatics." Anger over the assassination of President McKinley by an avowed anarchist led to the Anarchist Exclusion Act of 1903. State laws like the California Alien Land Law of 1913 made it illegal for immigrants to own property in the state, effectively excluding non-natives from participating in the economy. Other laws and policies targeted Filipinos, Indians, Mexicans, and other groups deemed a threat to American culture and racial "purity." In an effort to restrict immigration to the well educated, a literacy test requirement was imposed in 1917.

Finally, the comprehensive Immigration Act of 1924 established a complex set of quotas limiting the number of people who could move to the United States based on the national origins of Americans as reflected in the census of 1890. The use of a thirty-year-old benchmark was quite deliberate: The goal was to sharply reduce the recent influx of immigrants from Southern and Eastern Europe in favor of the Northern Europeans who had dominated the immigration rolls prior to that date. This baldly discriminatory quota system remained in place for more than forty years, when the Immigration and Nationality Act of 1965 set forth a looser set of numerical limits by hemisphere rather than by nation. One result of this shift: a new influx of immigrants from Latin America and Asia over the past fifty years, fueling what has now become the latest "immigration crisis" in our nation's history.

So Emma Lazarus notwithstanding, the United States has perpetually erected barriers to entry. And yet immigration to our shores has been almost impossible to stop. People have continued to come despite the intense efforts over centuries to reverse the trend.

Legal or Illegal?

It's easy to imagine that, in the past, most immigrants to our shores immigrated legally and that out-of-control illegal immigration is a modern condition. It turns out not to be true. Despite the hostility directed at specific categories of immigrants and the repeated attempts to legally exclude particular groups of outsiders, for the first century of US history there was no national system for monitoring and controlling the flow of people across our borders. Some port inspectors examined and recorded data from the manifests of incoming ships, which included the names and numbers of immigrants, but the information was purely for statistical purposes. When particular groups—members of specific nationalities or those with mental and physical illnesses, for example—were targeted for exclusion, port officials might seek them out and refuse admission to them, but enforcement of these rules was haphazard. Between the establishment of the famous immigration facility at New York's Ellis Island in 1892 and the start of World War II in 1914, twenty-five million immigrants arrived there; fewer than 1 percent were ever excluded by officials.[3]

No passports, visas, or other documents were required for immigration to America. In fact, until 1918, the United States didn't even *issue* passports except during times of war. There was no national immigration bureaucracy until 1891, when a Bureau of Immigration was established within the Treasury Department; not until 1924 was a border patrol created, and in the same year the first system requiring would-be immigrants to obtain visas from a consular office in their home country was established.

Thus, throughout the nineteenth century and well into the twentieth century, the vast majority of immigrants to the United States did not have to obtain documentation or follow any other legally prescribed process. They simply booked passage on a ship and stepped off the gangplank into American society. And during much of this period, with the national economy rapidly growing and industrializing, the demand for skilled and unskilled immigrant labor was so great that many newcomers were recruited for jobs right on the docks.

So there turns out to be nothing new about "illegal immigration." During the early decades of the twentieth century, when the national quota system and other legal restrictions on immigration were finally established, difficulties and irregularities in enforcing the laws quickly led to tens of thousands of immigrants entering the country outside the legal process. As early as 1925, the Immigration Service estimated that 1.4 million people were living in the United States in violation of immigration laws.

In 1929, a special law called the Registry Act was passed to provide a form of amnesty to immigrants "of good character" who were in the United States illegally. Over the next thirty-five years, over three hundred thousand of these "illegal immigrants" paid a small fee to have their status normalized. Unsurprisingly, the law was applied unevenly; the vast majority of those deemed "of good character" happened to be of Western European or Canadian origin.

So while many Americans think that their ancestors "followed the laws" when they immigrated to this country, it's not likely to be true. For millions of our ancestors, there were no immigration laws and no legal procedures to follow. And for millions of others, the laws and procedures that later existed were overlooked, skirted, or waived. Some of today's most passionate anti-immigrant crusaders are probably themselves a product of this kind of extralegal immigration. President Trump, who rails against illegals and has accelerated deportations of the undocumented, is himself the beneficiary of this unenforced system. His grandfather immigrated from Germany in the 1860s. Given the lack of law enforcement or structure at the time, his own grandfather might be considered an illegal by today's standards.

Having laws and procedures governing immigration is of course important, especially given the very real terrorist threats against our nation. And the issue of undocumented residents should be addressed. But the often-heard demands that today's immigrants "simply obey the laws" ignore the fact that the laws about immigration have actually been continually changing—and that codifying and enforcing those laws is far from a simple matter.

Conflict and Creativity

The reality, then, is that America's status as a nation of nations, drawing people from around the world with diverse cultural, linguistic, political, economic, religious, and personal backgrounds, has always been a source of both conflict and creativity.

Some Americans worry that fundamental cultural characteristics of some of today's newest immigrant communities are posing unique challenges to the traditional process of assimilation. They fear that Muslims from the Middle East represent a religious tradition that is basically incompatible with or even overtly hostile to the Christian faith that the majority of Americans espouse; they worry that the poverty of many migrants from Central and South America will drag down the wages and lifestyle of American workers; they fret that newcomers from African and Asian cultures that most Americans know little about will simply be unable to fit into our traditional way of life. Welcoming immigrants has always been a social and cultural challenge, even when they came from countries like Sweden, Ireland, or Poland; it can be even more difficult when they hail from more exotic places, like Rwanda and Belize, Bangladesh and Cambodia.

It seems likely that much of the pushback against welcoming immigrants stems from this generalized worry about social change. Perhaps this explains the results of a recent study by Maureen Craig and Jennifer Richeson, two psychologists from Northwestern University.[4] Wondering about the impact of the rising minority population on the political attitudes of white Americans, they conducted two simple studies. In one, a sampling of politically unaffiliated white Californians were given an article reporting that the state had become a minority-majority state, while others were given an article with a theme unrelated to race or ethnicity. In the second study, some respondents read a press release predicting that the United States will soon become a minority-majority nation, while others read a press release about a story with no racial implications. The researchers then asked all the respondents to describe their political ideologies.

In both studies, the respondents who'd been primed to think about their status as members of a white minority described themselves as more conservative than those who had not. In other words, thinking about diversity—and about the new demands it may place upon them—appears to cause at least some white people to shift right on the political spectrum, moving toward conservative attitudes associated with protecting and defending the status quo rather than embracing change.

Fears related to unwelcome cultural changes help explain the tendency of politically conservative Americans to view immigration as primarily a problem rather than a benefit to our nation. A Pew Research Center survey from May 2015 asked respondents to complete the sentence, "Immigrants today _____ the country" by choosing either the word *burden* or *strengthen*. Americans as a whole opted for *strengthen* by a 51 to 41 percent margin. (The remainder offered some other answer or said they didn't know.) But those who identified themselves as Republican lined up the opposite way, choosing *burden* rather than *strengthen* by a 63 to 27 percent margin.[5]

Of course, conservatives are not wrong when they worry that demographic change is likely to produce social and cultural change. Allowing immigration and empowering diverse groups to participate fully in the American experience *will* bring changes to our society. I'm convinced that the changes will be overwhelmingly for the better—and that even those who today are most fearful will end up benefiting in the long run. Still, there's no doubt that many Americans are nervous about the demographic and social changes happening around them...and consequently want to turn back the clock on diversity.

It's important to recognize that fears about social change driven by immigration aren't brand-new. America's steadily rising tide of diversity has always been viewed with suspicion and anxiety by those who consider themselves part of the national mainstream.

Every Irish American has heard the tales of the "No Irish Need Apply" signs once posted outside hiring halls; spend a few minutes searching nineteenth-century newspaper archives, and you'll find editorial cartoons depicting Irish immigrants as chimps or baboons. (African Americans are not the only people to have been subjected to this kind of vicious and ignorant stereotyping.)[6]

But it's not necessary to travel back a century or more. Go back just two or three generations, when even groups that today are firmly in the mainstream were considered dangerous outsiders likely to undermine the American way of life. World War II and the Holocaust were already history when Elia Kazan directed *Gentleman's Agreement* (1947), depicting the widespread prevalence of anti-Semitism in America. Baseball legends Joe DiMaggio and Yogi Berra were rising stars in the 1940s when sportswriters routinely referred to them using callous slurs like "spaghetti bender" and "garlic eater" and speculated as to whether Italians could have the native intelligence to succeed in sports over the long term.

The point is that it's simply not accurate that today's conflicts over immigration, assimilation, cultural differences, and the value of diversity reflect the dangers inherent in a new and radical movement to open America's doors to newcomers. We've been experiencing the same kinds of conflicts for generations—once when the newcomers were Irish, Dutch, and German; later when they were Italian, Polish, and Russian; and now, today, when they are Dominican and Guatemalan, Vietnamese and Kenyan.

This history of conflict has produced enormous pain and struggle for countless Americans on all sides of the thin lines that divide us. Millions of talented, hardworking young people from disfavored groups were denied places in schools and colleges, passed over for jobs they could have excelled in, turned away when they sought apartments or homes in good neighborhoods, and had their friendships and romances broken up by families unwilling to accept an unfamiliar face around the dinner table. And on the other side of the line, schools, businesses, neighborhoods, community organizations, government agencies, and many other institutions that could have benefited from the energy and intelligence of these diverse newcomers were deprived of those strengths and accomplished far less as a result. When we allow our society to be divided by lines of race, nationality, ethnicity, religion, and culture, we all lose.

Yet through it all, human beings have persevered. Immigrants have identified cracks in the walls of prejudice and then used their special gifts to blow those cracks wide open. Once they've gained a foothold in the institutions that once tried to exclude them, they've taken advantage of their unique perspective as outsiders to bring fresh, often brilliant, contributions to America.

In chapter two, we mentioned just a handful of the business innovators and company founders who have enriched our economy. Countless other immigrants have brought incredible social, cultural, scientific, and intellectual innovations to our country. It would be impossible to name them all, but a few, almost random, examples will serve to illustrate the breadth and variety of our immigrant hall of fame. They include songwriter Irving

Berlin (born in present-day Belarus), filmmaker Frank Capra (Italy), physicist Albert Einstein (Germany), architect I. M. Pei (China), painter Willem de Kooning (Holland), designer Diane von Fürstenberg (Belgium), inventor Igor Sikorsky (Russia), civil rights activist Stokely Carmichael (Trinidad), jurist Felix Frankfurter (Austria), scientist William Shockley (Britain), Secretary of State Madeleine Albright (Czech Republic), economist Amartya Sen (India)...and many, many others.

As these examples of immigrant success indicate, despite the continual tensions and setbacks that have plagued our national quest for diversity, the American experiment has often worked astoundingly well. Alongside our tradition of xenophobia, intolerance, suspicion, and bigotry against outsiders, we've also forged a tradition of gradually increasing acceptance of diversity. Over time, people from one ethnic, racial, and cultural group after another—Southern and Eastern Europeans, Roman Catholics, Jews, Mormons, Hispanics, and Asians—have fought their way into the national mainstream, enriching our society in the process. African Americans, though still shortchanged economically, politically, and socially, have overcome at least a portion of the impediments that once limited their contributions.

One of the most striking examples of how immigrant groups once regarded with fear and suspicion have gradually attained complete acceptance as part of the American fabric is the story of Italian Americans. Partly because of their Mediterranean origins (as contrasted with the Northern European roots of America's Anglo-Saxon founders), partly because of their Roman Catholic religious heritage (unlike the Protestant faiths embraced by the Pilgrims, Quakers, and Anglicans who dominated American society during our first few generations after independence), the Italians who flooded our shores during the 1880–1920 period were shunned and feared. Often they were caricatured as uneducated, violence-prone, even semihuman. In one typical 1893 editorial, the *New York Times* characterized Italy as "the land of the vendetta, the mafia, and the bandit."[7] Harsh immigration restrictions imposed in the 1920s were motivated largely by the desire to stem the influx of Italians. I've already mentioned the lingering sense of contempt and mistrust that shadowed even accomplished Italian Americans like Joe DiMaggio and Yogi Berra as late as the 1940s.

Then things started to change. Inevitable generational transitions played a role: The children of Italian immigrants who arrived in the 1880s and 1890s grew up studying English in American classrooms, watching the same early moving pictures in the nickelodeons with their American friends, and playing stickball in vacant lots in American towns and villages. As midcentury approached, they'd become thoroughly Americanized—the same process of cultural change virtually every immigrant group has experienced.

The outbreak of World War II also played a role. During the early months of the war, Italian Americans who had not become citizens were officially classified as "enemy aliens"—after all, Mussolini and his countrymen were allies of our archenemy Hitler. But by 1942, it had become apparent that almost no Italian Americans harbored any traitorous intentions. So President Roosevelt, eager to enlist yet another demographic group as enthusiastic supporters of the war effort, dropped the "enemy aliens" label, and news media wrote about the half million Italian American kids who were fighting heroically for Uncle Sam against the fascists.[8] It's tragic that the same sensible logic wasn't applied to the loyal Japanese Americans on the West Coast who were interned during the war.

By the end of the 1940s, America had largely embraced its immigrants from Italy as full-fledged participants in the American dream. DiMaggio was the nation's greatest sports hero, Sinatra its top musical idol. Today, with Italian Americans like

Antonin Scalia and Andrew Cuomo, Sam Palmisano (IBM) and Patricia Russo (Lucent), writers Gay Talese and Richard Russo, and movie directors Francis Ford Coppola and Martin Scorsese playing prominent roles in our national politics, business, and culture, it's hard to remember a time when people with names and backgrounds like theirs were scorned and ignored.

What happened with the Italians has happened with the Irish and the Germans, the Greeks and the Jews in different ways and over different time frames. History tells us that eventually it will happen with the Dominicans, the Kenyans, the Afghans, and the Hmong.

Furthermore, our story of inclusion doesn't apply only to immigrant groups. In recent decades, we've increasingly moved as a nation toward accepting the idea that people who embody diversity in ways other than their ethnicity are also important contributors to our national story. In the last fifty years, women, gays and lesbians, bisexuals, transgender individuals, people with disabilities, and other groups once marginalized or rejected have made unprecedented strides toward equality and the realization of the American dream.

But the quest to create an America that embraces people of *every* kind and takes full advantage of their talents, insights, and creative energies is far from over. Now we may better understand the fragility of the balance. There's a real risk of backsliding—a danger that the progress we've made so far will be dissipated and lost. If the American commitment to honoring true diversity is abandoned or seriously weakened, we'll suffer as individuals, deprived of the exciting presence of fellow humans with so much to contribute to our minds and spirits. Even worse, we'll suffer as a nation, our economic and social creativity profoundly damaged by our failure to capitalize on the gifts of a large portion of our fellow Americans.

It's a mistake we can't afford to make.

5. Demographic Destiny

As you discover what strength you can draw from your community in this world from which it stands apart, look outward as well as inward. Build bridges instead of walls.

Sonia Sotomayor, My Beloved World

In the 1980s and early 1990s, Japan was an emerging global superpower that many experts predicted might dominate the world economy in the twenty-first century. So certain was Japan's march to hegemony that many American high schools taught children Japanese as an important survival tool for the years ahead. Experts on sociology, psychology, and anthropology authored studies explaining why Japan's unique national culture—nurtured through centuries of near isolation and a deliberately fostered sense of unity and homogeneity—gave the country powerful competitive advantages in technology and business.

Yet Japan did not become a dominant global superpower; its growth sputtered and slowed, and the country has suffered nearly two decades of sustained recession. Why? It turns out that the very mores that define Japan may be its undoing. The Japanese failure to embrace and leverage diversity of any kind has had drastic consequences, especially as the country ages. Its unwillingness to welcome immigrants, to accept cultural and ethnic diversity, and above all to fully empower its millions of highly educated women in the workforce and in politics have all hindered growth. The demographics of Japan have come to dictate its economic destiny.

With one of the world's lowest birth rates, Japan has a shrinking population. Demographic experts predict it will fall from 128 million in 2010 to 87 million in 2060—a decline of one-third. The workforce is expected to shrink at a similar pace, which means the number of productive employees generating wealth to support a growing number of aging pensioners will continue to dwindle, creating incredible stress on the nation's economic and social fabric.

Compounding the challenge, Japan's laws governing naturalization for those of foreign ancestry are among the strictest in the world. So are the rules concerning work permits and residency visas. As a result, just 1.6 percent of Japan's population consists of foreign nationals, the third-lowest rate among nations belonging to the Organisation for Economic Co-operation and Development (OECD); only Poland and Slovakia rank lower.[1]

Japan's failure to welcome newcomers from abroad might not matter if the nation was growing from within. But just the opposite is happening. Jared Diamond, a Pulitzer Prize–winning professor of geography at UCLA, has described Japan as "the world's most homogeneous large country" and observed:

This rejection of immigration not only bodes ill for the future of Japan's retirement system, but also deprives the country of the pool of workers, artists, scientists and inventors that immigrants represent for the U.S., Western Europe and Australia...Differences in immigration policies contribute directly to the big gap between the U.S. and Japan in Nobel Prizes. The U.S. leads the world in those awards, while Japan wins few despite high government outlays for science.

Scientific advances are essential to a technology-based econ-
omy. Thus, while immigration creates big problems, lack of it
creates bigger ones.[2]

Japan's insularity has proved disastrous economically. Without an immigrant population, as the nation's demographics collapse, Japan continues to fall into a deeper and deeper economic
hole.

But restrictive immigration isn't Japan's only serious problem.
Its failure to integrate women into the economy has had an even
greater negative impact. Japan has millions of highly educated
women; the college graduation rate for the country's females
rivals that of any country in the international surveys conducted
by the OECD. But many of those bright women are discouraged from bringing their talents to work. Japan's rate of female
participation in the workforce is just 63 percent, far behind that
of other developed countries. When Japanese women start their
families, *70 percent* drop out of work for a decade or longer, many
permanently. And few women manage to sustain careers that lead
them to the upper echelons of corporate leadership. Just 1 percent
of Japanese senior executives are women, compared to 9 percent
in China, 15 percent in Singapore, and 4 percent in the United
States.[3]

A similar dearth of female participants marks the Japanese
political sector. Women hold just 8 percent of seats in the lower
house of the Diet, the equivalent of the US House of Representatives. A 2013 report by the World Economic Forum ranked the
country 105th out of 136 nations for gender inequality and 120th
for women in legislative offices.[4]

The forces preventing women from fully participating in
the workforce are numerous. Ambitious white-collar workers
in traditional Japanese corporations are expected to work ten

to twelve hours per day, even when there isn't enough work to keep them busy, in order to demonstrate their almost cultlike dedication to company and work. Those long workdays are often followed by hours of drinking in downtown bars, engaged with their colleagues and bosses in sessions of *nominication*—a coined word that blends *nomu*, the Japanese word for drinking, with the English word *communication*. At 11:00 p.m., the Tokyo subways are often filled with groups of sodden, black-suited salarymen, heading home for a few hours' sleep before restarting the ritual in the morning. This isn't a way of life that is welcoming to women, particularly those who want to have children. And corporate employment policies make matters worse. Japanese women earn seventy-two cents for every dollar earned by a man in a comparable job, a gap that increases during the childbearing years, reflecting an unwritten policy that economist Laura Tyson has called the "motherhood pay penalty."[5]

In the few Japanese fields dominated by women, the vast majority of employees are classified as part-timers, despite the fact that many of them work forty hours a week or more. At KDDI Evolva, a subsidiary of Japan's second-largest phone company, just 8 percent of the fifteen thousand call center workers are considered full-time. Machiko Osawa, a career expert at Japan Women's University, says that "nonregular" employees like these—68 percent of them women—suffer from the false perception that few are primary breadwinners for their families. The part-time workers earn an average of 38 percent less per hour than full-timers and receive none of the lavish benefits, such as subsidized meals and commuting allowances, that most full-timers enjoy. And since courts refuse to grant them the career protections routinely accorded to full-timers, they are subject to wage cuts, hour reductions, and layoffs at their employers' whim.[6]

The list of barriers facing women at work is long. Tax and

pension regulations are written in such a way as to reward single-breadwinner homes while penalizing two-income families. Childcare centers—until recently a government-monopolized service—are of poor quality and have long waiting lists. When they face obstacles like these, it's no wonder many Japanese women have found it easier to acquiesce to traditional cultural norms that relegate females to limited roles as mothers and homemakers.

The failure to take full advantage of the productivity and creative talents of women has negatively impacted Japan's economic growth. Coupled with the country's low fertility rate, the dearth of female workers has contributed to the alarming shrinkage of Japan's workforce. Declining productivity and lower GDP make it increasingly difficult for the nation to support a large and growing population of aging pensioners, leading to further economic and social stress.

More subtly but no less profoundly, Japan's culture of conformity, driven by cultural anxiety and conservative values, has limited the nation's ability to craft innovative solutions to the business and social challenges of our time.

Today some Japanese political leaders are belatedly struggling to overcome their diversity shortfall. In a 2013 speech before a council of the OECD in Paris, Prime Minister Abe observed, "Turning our eye to the world beyond Japan, we find a great number of non-Japanese who are brimming with ability...I wish to have such people more actively engaged within Japan."[7] Cynical observers of Japanese politics have noted that Abe tends to talk more candidly about the need to expand immigration when addressing foreign audiences than when speaking before his fellow Japanese, whose xenophobic attitudes are well documented. Yet even some politicians who once denounced foreign immigrants as threats to the Japanese way of life are shifting their rhetoric. The conservative writer and former governor of Tokyo Shintaro Ishihara has come out in favor of liberalized immigration laws, adopting the slogan "Population is power."[8]

Abe has also urged that, by 2020, 30 percent of all leadership roles in Japanese government and business should be held by women. To support and encourage Japanese women workers, Abe has been speaking in public about cultural and practical factors like the availability of adequate childcare and the social stigma attached to breastfeeding in public. The importance of increasing female participation has been spotlighted by a number of well-publicized reports. A Goldman Sachs analysis calculated that raising the percentage of women with jobs could add eight million people to the nation's shrinking workforce and boost GDP by 15 percent.[9]

Unfortunately, few Japanese business or political leaders have signed on to Abe's campaign to increase diversity. Keidanren, the nation's leading business organization, has refused to even participate in surveys seeking to ascertain the number of women on corporate boards, recognizing that quantifying the problem would be a first step on the path to addressing it. In 2014, out of five thousand foreigners seeking political, ethnic, or religious asylum, Japan accepted a grand total of just eleven. And during the massive refugee crisis of 2015 spurred by strife in the Middle East, some Japanese leaders called for measures to make the country's immigration system even more restrictive—if such a thing were possible.[10]

Thanks to foot-dragging by business and political leaders as well as the cultural resistance so embedded in the Japanese system, analysts say there's virtually no chance Abe's ambitious goals for achieving a more diverse national workforce will be met. However, the effort seems to be working for him politically—in 2014, Abe was reelected prime minister in a landslide. And more than ever before, Japanese women are warming to the idea of working outside the home. In 1979, 70 percent of women said that men should be breadwinners and women should "take care of the home." By 2012—influenced, no doubt, by Japan's economic slowdown and the increasing financial pressures faced by families—that number had fallen to 50 percent.[11] It seems that significant factions of the Japanese people are ready to accept the idea of diversity. It remains to be seen whether the nation's leaders are prepared to take the practical steps to turn that idea into reality.

Collectively, the Japanese understand and recognize the economic benefits to greater diversity, and they desperately need to grow the economy. And yet entrenched social norms and fear of change have held them back. It's an important cautionary tale for the United States. Japan may seem like a faraway and alien land to us, but their challenges are not that dissimilar from our own. We are a much more diverse nation and we have embraced diversity to a degree most Japanese would find unimaginable, but given the changing demographics of our nation and world, we risk a similar economic failure if we turn our back on the demographic reality around us. Like the Japanese, we, too, may find that our demographics are our destiny.

The Changing Face of America—and of Humankind

For the first one hundred fifty years of our nation's history, the geographic isolation and size of the United States made it relatively easy for us to amass wealth and power on a global scale without addressing all the challenges of diversity. Of course, we had big diversity issues to deal with, especially the overarching problem of racial prejudice, embodied first in the national crime of slavery and then in the decades of battle over Jim Crow laws and other policies and practices that denied freedom and equality to a vast cohort of our fellow Americans. But as a continental power shielded by two oceans, the United States had the luxury of distancing itself from the intense cultural and social conflicts that had long raged within Europe and Asia. When immigrants from those lands arrived, we expected them to shed old allegiances to crown, church, ideology, or party and become Americans, committed to building a new land of economic opportunity and individual freedom—central tenets of the American dream.

And for the most part, that's exactly what those newcomers did. For one hundred fifty years, the doctrine of the "melting pot" ruled. United in our shared acceptance of that American dream, we created a cultural, political, and social landscape tacitly dominated by the Anglo-Saxon mores of our nation's founders, including a belief in laissez-faire capitalism, individual initiative, and what sociologist Max Weber dubbed "the Protestant work ethic."

For most of our nation's history, the population was overwhelmingly white. For example, the 1900 census showed that 87.9 percent of the population was white, with practically all the remainder (11.6 percent) classified as black (or "Negro"). What's more, this breakdown tends to *overstate* the diversity of most parts of the United States, since, until at least 1910, the majority of American blacks lived in the formerly slave-holding states of the Deep South. Thus, as far as most Americans were concerned, the United States was simply a white country; to the extent that issues of racial diversity were even considered, the "Negro problem" was viewed largely as a regional issue of moral importance but one with minor impact on the national political agenda.

The twentieth century brought dramatic demographic change. When the United States entered World War I, an explosion of military-related industry in the North triggered the so-called Great Migration of Southern blacks to Northern cities like New

York, Boston, Chicago, Detroit, and Cleveland. Over the next few decades, the black population percentage in cities and states across the North increased sharply.

After the restrictive national quotas that had dominated immigration policy since 1924 were lifted in 1965, a different wave of demographic change swept over America. Spanish-speaking people from Mexico, the Caribbean, and Central and South America moved to the United States in unheard-of numbers. Asian immigrants from China, Japan, India, and many other countries also arrived in large numbers.

With Latinos and Asians flocking to the United States while the black share of the population remained level or increased slightly, the relative dominance of whites steadily fell. By 1980, non-Hispanic whites represented 79.6 percent of the population. By 2010, they were just 63.7 percent. In that 2010 census, blacks claimed 12.6 percent of the population, Hispanics 16.3 percent, and Asians 4.8 percent; about 3.5 percent fell into other categories. Four states (Hawaii, New Mexico, California, and Texas) had become minority-majority states, in which racial or ethnic minorities, taken together, made up a majority of the population. Thirteen of the forty largest metropolitan areas in the United States are also minority-majority districts.

As a natural outgrowth of these trends, interracial marriages are also increasing, producing growing numbers of children who are biracial or multiracial. Experts believe they constitute somewhere between 3 and 7 percent of the population and are likely to reach 10 percent by 2020.[12] The exact numbers are unclear, partly because demographers have only recently begun to study the question and partly because there is no generally accepted way of classifying these "both/and" Americans. But this new, increasing segment of the population is further altering the ethnic face of America by creating a large group of citizens who can't easily be fitted into a neat demographic box and therefore labeled with a reductive stereotype.

The result of all these changes is that it's no longer possible for white Americans to view themselves as "normal"—the default racial category that once seemed to define "Americanism." And the trends of the twentieth century are not abating. The US Department of Commerce predicts that, between now and the year 2050, fully 85 percent of the nation's population growth will come from nonwhite ethnic groups. Depending on future birth rates and immigration patterns, the entire country is projected to become minority-majority sometime between 2041 and 2046.

But ethnic and cultural changes aren't the only transformations to the landscape of what is American. As the nation becomes more tolerant of variations in gender identity and sexual orientation, more Americans will undoubtedly come out of the shadows, or closets, and identify themselves as who they really feel they are. In 2014, social media giant Facebook, then with 1.3 billion active monthly users, launched a new list of fifty-six additional categories for gender identity in the United States. In explaining why, Alex Schultz, the company's director of growth, explained, "It was simple: Not allowing people to express something so fundamental is not really cool, so we did something. Hopefully a more open and connected world will, by extension, make this a more understanding and tolerant world."[13] If Facebook could identify fifty-six categories of gender identity, there are clearly limitless numbers of racial and ethnic categories possible. (Facebook does not ask users to identify race or ethnicity.) My own children are biracial, French, American, Jewish, Catholic, and practice Eastern meditation. What box could contain the many facets of what makes them who they are? What's more, my children are hardly anomalies. As the nation has diversified, identity has become infinitely more complex. The mind boggles.

Obviously, dramatic demographic shifts are not exclusive to the United States. Global statistics on the changing world population, labor force, and consumer population all point toward the declining hegemony of the white male and the steady rise of people of color, women, young people, and other once-marginalized groups to greater numerical prominence—which of course is leading, over time, to increased economic, social, and political clout.

As of 2015, the estimated 7.3 billion humans on earth are mostly Asian—around 60 percent of the global total. Africans represent the second-largest population, numbering about 15 percent. Europe has 12 percent, Latin America about 9 percent, and North America (the United States and Canada) just 5 percent.[14] But these already unbalanced numbers are going to become far more skewed in the future, with population growth rates in Asia and Africa far higher than anywhere else in the world. (Many countries in Europe are experiencing an actual *decline* in their populations.)

These demographic trends underlie and support the economic and political growth of places that were once among the world's poorest, including China, India, Latin America, Africa, and the so-called MINT countries (Mexico, Indonesia, Nigeria, Turkey). Not only are the continents of Asia and Africa growing in sheer numbers, they are also rapidly developing, with tens of millions of their inhabitants moving from poverty to middle-class status every year. As the peoples of these once-poor continents become more affluent, they produce a larger and larger economic force. At the same time, they continue to send immigrants seeking educational and work opportunities around the world, contributing to even more demographic shifts.

All of this poses huge challenges for everyone, especially for those leading businesses, government agencies, and other organizations. These changes create natural stresses—social, cultural, psychological—while also offering vast opportunities. On the whole, it helps explain why diversity is more of a hot-button issue for Americans (and people around the world) than ever before.

The World at Our Doorstep

More and more, American businesspeople find themselves working closely with customers, suppliers, partners, and colleagues beyond US borders—which means the ability to cope with racial, ethnic, linguistic, and cultural diversity is an increasing prerequisite for business leadership.

Other factors, such as technological innovation, are amplifying the power of these demographic changes. Instantaneous global communication, relatively quick and easy travel, and cheaper, more open international trade make it easier for companies to compete across borders. The creation of free-trade regions linking countries around the world and lowering legal, regulatory, and tariff barriers to international trade is encouraging further globalization of markets. So is the continuing trend of outsourcing business functions to countries where labor is more affordable, land is cheaper, and regulation is more flexible. Today, not only manufacturing but product design, customer service, and many other operations of multinational businesses are shipped to locations abroad.

The lower bars to entry to international trade work both ways, of course. US-based companies are selling increasing shares of their products in the rapidly expanding markets of Asia, Latin America, and Africa. At the same time, companies from those regions are selling their wares to customers in the United States. This means that American corporations, which dominated the world economy for decades in the wake of World War II and the devastation it wrought, now need to be able to respond to challenges from anywhere in the world more quickly and nimbly than ever.

Furthermore, now that US employers are no longer the only game in town, the global war for talent is intensifying. Managers who know how to run operations and sell goods and services in Asia, Latin America, and Africa are increasingly in demand; the best are the subject of bidding wars by top organizations based everywhere from Tokyo to Omaha, Frankfurt to São Paulo. Your next boss could be an American with managerial experience in South Africa, Dubai, Venezuela, or Malaysia—or a manager born, raised, and educated in one of those countries.

American companies—even those that do most of their business in the United States—can no longer pretend that "non-mainstream" markets are negligible. In this new, more diverse, and ever more complex world, both inherent and acquired diversity are crucial resources for companies, countries, and societies that hope to compete. For businesses that need to sell their wares to customers around the globe, the ability to empathize with and meet the needs of people from enormously diverse backgrounds will spell the difference between success and failure. Evidence is mounting that managers who understand the "pain points" in traditional products and services from an outsider's perspective are better able to innovate creatively, simply because they are better able to understand and adapt to the varied points of view that *must* be taken into account in strategic thinking for the twenty-first century.

In my work on these issues with a range of big companies, a few really stand out. In 2013, I had the privilege to work with health-care device maker Covidien (now part of Medtronic) and José "Joe" Almeida, its Brazilian-born CEO at the time. Joe was passionate about advocating diversity. He saw diversity as a marketplace differentiator, and under his watch, the company made massive strides. When I met Joe, he had already made a commitment to his investors and employees that he would drive greater global growth and marketplace innovation, but he hadn't yet focused on the people and diversity implications of these goals. In our first conversation, that quickly changed. As Joe and I talked, he realized how more diversity and inclusiveness from his leadership team would help power the company. After all, if leaders fail to enable everyone to surface ideas and allow the ideas of women or minorities to go unheard, how can they ensure that the best thinking and innovation for the marketplace will become reality?

Joe vowed to improve both representative diversity at key levels and the culture and climate in leadership. He publicly stated those goals in town hall meetings with the whole company and commissioned us to help bring the goals to life.

As a first step, Joe asked me and my team to conduct an in-depth research study to better understand the barriers to progress. Our surveys and focus groups revealed a direct connection between how leaders enabled a "speak-up culture" and how successfully women and minorities advanced. Leaders who fostered more inclusive teams, where everyone felt more welcome and able to contribute, enjoyed better business results. But overall, there was work to do in ensuring that all Covidien leaders understood how to unlock the insights from their teams and create an environment where everyone could succeed.

One initiative we led helped achieve Joe's goals in tangible ways. We surveyed employees to identify a handful of exceptional, inclusive leaders at Covidien locations around the world who were already excelling in the market by empowering and building diverse teams. Then we conducted a long series of in-depth interviews with those leaders to uncover how they operated. We looked for commonalities and strategies that seemed to work and codified them so their peers could study exactly what they did that worked so well.

It turned out that the secrets of these inclusive leaders weren't very complicated. The best leaders did some incredibly simple but powerfully effective things. Many devoted long hours to getting to know each person on their team. They met often and talked not just about work but about their families, their goals, their passions. These relationships allowed the leaders to solicit the best feedback and input from those individuals. And when leaders made that kind of effort with employees of a different gender or ethnicity, the work bore even greater fruit. Having gotten to know people personally, leaders could recognize when someone wasn't happy or was getting sidelined in a meeting and rectify the situation. Perhaps most interesting, the leaders who spent the most time focused on supporting and getting to know their teams experienced the best financial results.

The analysis of good, inclusive leadership at the company established the foundation of a model for training and encouraging others to do the same. Thanks to positive peer pressure, peer-to-peer training, and a sustained focus on inclusion, in a short time Joe saw a measurable impact on employee engagement, creativity, and innovation.

I recently had the privilege to meet with a group of leaders who had been part of the Covidien program at the time. They all told me they had been changed by the experience and were building on that success and momentum in the new merged company.

Business leaders from the United States and around the world have much to learn from efforts like these. Most important, American executives must understand that true diversity is *not* simply about meeting numerical quotas. Nor is it about the old vision of a melting-pot America where people of varied backgrounds became homogenized components of a single monolithic culture. It's about creating a climate in which people who cross traditional lines in many directions are able to feel accepted and appreciated when they share *everything* that makes them who they are.

The Politics of Diversity: Leading in a More Complicated World

Political leaders, too, must learn to respond to the changing demographics of America. They can no longer continue to appeal solely to narrow demographic blocks. In the past, gerrymandered election districts and low voter turnout (especially in midterm elections) have allowed some politicians to get away with doubling down on familiar divisions along lines of race, gender, and class. When group identity lines are rigid and people rarely venture outside those lines, identity politics pays dividends, especially for certain political leaders who belong to the dominant demographic group. That clearly happened in the 2016 election of Trump.

Thinly disguised appeals to racial prejudice have long been a staple of partisan politics. Indeed, some political operatives have more or less openly boasted about their ability to evoke racial anxieties and resentments through the artful use of code words. Way back in 1981, consultant Lee Atwater explained in a shockingly callous and offensive interview how the language of anti-black politics had evolved over the years:

> *You start out in 1954 by saying, "Nigger, nigger, nigger." By 1968 you can't say "nigger"—that hurts you, backfires. So you say stuff like, uh, "forced busing," "states' rights," and all that*

stuff, and you're getting so abstract. Now, you're talking about cutting taxes, and all these things you're talking about are totally economic things and a by-product of them is, blacks get hurt worse than whites... "We want to cut this" is much more abstract than even the busing thing, uh, and a hell of a lot more abstract than "Nigger, nigger."[15]

The impact of Atwater's approach was far-reaching, and the effects can still be seen today. Atwater himself was a master of using white racial anger on behalf of political candidates. Working for presidential candidate George H. W. Bush in 1988, Atwater vowed he would "rip the bark off the little bastard," referring to opponent Michael Dukakis. Atwater achieved his goal in part through an infamous ad blaming Dukakis for crimes committed by Willie Horton, a Massachusetts convict who'd escaped while on furlough from prison. At the time, all fifty states had similar furlough programs, so attacking the governor for the Massachusetts program was arguably unfair. But Atwater pledged to make Willie Horton into Dukakis's "running mate," and he created a campaign ad using the most frightening picture available, showing Horton after several weeks in solitary confinement, looking crazed and deranged, with an untrimmed Afro and bristling beard. The ads helped crush Dukakis's candidacy, and for decades afterward politicians lived in terror of being "Willie Horton'ed" by their opponents.[16]

Similar appeals to racial fear and anger have been employed by other politicians over the years. In 1990, consultant Alex Castellanos, sometimes called "father of the modern attack ad," helped North Carolina senator Jesse Helms win a tight reelection race against an African American opponent with his notorious "white hands" commercial, in which an angry white worker crumples up a job rejection letter that he has received, according to the narrator, because "they had to give it to a minority."[17]

These thinly disguised racial messages—sometimes referred to as "dog whistles," since they send signals that are particularly audible to those whose ears are trained to hear them—have been subject to increasing criticism over the years. Yet some politicians continue to employ them.

In early 2016, Maine governor Paul LePage described the causes of his state's heroin epidemic this way: "These are guys with the name D-Money, Smoothie, Shifty—these type of guys that come from Connecticut and New York. They come up here, they sell their heroin, then they go back home. Incidentally, half the time they impregnate a young white girl before they leave, which is a real sad thing because then we have another issue that we've got to deal with down the road." Later, LePage tried to deny that his remarks had any racial overtones: "I don't know if they're white, black, Asian," he said. "I don't know."[18] However, it's doubtful that LePage would have made comments like this if he'd been accustomed to running for office in a state with more electoral diversity: Maine's population is 95 percent white, and African Americans amount to just around 1 percent of the total.

Perhaps no one has used dog whistles to greater effect than Donald Trump, who throughout his campaign didn't hesitate to employ attacks on Mexicans, Muslims, and other minorities. When Trump criticized opponent Jeb Bush for "speaking Spanish" during a visit to McAllen, Texas, Bush shot back, "Those are dog whistle terms; he knows what he's doing. These are very divisive terms. If we're going to win elections, we need to be much more open, open and optimistic, rather than sending signals that prey on people's angst."[19]

Trump may have won but Bush was right about the future of

electoral politics in the United States. With more and more people claiming mixed-race identities or crossing dividing lines through acquired diversity, and, in particular, as the pressures exerted by demographic change continue to mount, the divide-and-conquer strategy will become increasingly ineffective.

America is on the verge of minority-majority status, and no national leader will capture the support of the electorate long term without embracing today's hugely important new voting blocks. This will be a massive challenge for leaders of both parties in the post-Trump world. Nevertheless, the practical political reasons for our leaders to accept and leverage difference are overwhelming.

Diversity is also crucial to our national effectiveness in shaping and executing public policies. In a world where the United States can no longer dictate terms to other nations, only embracing both inherent and acquired diversity will enable our leaders to understand and empathize with the aspirations of people everywhere and therefore work with them more effectively. A diverse US State Department will be in a better position to address issues ranging from youthful revolts in the Arab world to gay rights in Russia and sub-Saharan Africa; a diverse Supreme Court will have the breadth of perspective to make wiser decisions regarding social issues from voting rights and entitlement reform to marriage equality and abortion.

A few pioneers are paving the way. In New York City, Mayor Bill de Blasio is walking a political tightrope few before him have attempted. A white man with a black wife and biracial children, he captured City Hall in 2013 by reaching across ethnic lines. In fact, many savvy observers credited de Blasio's victory in a hotly contested Democratic primary race to a television commercial featuring his son, Dante. Looking directly into the camera, fifteen-year-old Dante—sporting a stylish, oversize Afro— praised candidate de Blasio's policy proposals, then concluded,

"Bill de Blasio will be a mayor for every New Yorker, no matter where they live or what they look like, and I'd say that even if he weren't my dad." The ad's appeal to inclusion struck a responsive chord in thousands of New Yorkers and helped sweep de Blasio to victory.[20]

De Blasio's commitment to diversity isn't just skin-deep. For years, he has sought to forge genuine connections across racial and ethnic lines, the better to grasp the challenges facing the marginalized and the poor in a city of millionaires. A typical story recounts how de Blasio, while serving as New York's public advocate, became close friends with Reginald and Katherine Wilson. De Blasio had visited the Wilsons, an African American couple living in a tenth-floor East Harlem apartment, during a 2013 tour of the neighborhood to discuss housing issues. Their meeting led to an impromptu sleepover and a lasting friendship. Since de Blasio has become mayor, the Wilsons have stayed in touch with him, occasionally offering advice on issues ranging from policing strategy to the threat of Ebola.[21]

De Blasio's acquired diversity has been a powerful political asset. However, as mayor, de Blasio struggled to establish policy consensus on some of today's most divisive issues. When the death of Eric Garner thrust police violence onto the front burner of New York politics, de Blasio assumed that the growing racial diversity of the police department would help ensure support for his reform efforts. (Since 2010, a majority of the officers patrolling New York streets have been racial minorities.) Some cops have indeed backed de Blasio's criticisms of police misconduct, but more have rejected them. "What it comes down to is that most cops are 'blue' before they're anything else," says retired NYPD detective sergeant Joe Giacalone. "That's what [de Blasio] failed to take into consideration."[22]

Thanks to controversies like this one, polls from late 2015, two years into de Blasio's mayoral term, showed his support among New York's white voters shrinking even as blacks and Hispanics remained in his corner. Ironically, the mayor—himself a white man—is being forced to hold neighborhood town hall meetings and community dialogues in an effort to build bridges with New York's white population. It's too soon to tell how successful these coalition-forging efforts will be. De Blasio's story illustrates the political power and importance of acquired diversity—as well as the challenges of applying it effectively in a polarized, fractious society.

Even as de Blasio struggles to pioneer his own path, other prominent national leaders, from Bernie Sanders to Nikki Haley, Elizabeth Warren to Cory Booker, are seeking their own ways to embody our nation's changing identity.

In the 2016 presidential primary race, Jeb Bush ran television commercials that started with an image of the American flag, then quickly shifted to the candidate, speaking Spanish as he praises the value of Hispanic culture. "Hispanics contribute every day more to our culture [and] are an integral part of the American dream," Bush says in the ads. Soon his Mexican-born wife, Columba, chimes in: "You know, but at the end it's just that, you know—faith, friends, and family." Some Latinos responded favorably, but other Republicans questioned whether the overtly ethnic appeal made Bush less "patriotic."[23]

Bush's rival Marco Rubio, a son of Cuban American immigrants, built a successful political career around his bifurcated image as an assimilated Latino with both a proud ethnic heritage and mainstream American tastes: "Celebrating Noche Buena with lechon asado—Christmas Eve with marinated pork—and then watching the Miami Dolphins on New Year's Day. Speaking Spanish on Univision, English on Fox. Riffing on rap and dancing to Cuban music."[24] Unfortunately for Rubio, this appeal failed to translate nationally during the 2016 presidential race.

The largely white Republican primary electorate failed to turn out for him, just as they failed to support Jeb Bush.

On the Democratic side, presidential candidate Bernie Sanders—a white Jewish man representing Vermont, one of America's whitest states—reached out to the leaders of the Black Lives Matter movement, increased minority representation on his campaign staff to more than 30 percent, and invoked his own Jewish heritage in an October 2015 speech in which he called for an end to anti-Islamic rhetoric and racial prejudice.[25] His efforts to embody diversity appeared to be sincere, but they were also politically expedient, since no Democrat can hope to win the party's nomination without significant minority votes.

Nikki Haley, the US Ambassador to the United Nations and former Republican governor of South Carolina, who is the daughter of Sikh immigrants, has spoken about how her own family was subjected to racial prejudice, describing how her turban-wearing father was trailed by uniformed officers while peacefully shopping in a local fruit market. Haley was credited for bringing white and black leaders together behind the drive to remove the Confederate battle flag from the grounds of the statehouse in the wake of a mass shooting at a historically black church. She has also refused to endorse the spate of antigay, so-called religious liberty bills that have been passed by legislatures in a number of Southern states. At the same time, she has reinforced her conservative credentials by criticizing Black Lives Matter for what she views as needlessly incendiary rhetoric.[26]

Massachusetts senator Elizabeth Warren, best known as an advocate for financial reform, embraced the Black Lives Matter movement and has spoken forcefully about topics such as the importance of diversity in the federal judiciary…even as she has come under personal criticism for repeating apparently erroneous family lore about her supposed Cherokee ancestry.[27]

Cory Booker, who grew up in the only black family in a middle-class New Jersey neighborhood, served as the youthful mayor of a racially and economically divided Newark and in 2013 became just the fourth African American elected by the voters to the US Senate (following in the footsteps of Edward Brooke, Carol Moseley Braun, and Barack Obama). Now he uses that position to address issues like education, economic opportunity, and criminal justice reform from a strongly pro-diversity perspective. "I don't want to live in a post-racial society," Booker says. "I want us all to always be a rich place where we celebrate our racial, ethnic diversity."[28]

Each of these politicians is experimenting with a new style of leadership—one in which ethnic, racial, and gender diversity coexists with traditional American values and a messaging approach they hope people of every background can support. In their varied ways, they represent the future of American politics.

Our economic success and social harmony increasingly depend on our ability to understand and respect one another in all our incredible diversity. It's a diversity that encompasses an amazing variety of human types our grandparents and great-grandparents might have been baffled to encounter. It includes people like . . .

• Erica Shindler Fuller Briggs of North Charleston, South Carolina, who is weary of explaining her mixed-race background to curious but sometimes ignorant people—like the man who criticized her for not knowing what he called "her native language," Spanish, even after Erica explained, "I'm not Latino." Or the shoe store clerk who announced, "I don't believe you're black—you're too pretty to be black."

• David Kung of St. Mary's City, Maryland, a math professor with a Chinese father and an Anglo mother, who was so relieved when the census forms were changed to let him check more than one box in the "race" category that he sat down and cried.

• Ali Berlinski, who describes herself as an "American Polish Filipina living in Spain," says her family "could very well be the United Nations," and jokes, "Being a biracial kid can be hard, especially when you have a white name and a face that screams, 'I give pedicures.'"

People like these, in all their uniqueness and individuality, are the future of America—and of our world.[29]

As our national diversity continues to grow, proliferate, and deepen, it won't be possible to hide our heads in the sand or push back against the demands for recognition and respect that once-marginalized groups are making.

A new America—and a new world—are already here. Rather than pretend they don't exist, let's discover what we need to do to make the most of them. In the twenty-first century, success will be attained by those individuals, organizations, and societies that have learned to turn diversity from a challenge into a powerful asset. We Americans should commit ourselves to ensuring that our country leads the way.

6. Bias Blindness

Whoever is careless with the truth in small matters cannot be trusted with important matters.

—*Albert Einstein*

When I first conceived this book, I was amazed to find that while American media are continually filled with stories about the struggles of being such a diverse nation, there have been very few books dealing with this national challenge and opportunity. My outreach to editors at top publishing houses in New York quickly revealed why. Many of the editors replied with remarks like "Everyone knows diversity is important and good. What is there to talk about?" They mostly seemed to feel that we had somehow solved the diversity problem—that in today's America, diversity has become such a central part of our identity that everyone "gets it."

Luckily, one editor felt differently, which is why you now have the opportunity to read this book. But those other book editors have a perspective shared by many Americans. In a country with a black president and unlimited opportunities for people of every background, what more is there to talk about?

Despite the lore that describes the United States as a melting pot that absorbs people of all backgrounds, America's relationship with diversity has never been easy. In the past century, we achieved significant progress in opening up economic and social opportunities to women and members of ethnic, racial, and religious minorities who were once excluded from the mainstream. Yet we have struggled to fully accept those changes.

We may not be fighting the biggest battles, as we did in the sixties and seventies, but our national commitment to diversity remains complex and controversial. Anxiety over the changing face of our nation has driven more restrictive immigration policies, laws prohibiting government offices from providing services to non-citizens or those who use languages other than English, and a backlash against affirmative action, women's rights, gay rights, and other assertions of value in diversity.

At the same time, many white Americans mistakenly assume that bias and the barriers it raises are a thing of the past, making continued efforts to encourage diversity unnecessary. It's actually quite rare today for people to acknowledge their biases or to say what they may really be thinking. But the fact that we don't talk about it doesn't mean it doesn't exist. In fact, we're facing an epidemic of *diversity denial*. It's a reality I personally struggle with because so many people in my own world seem to defy this trend, but the data proving the point is overwhelming. The truth is that many Americans find it difficult to see or acknowledge the very real obstacles confronted by minorities and women. Because we largely deny that racism still exists, we have never fully come to grips with our history of institutionalized racism. After the civil rights battles of the 1960s were won, there was no truth and reconciliation commission to help Americans heal the wounds; no systemic, thoughtful approach to recovering and moving on from centuries of conflict; no reparations paid to undo, at least partially, the oppression and exploitation millions of Americans had suffered. So it should not surprise us that we find ourselves today reliving the battles many Americans thought were settled.

Donald Trump's hostility toward minorities—expressed through his denunciations of Mexican immigrants as drug dealers and rapists, his efforts to ban Muslims entering the United States, and his long history of questioning Barack Obama's citizenship and religion—clearly appeals to some aggrieved white voters who saw Trump as the only leading figure willing to speak the truth. At least one poll during the 2016 election found that more than 60 percent of Trump's supporters agreed that Obama was neither American born nor a Christian—both generally considered "fringe" beliefs with no factual basis.[1]

Of course, Trump drew support from women as well as men, and their motives were surely varied. But as journalist Eduardo Porter put it, "By far [Trump's] most solid support comes from less educated, lower-income white men."[2] Trump's complaints that Americans are no longer "winners" took on a racial and ethnic tinge in this context.

Thus, when Trump spoke of "taking our country back," many among his supporters and his detractors assumed he was referring to taking it back from a "foreign-born" black president and from the demographic trends that are transforming America into a minority-majority nation. After his election, many on the left seemed surprised, even shocked, by Trump's win. But there's really nothing shocking about it. He tapped into widely held attitudes that have been there all along, albeit under the surface. Many Americans are intensely suspicious of and uncomfortable with the diverse nation we've become.

It's not just in politics where this is evident. Rosalind Brewer was one of the most successful black women executives in the United States. As the former CEO of Sam's Club, one of the country's most important retailers, she oversaw six hundred fifty stores and tens of thousands of employees. In a 2015 CNN interview, Brewer talked about her commitment to ensuring diversity on her leadership team and among her suppliers. After all, women and minorities make up a significant part of the Sam's Club customer base, and it's to be applauded that Brewer uses her position of influence to make sure people of every background have a chance.

Brewer's remarks were pretty innocuous. "My executive team is very diverse, and I make that a priority," she told interviewer Poppy Harlow.

> *I demand it of my team and within the structure. And then, every now and then, you have to nudge your partners, and you have to speak up and speak out. And I try to use my platform for that...I try to set an example. I mentor many women inside my company and outside the company because I think it's important...*
>
> *I talk to my suppliers about it. Just today we met with a supplier, and the entire other side of the table was all Caucasian male. That was interesting. I decided not to talk about it directly with [the supplier's] folks in the room because there were actually no females, like, levels down. So I'm going to place a call to him.*[3]

Both Brewer's comments and her actions as CEO reflect the values of most American business leaders today who recognize the usefulness of building teams that include both genders and every ethnic and racial group. But the explosion of online vitriol in response to Brewer's remarks made clear the massive divide that remains on issues like this. White shoppers took to social media to decry her comments as racist and antiwhite, using the hashtag #BoycottRacistSamsClub. To many, the idea that Ms. Brewer was helping to promote minority employees meant she was discriminating against whites. One Twitter user wrote, "As a White person I need a safe space from racist blacks. I do not feel safe at Sam's Club." To his credit, Doug McMillon, the CEO of Walmart (which is the parent corporation of Sam's Club), immediately defended Ms. Brewer as having articulated some important goals of the company, not merely her own ideology, and expressed complete support for her.

I was blown away by this incident. It's hard to imagine a similar backlash to the same comments if they had been made by a white male leader. But articulated by a black female, the effort to promote diversity was threatening to some whites. They seem to view diversity as a kind of zero-sum game. Of course, promoting diversity doesn't mean excluding or discriminating against whites, but that view persists. No matter how open we think we are as a nation, in reality we remain deeply divided along racial lines.

Despite the undeniable progress we've made in some areas, we are still far from an all-inclusive nation. We're now at a crucial crossroads, facing the question: Are we ready at last to live up to our national creed of *e pluribus unum*, or will we turn our backs on that proud heritage and surrender to xenophobia, narrow-mindedness, and fear?

Seeing in Black and White

For many Americans, the election of our first black president signaled the historic completion of a long and painful journey. Some pundits announced the arrival of a post-racial era in America—one in which true meritocracy had finally conquered distinctions of race, gender, generation, and culture. The inauguration of Barack Obama meant: "Problem solved."

But after two terms of Obama's presidency, many Americans were disillusioned. His presidency brought out both the best and the worst in us. And in a way, the advent of social media, which has exploded in the years since Obama became president, has helped to lay bare what has been hidden behind a veil of political correctness for most of my lifetime. It has emboldened people to say what they've always really thought, and some of those thoughts are extremely ugly. America appears divided between those willing to recognize, acknowledge, and dismantle our remaining discriminatory barriers and those who deny their very existence. It's one of the big causes of our national polarization and of the enormous difficulties in forging and implementing commonsense solutions to our economic and social challenges.

The widely publicized deaths of Trayvon Martin, Sandra Bland, Eric Garner, Michael Brown, Tamir Rice, Laquan McDonald, Walter Scott, Freddie Gray, and others symbolize these profound divides. In addition to exposing serious biases in policing, these tragedies shed much-needed light on the biases black Americans deal with every day. Triggered by these episodes, the Black Lives Matter movement has surged into a powerful national political and social force. Founded by three women—Alicia Garza, Opal Tometi, and Patrisse Cullors—Black Lives Matter has been hugely effective in raising public awareness of the real challenges faced by black Americans. Like the civil rights movement of the 1960s, the feminist movement of the 1970s and '80s, and the gay rights movement of the 1990s, Black Lives Matter has sparked controversy and resistance. Not everyone would agree with all of its positions or its tactics, but it has served America well by putting some important issues about racial and social justice and inclusion on the national agenda for the first time in many years.

Consider the economic realities surrounding race. Black Americans face daunting odds. The 2000 census showed that a black family with an income of $60,000 or more is more likely to live in a poor neighborhood than a white family with an income of $20,000.[4] Think about what that means in terms of access to good schools, health-care facilities, libraries, parks, museums, and other valuable amenities that improve one's quality of life and help make personal advancement possible.

Another startling number: As of 2009, the ratio of average family wealth held by white families to that held by black families was 19 to 1—a significantly *worse* ratio than at any time during the previous fifteen years. (Hispanic Americans didn't do much better: The ratio of white family wealth to that of Hispanic families was about 15 to 1.)[5] Think about the huge disadvantage this places on a young person growing up in a black family, with access to just a fraction of the resources that many white youngsters take for granted.

Add to this the disproportionate arrests and imprisonment of black Americans, and you have cemented the barriers to accessing the American dream for a substantial segment of our society. Sadly, it's taken a series of horrific incidents, many of them caught on film, and a well-coordinated political movement to create a general awareness that significant, entrenched racial bias persists.

Perhaps not surprisingly, Black Lives Matter has triggered a backlash not too dissimilar from the reaction to Rosalind Brewer's comments about diversity at Sam's Club. Conservative politicians like Mike Huckabee and media personalities like Glenn Beck have promoted the opposing slogan All Lives Matter. In August 2015, Beck organized an All Lives Matter rally in Birmingham, Alabama, that reportedly was attended by twenty thousand people.

A slogan like All Lives Matter seems innocent and inclusive enough. But in reality it's shorthand for a denial of the racial disparities that the Black Lives Matter protests are meant to shed light on. Many white Americans chafe at the idea that minorities suffer disproportionate challenges. They themselves feel aggrieved and deprived. The fundamental problem with All Lives Matter is its disingenuousness. It purports to promote unity while in fact it promotes denial of the very real and unique issues black Americans continue to face.

It's sad but unsurprising that when activist Mercutio Southall Jr. interrupted a Donald Trump campaign rally in Birmingham, Alabama, with shouts of "Black lives matter," the crowd responded with chants of "All lives matter"—and with a violent assault on Southall. CNN video cameras captured images of Southall being kicked and punched by Trump supporters. On Fox News the next day, Trump seemed to justify the attack. "Maybe he should have been roughed up, because it was absolutely disgusting what he was doing."[6]

Of course, all political campaigns have to deal with protestors and hecklers. Most manage to do so without resorting to brutality.

Many in law enforcement have also taken issue with Black Lives Matter and continue to resist demands for change. At the December 2014 funeral of a New York City policeman, many officers angrily turned their backs on Mayor Bill de Blasio in retaliation for his statement expressing empathy for black families who feared the police. Subsequently, many in law enforcement, including FBI Director James Comey, speculated that widespread criticism of police tactics could lead to a "Ferguson effect" that would embolden and empower criminals. (In fact, crime statistics strongly suggest that the Ferguson effect is basically a myth.)[7] It's also widely believed that NYPD officers went on an unofficial, unspoken strike in retaliation for the mayor's remarks. In the months following the murder of two police officers in New York City in the summer of 2015, summonses and tickets issued by officers fell by 94 percent and overall arrests dropped by 66 percent.

Under the circumstances, black Americans can't be blamed for wondering, "What will it take for our grievances as a community to be taken seriously by the rest of the country?"

These gulfs in perception and perspective are significant and measurable. A Pew Research study found that 80 percent of black

Americans felt the police shooting of an unarmed teen raised "important issues about race"—but just 37 percent of whites agreed.[8] A similar 2014 survey timed to coincide with the fiftieth anniversary of the Civil Rights Act of 1964 found that few white Americans believe that unfair treatment of black citizens is still prevalent in their communities. While 54 percent of blacks (and 40 percent of Hispanics) said they'd seen biased behavior while on the job, just 16 percent of whites agreed. Similarly, while 48 percent of blacks (and 30 percent of Hispanics) reported biased treatment in connection with elections and voting, only 13 percent of whites shared that perception.[9]

The problem for the nation is how we will make progress if we're unwilling to acknowledge the problem.

Color Blindness: When Denial Becomes a Form of Racism

Many white Americans claim that they believe in and practice "color blindness" in their interactions with people from varied backgrounds. Unfortunately, we are fooling ourselves; practically all Americans (I absolutely include myself here) harbor biased attitudes that lurk just below the surface of consciousness. But even if it were true that most white Americans are color blind, this wouldn't necessarily be a good thing. It may seem counterintuitive, but because color blindness denies the reality that people of color face significant obstacles in our society, it is actually a kind of racism.

I think in some ways I was color blind as a young person. I had close, loving relationships with people of many races and backgrounds, and I thought nothing of it. But as I got older, I realized that it wasn't possible to ignore the inevitable issues of race between us. Fortunately, as I mentioned earlier, my school stepped in at a critical time to encourage me and my fellow students to consider the implications and challenges of difference. I learned that acknowledging difference in order to honor the experience of another person and learn from it is fundamental to building bridges and crossing lines. I'm profoundly grateful for the opportunity because it taught me not to fear the conversations but to welcome them. And I've been having those conversations ever since.

But sadly, we have not valued this open dialogue nearly enough, and in its place has risen a virulent and insidious willful blindness. The All Lives Matter backlash is a good example of how this subtle form of denial works. The All Lives Matter movement exists to deny the validity of the complaints offered by the Black Lives Matter movement. In effect, this supposedly color-blind slogan tells people of color, "Your children are *not* at risk of harm at the hands of police officers—no matter what the statistics and the tragic news stories indicate. And so your demands for change and justice must be ignored." In a country where, in fact, black lives are routinely treated as if they do not matter—or at least matter much less than white lives—this message is false, cruel, and divisive.

The misguided commitment to color blindness—as well as its corollaries, "gender blindness," "sexual orientation blindness," and other similar forms of willful ignorance—grows out of the desire to believe that bias, discrimination, and injustice are things of the past. The allure of this myth is understandable. Naturally we Americans want to cling to the belief that our country is the land of opportunity where everyone can get a fair shake. But to accept this belief is to tacitly deny the barriers others face, making it impossible to build trust across dividing lines.

Many people feel deeply threatened by the ideas that our

nation is not a true meritocracy and that there is automatic privilege that comes with race. We all like to think we've earned everything we have and that we're all the same. But it's simply, empirically untrue. As a white person, I have had and continue to have the privilege my majority status accords me. I absolutely don't know what it's like to encounter discrimination every day. But on a human level I can acknowledge the challenges faced by minority Americans and I can take part in honest dialogue about them. It's essential to our future that we all do this. Continuing to deny the reality of millions of our fellow citizens is as tragic as it is misguided.

Some of America's most powerful political and business leaders—people who, in other circumstances, have shown themselves to be intelligent and capable—have fallen into this trap. Larry Summers is a noted economist with a distinguished career in public service, including stints as the chief economist of the World Bank, secretary of the Treasury in the Clinton administration, and president of Harvard University. But his brilliance didn't serve him well in 2005 when he suggested at an academic conference that "innate differences" between men and women might explain why relatively few women have successful careers in math and science. In fact, of course, a significant body of research has substantiated what thousands of women have observed through painful personal experience—that major social, economic, organizational, attitudinal, and political barriers discourage girls and women from pursuing educational opportunities and career pathways in the so-called STEM fields of science, technology, engineering, and mathematics. Whenever the topic arises, I remember one of my early math teachers who never *once*, the entire year, called on a girl in my class unless it was to embarrass her.

It might be comforting to blame "innate differences" rather

than institutional barriers. After all, that belief exonerates those in power from any responsibility to recognize and work to reduce those barriers. But while the belief in a gender-blind society might be comforting, it's far from accurate—which Summers certainly should have known. The uproar that followed his remarks was entirely predictable and understandable.

In 2014, Satya Nadella, the newly elevated CEO of Microsoft, made some awkward remarks that appeared to dismiss the seriousness of the gender pay discrepancy in high-tech industry when he responded to a question from interviewer (and college president) Maria Klawe at a conference: "It's not really about asking for the raise, but knowing and having faith that the system will actually give you the right raises as you go along." His comments made the front pages of many papers, and many women reacted strongly on social media.

To his credit, Nadella later apologized for his remarks, saying, "I answered that question completely wrong. Without a doubt I wholeheartedly support programs at Microsoft and in the industry that bring more women into technology and close the pay gap...And when it comes to career advice on getting a raise when you think it's deserved, Maria's advice was the right advice. If you think you deserve a raise, you should just ask."[10] It's worth noting that Microsoft has recently taken an industry-leading stance on diversity by proactively auditing and equalizing the pay of their female employees.[11]

The most recent leader to fall into this trap is Michael Moritz, chairman of Sequoia Capital and one of the most prominent figures in the world of Silicon Valley venture capital. Asked in a Bloomberg interview why his firm has no women investing partners, Moritz proceeded to claim that Sequoia is "blind to somebody's sex, to their religion, to their background"—which of course leads to the obvious question: If this is so, how has

Sequoia managed to avoid hiring any women? Moritz then compounded the problem by claiming that his firm would be happy to hire women, but adding, "What we're not prepared to do is to lower our standards," clearly implying that women, as a group and as individuals, are less capable than men.[12]

In a way, Moritz's comments performed a valuable public service. They plainly revealed the underlayer of bias that lies just below the surface of claims to be "blind" to issues of diversity. In a world where people from different backgrounds do *not* have the same opportunities to excel, "blindness" simply isn't good enough—and claiming blindness is really a subtle way of clinging to the injustices built into the status quo. As psychologist Monnica T. Williams, director of the Center for Mental Health Disparities at the University of Louisville has put it, "Colorblindness has helped make race into a taboo topic that polite people cannot openly discuss. And if you can't talk about it, you can't understand it, much less fix the racial problems that plague our society."[13]

Everyone's a Little Bit Racist

When the puppet musical *Avenue Q* hit Broadway in 2003, the irreverent song "Everyone's a Little Bit Racist" stirred up controversy with its cheeky lyrics. The words hit a nerve because they are largely true. We all carry real biases that impact everything we do, individually and collectively. Most of those biases are unconscious. Today relatively few Americans harbor conscious hostilities toward people of differing racial, ethnic, or religious backgrounds. The vast majority share Dr. Martin Luther King Jr.'s dream of a nation where people "will not be judged by the color of their skin but by the content of their character." Most of us would like to believe that we carry out that credo in our daily lives and actions—that we relate to other people based solely on their behavior and never on biases, prejudices, or stereotypes.

Unfortunately, it's probably not true. Even people with strongly egalitarian value systems and a strong personal commitment to color-blind attitudes hold unconscious biases that impact their thoughts, emotions, and reactions—and, inevitably, their behaviors. I include myself in this company, of course.

Conscious and unconscious biases have a profound effect on our society and are part of a complex tapestry of challenges all women and minorities face. For example, in health care, studies have shown that black patients receive less adequate care than white patients for chronic illnesses such as diabetes and heart disease, contributing to persistent disparities in life expectancy and overall health.[14] Shop owners and other retailers routinely track, question, and otherwise harass customers of color, despite studies that show they are no more likely than white customers to commit offenses such as shoplifting.[15] Experiments have revealed that job applications bearing "black-sounding" names like Jamal and Taisha are routinely discarded by human resource officers at far higher rates than *identical* applications with "white-sounding" names like Peter and Katherine.[16] And despite laws against discrimination in housing, many real estate brokers still engage in "steering" practices that shunt prospective home buyers or renters toward specific neighborhoods based on their race.

One of the most striking demonstrations of the persistence of these unconscious biased responses is found in the research of Project Implicit, founded in 1998 by Tony Greenwald from the University of Washington, Mahzarin Banaji from Harvard University, and Brian Nosek from the University of Virginia. The project studies what it calls "implicit social cognition—thoughts and feelings outside of conscious awareness and control." To capture these unconscious responses, the scientists developed the

Implicit Association Test (IAT). It's a simple ten-minute test, administered by computer, that requires participants to rapidly associate a random assortment of "good" words (such as *joy*, *wonderful*, and *laughter*) and "bad" words (such as *agony*, *evil*, and *failure*) with faces that appear on the screen.

To test unconscious attitudes regarding race, for example, the IAT shows both black and white faces. The objective: to observe whether there is a measurable difference in the ease with which test-takers associate "good" words and "bad" words with black faces and white faces. A person with an unconscious bias against black people is able to associate a black face with a "bad" word more quickly and easily than a black face with a "good" word—and the reverse with a white face.

In the years since Project Implicit was launched, over fourteen million such tests have been administered. The results are clear: When the data are aggregated by state and charted on a map, researchers find that white people in every state of the Union are unconsciously biased to some degree. There are regional variations, such as implicit bias levels appearing stronger in the states of the Southeast and East. But as one journalist puts it, "Looking at a map like this one tells us something pretty crucial to our understanding of racial bias: It is everywhere, from north to south, from Maine to California. It is present among liberals and conservatives, men and women, young and old."[17]

The experts at Project Implicit have expanded their research to include tests that measure other forms of implicit bias—for example, in relation to Asians, Arabs, disabled people, and adherents of various religions. They've even found ways to test unconscious attitudes regarding the connection between women and various occupations that could be stereotyped as either "feminine" or "masculine."

If you're intrigued by this research, you can visit the website of Project Implicit and take one or more tests yourself.[18] You're likely to find the results eye-opening and perhaps distressing. That's what happened to Mahzarin Banaji—one of the founders of Project Implicit—when she took the test about women and careers. Her test results showed that she unconsciously linked images of females with home life rather than professional work, despite the fact that she herself had overcome such prejudices in pursuing her career in social psychology. Her spontaneous reaction to the results? "I thought to myself: Something is wrong with this damned test."[19]

Finding Our Way

Although we may not like discovering that we tend to harbor biased attitudes, a bit of reflection suggests why this is so—indeed, why it is practically inevitable. We live in a society that for centuries has been permeated by stereotyped ideas, images, and attitudes. They're woven into the fabric of our lives—into our educational system, our news media, our sources of entertainment, our economic and political structures, and our social and family lives.

Many of these are beginning to change, to reflect the more inclusive attitude toward diversity that millions of Americans now accept. But change comes slowly. Meanwhile, decades of immersion in once-traditional ways of thinking can't help but leave a deep imprint on our minds and hearts. It's that imprint that is reflected in the results recorded by Project Implicit—and that continues to influence the spontaneous emotional and psychological responses triggered by events in our daily lives.

This poses a serious challenge to people who want to embrace diversity and enjoy its benefits. It means that accepting diversity requires us to change habitual ways of thinking, feeling, and reacting. It doesn't happen overnight, and the difficulty of achieving it goes a long way toward explaining the personal and social stresses we often feel in regard to the subject of diversity.

In the last few years, many American companies have spent small fortunes trying to retrain people from their unconscious biases. We'll explore more in a later chapter why this is not the most effective strategy. But many of us, like Mahzarin, would like to rid ourselves of these biases and prevent our children from inheriting them. How can we find ways to do this?

Psychologist Monnica T. Williams, whom I quoted earlier in this chapter, recommends that we practice thinking in terms of *multiculturalism* rather than color blindness. This means recognizing, understanding, and celebrating diversity in all its forms—including differences in race, ethnicity, gender, religion, and sexual orientation. It means striving to comprehend what is meaningful, unique, and important in all these differing backgrounds and acknowledging the reality that many people have suffered as a result of conflict among diverse groups. And it means taking specific steps to deliberately nurture our own multiculturalism, including

- recognizing and valuing differences;
- teaching and learning about differences; and
- fostering personal friendships and organizational alliances.[20]

If you're thinking that multiculturalism as described by Williams sounds a lot like the acquired diversity I have focused on in this book, you're right—the two concepts have a lot in common. And the steps Williams recommends to nurture multiculturalism are useful in the process of enhancing your acquired diversity, too.

There is also evidence that parents can assist future generations in coping with and avoiding some of the unconscious biases that seem to arise so easily. In their book *NurtureShock*, journalists Po Bronson and Ashley Merryman looked at how racist views (as well as other negative traits, such as excessive aggression and cruelty) emerge in children.

One surprisingly powerful force helping to fuel the development of bias is simple silence. While the majority of nonwhite parents discuss race with their children, 75 percent of white parents never do.[21] Researchers who studied this phenomenon found that children raised in families where the parents never discussed race were more likely to draw negative conclusions about people different from themselves. This bias arose despite deliberate efforts to reduce or discourage it, such as providing the children with *Sesame Street* videos highlighting multicultural communities and families. In the absence of explicit parental conversations about race, these videos did nothing to educate children about the fact that people of every skin color and heritage are equal, worthy, and valuable.

The conclusion is obvious. In raising children, just as in adult society, "color blindness" as an ideal is both illusory and misguided. As parents who want to contribute to a world in which people of all backgrounds are respected and honored, our mission is clear. Don't ignore diversity when communicating with your kids. Instead, talk about it and teach your children to appreciate it. It's a lesson that all of us still need to learn.

My daughter Stella, who is biracial, was in nursery school when she pointed out to me that her skin was "browned" and mine was not. I was shocked that she had noticed racial differences at such a young age, and it was apparent that the subject had come up at school. While my husband and I have always worked hard to ensure she's in a diverse school environment, her French nursery school on the Upper West Side was entirely white that year. And as the white parent of an adopted black child, I certainly expected race to be a topic in our family and was prepared to talk about it, but in that moment I wasn't sure what to say, and I braced myself for something difficult. I thought of my grandmother, who would lower her voice and whisper when pointing out that a particular neighborhood had become "all black." After a moment, though, I realized that Stella had no judgments about being "browned"—she was just stating a fact, that her skin was darker than mine. So we talked about why she doesn't look like me and why that was because she was in someone else's tummy. Then we talked about how beautiful her skin is and how people are all different. And then we moved on.

Now, to be crystal clear, I'm not at all claiming I handled it perfectly, and I'm sure that when this book comes out I will face a barrage of criticism for many things. The subject of race and color has come up since, and it will most certainly come up many times in our lives. I believe it's important to honestly acknowledge who we are and to be truthful with our children about it. We don't have to be identical or deny our differences to respect each other.

I believe that if everyone spent more time asking those who are different from us to help us understand their experience, or simply acknowledged when we're uncomfortable, we might go a long way toward thinning the lines between us. The lines are real, and to deny them is dishonest. We must instead admit that they are there and that we are all complicit in reinforcing them, then work like hell to take them apart. Only then can we make progress through truth, sincerity, and humanity.

7. Outspread Wings

The outspread wings of the American eagle are broad enough to shelter all who are likely to come.
— *Frederick Douglass, "Our Composite Nationality"*

In November 2015, a group of armed militants attacked the city of Paris, killing more than a hundred innocent civilians at a concert hall and in cafés and restaurants. Almost immediately, anti-immigrant sentiment exploded in the United States. On cable news shows, hosts and guests made wild generalizations about all Muslims, insisting they were either violent extremists or tacit supporters of terrorism. Comedian Bill Maher used the word *barbaric* to describe the tenets of Islam. Within a week of the attack, dozens of US governors and mayors issued statements that they would bar any Syrian immigrants or refugees from entering their jurisdictions—positions they had zero legal authority to enforce. (This despite the fact that none of the Paris attackers appear to have been Syrian refugees. As of this writing, all the attackers who have been identified have proven to be European nationals, although one seems to have been carrying a fake or stolen Syrian passport.)[1]

Presidential candidates Donald Trump, Ben Carson, and others proposed even more extreme ideas to shut down mosques, create a database to track all Muslims in the United States, and even to halt the entry of Muslims into the United States altogether. One of the most egregious of the many appalling public statements came from David Bowers, mayor of Roanoke, Virginia. In a memo explaining why Syrians were not welcome in his city, he used the internment of Japanese Americans during World War II as a model for how we should manage apparent threats from foreigners.[2] (For the record, not only the vast majority of historians but also virtually all American political leaders have acknowledged that the internment was one of the most shameful episodes in our nation's history, as recognized by President Ronald Reagan when signing a 1988 act providing restitution for some of its surviving victims.)[3] Bowers eventually apologized for what he said were "unwise and inappropriate" statements, but the damage was done.

When I started this book, I wanted to write a positive account of promise and possibility. I felt compelled to tell a different side of the diversity story than the one we hear on the news every day. I feel very optimistic that we can overcome our differences and make real progress as a nation. And yet, in the time I have been writing, the vitriol and policy around immigration has hit a level of intensity I can't remember in my lifetime. In reality, we may be further apart on immigration than we are on any of the other issues currently dividing our politically polarized nation.

My high school classmate Sandra Grossman is one of America's leading immigration attorneys. The clients whose rights she has defended range from a female professor from Iran's University of Tehran who'd been persecuted for her political views in her homeland and later overstayed her American visa—Grossman's first case as a student at Georgetown University—to Joey Alexander, an eleven-year-old jazz piano prodigy from Jakarta, Indonesia, whose amazing musical talent enabled Grossman to successfully petition for him to receive a special O-1 visa granted only to individuals with "extraordinary ability."

But none of the legal and personal challenges that Grossman has faced have shaken her as deeply as when she first visited the Department of Homeland Security's "family detention" center in Artesia, New Mexico, in 2014. "They called it a 'family detention center,'" Grossman recalls, "but it was a jail. People were not free to come and go, and there were barbed-wire fences surrounding the buildings."[4] The average age of the children held at Artesia was six. The conditions at Artesia were so appalling that Grossman, who has "seen it all," felt shocked and heartbroken. Detainees reported sleeping eight to a room, receiving inadequate food and minimal opportunities for exercise, recreation, schooling, or medical care. American citizens convicted of heinous crimes are rarely treated so shabbily.[5] Yet the prisoners at Artesia whom Grossman and a cadre of other immigration attorneys met in order to provide them with legal services were overwhelmingly women and small children fleeing serious threats of gang violence and domestic abuse in their homelands in Latin America—desperate refugees facing life-and-death choices.

Contrary to popular assumption, the majority of immigrants currently arriving at the southern US borders have little in common with the poor Mexicans who illegally entered the country in large numbers over the last twenty-five years. In fact, since the US economic collapse of 2008, the flow of Mexicans seeking economic opportunity here has slowed dramatically. Today many of those seeking entry from Latin America are women and young children fleeing gang violence in countries like El Salvador and Guatemala, where entire town and regional governments have been taken over by armed bands dedicated to extortion, robbery, and murder. Others are victims of domestic abuse that local authorities are helpless to prevent. "Under established laws," Grossman explains, "individuals who suffer domestic abuse or who are targeted by gangs due to their relationship with a family member, for example, may qualify for protection in the US. They must also show that their own governments are unwilling or unable to help them, as well as meeting a host of other criteria. But most of the women I met with were very clear about one thing: If they were forced to go back home, they and their children would be subject to violence and even death."

Conditions in their home countries are so extreme, so perilous, that women like these are willing to brave not just the treacherous journey north but the harsh treatment they receive when they reach the borders of the "land of opportunity." Many are held for days in unheated border facilities known as *las hieleras*— the freezers—where there have even been reports of babies dying in their mothers' arms.

Those that made it to the detention centers in places like Artesia faced months of uncertainty in environments recognized as completely inappropriate for children. Grossman explains that a federal judge in California found in 2015 that Artesia and other facilities like it violated a nationwide agreement on minimum standards for detaining children. Lack of schooling, limited food, and filthy conditions were widely documented.

"Applying for and obtaining asylum is an extremely difficult process," Grossman says. "Persons expressing a fear of persecution will be turned back at the US border unless they can pass an initial 'credible fear' interview. If they pass, they are placed in removal proceedings before an administrative judge from the Department of Justice. Without legal defense, the women and children detained at Artesia often did not have a chance, even if their persecution claims were valid."

Those at Artesia who passed the credible fear test might be released on bond to await a final hearing months or years in the future—although Grossman reports that would-be immigrants were sometimes asked to pay exorbitant bonds of $20,000 to

$30,000 rather than the typical $1,500 demanded of a criminal suspect not regarded as a flight risk. Some were forced to wear ankle monitor bracelets to enable authorities to track their whereabouts, adding a visible stigma to the widespread social prejudice they already faced as "illegals."

The harsh treatment at the border was intentional. The program was designed by the Obama administration to be so awful as to deter future refugees from coming. Jeh Johnson, the secretary of Homeland Security, told a Senate committee in 2014, "Our message to this group is simple: We will send you back."[6]

The trouble is, Grossman explained, "He was stating a policy that violates national and international law. And that policy is the reason we were holding toddlers in jail cells without adequate food or schooling, and failing to give their parents a fair opportunity to work with attorneys to present their cases before a judge." In Grossman's judgment, the refugees arriving here are not breaking the law or arriving as "illegals." It was in fact our own federal government, not the would-be immigrants, violating the law. "US asylum laws are very clear," Grossman says:

> *Any person who is facing persecution at home due to race, nationality, religion, political views, or membership in a particular social group is legally entitled to seek asylum in this country. And the US government is explicitly forbidden to force such asylum seekers to return home. The same rights are also protected by international laws like the UN Convention against Torture.*

Grossman isn't advocating a policy of open, uncontrolled borders. "We are a nation of laws," she says:

> *We do have to respect the immigration laws and protect the integrity of our national borders. And we have to be fair to the*

people who have been waiting in their homelands to get visas and other documents needed to enter the United States legally. But by the same token, we have to apply the laws on our books. And that's where the Obama administration has fallen short. They wanted to strengthen their case for immigration reform by showing that they were "tough" on border issues. But they ended up crossing the line by actually violating not just the laws but the ideals that are supposed to guide American immigration policy.

Recent court rulings have affirmed Grossman's argument and the government's responsibility to abide by immigration laws. In November 2014, a federal judge ordered Artesia closed. The administration complied mainly by transferring the women and children detained there to a similar facility in Texas. A series of searing articles detailing the appalling conditions at the center triggered action from Congress. A group of thirty-two lawmakers wrote to the president asking for another approach. The letter's lead author, Rep. Zoe Lofgren (D-CA), said, "While closing the Artesia facility is a step in the right direction, the fact remains that shifting women and little children from one detention center to another does little to mitigate the serious concerns regarding family detention that members of Congress, including myself, have voiced to the administration but have yet to receive a response."[7]

The Obama era, while troubling on this front, looks positively quaint compared to the aggressive pace of deportations under Trump.

The legal barriers that we Americans are placing in the way of those seeking to enter our country are still enormous. And as the ever-changing political climate evolves, the public anxiety, fear, and anger directed at immigrants have ratcheted up by several notches. Nightly images of thousands of refugees from Syria and Iraq seeking asylum in Western Europe from the violence of ISIS, the so-called Islamic State, have sparked worries about the impact on the United States from an influx of Middle Easterners with unfamiliar languages, customs, and religions—as well as fears that some of the immigrants, many of them victims of terrorism, might themselves harbor terrorist ambitions.

"Immigrants are an easy target," Grossman observes. "They don't have the power to vote and are often afraid to defend themselves. They live under the radar. When you blame people who are not Americans for the problems we face in this country, you are taking an easy out."

Grossman's commitment to defending the rights of refugees is intensely personal to her. Her father, a student activist in Chile under the Allende regime, was forced to go into hiding in 1973 after the coup that brought Augusto Pinochet to power. His father, David Grossman—Sandra Grossman's grandfather—was detained, questioned, and tortured by officials of the junta. With help from the Dutch embassy in Chile, Sandra's young parents fled to Holland, where they lived for almost a decade and where Sandra and her sister were born. In 1982, when their father was offered a job as a professor at Washington College of Law, the family moved to the United States. Sandra Grossman became a proud US citizen in 1995 at the age of twenty-one—and a crusading attorney a few years later.

"So not only am I myself an immigrant to this country," Grossman says, "but so were the members of my whole family—and my parents were also political refugees." Assisting the next generation of asylum seekers is Grossman's way of giving back to her adopted homeland—by pushing it to live up to the high ideals of tolerance, acceptance, and diversity that are supposed to define it.

It's a sad reality that attorneys like Grossman have so many tough battles to fight on behalf of the kinds of people America was founded to welcome. Our nation's openness to accepting immigrants—always partial and fluctuating thanks to the shifting tides of political and social change—has recently suffered a series of painful setbacks.

Of course, our political leaders on both sides of the aisle continue to pay lip service to the ideal of America as a country that welcomes people from around the world. The Republican immigration-reform principles released in January 2014 noted the thousands of foreign students studying at US universities and called for retaining "these exceptional individuals to help grow our economy."[9] From his perch as leader of the Democratic Party, President Obama said in his 2014 State of the Union speech, "When people come here to fulfill their dreams—to study, invent, contribute to our culture—they make our country a more attractive place for businesses to locate and create jobs for everybody."[10] But at the same time, the Obama administration was responsible for imprisoning women and children at the border. Republican anti-immigrant rhetoric may be particularly dramatic, but neither party has lived up to the ideals of a welcoming nation they publicly espouse.

Fears and confusion stoked by the media and opportunistic political leaders have obscured the facts about immigration—the benefits it provides to our economy and the social and cultural richness that immigrants add to the American mosaic. As a result, US immigration policy has become a highly charged political issue. And as Sandra Grossman's experiences show, our readiness to welcome those who seek to contribute to our nation has become less and less certain.

Immigration and American Success

When we hear the word *immigrant*, most of us imagine someone destitute and desperate. But changing economic and social trends are continually altering the mix of people who seek to join American society, and the stereotype of the penniless Mexican as the typical newcomer to the United States is badly outdated.

"In recent years," Grossman notes, "many of the Latin American immigrants I've worked with have been well-educated, prosperous business owners and professionals from countries like Venezuela, Mexico, and Ecuador. Some have sought asylum in the United States for political reasons. Others have obtained work-related visas, created companies, and made substantial investments here. Far from being poor or a drain on the economy, I've heard that these hard-working immigrants are driving an increase in property values in places like Miami!"

Grossman's anecdotal observation is borne out by statistical evidence. Research shows that immigrant families have average incomes around the same as those enjoyed by native-born American families (though of course, some are higher, some lower). Almost half of all immigrant workers are in white-collar occupations, and 46 percent have at least some college education. As a result, fears that immigrant workers are likely to drag down overall wage rates in the United States are basically unfounded. A thorough analysis of research into this question by the Economic Policy Institute concluded, "The most rigorous work on the effect of immigration on wages finds extremely modest effects for native-born workers, including those with low levels of education."[11]

To the extent that incoming workers *do* impact US labor markets, the effect is largely due to the failure of political leaders to pass comprehensive immigration reforms that would allow all residents in this country to obtain legal status and documentation. Lacking "papers" that give them a foothold in the United States, workers in the shadows have no bargaining power and therefore can be exploited by unscrupulous business owners. Reforms to immigration rules would prevent such abuse, create more opportunities for US workers, and help protect the rights of all workers, immigrants and natives alike.

So the stereotypes of immigrants as poor, lacking skills, and depressing overall wages are generally false. In fact, immigrants contribute enormously to the US economy. They constitute 16 percent of the national labor force and 18 percent of small business owners, and they generate 14.7 percent of total national GDP—all figures that *exceed* their numerical share of the US population, which is around 13 percent.[12]

The value that immigrants contribute to our economy goes beyond these numbers. Many immigrants are inventors or entrepreneurs, and the best ones excel at math and science at a time when companies are crying out for those skills. In 2013, 303,000 patents were filed in the United States. Of that total, more than half—51 percent, to be exact—were issued to non-US citizens of foreign origin. Foreigners on American soil are also responsible for an outsize share of the business start-ups in this country. The Kauffman Foundation found that foreign-born entrepreneurs have launched more than half of the new ventures in Silicon Valley.[13] And from those acorns, many giant oaks have already grown. More than 40 percent of Fortune 500 companies (a total of 204 of America's biggest businesses) were founded by immigrants to the United States or by their children.[14] In total, immigrant-owned companies in the United States today generate more than $775 billion in annual revenue and employ more than one out of every ten American workers.[15]

Thus, immigrants to America contribute huge amounts of personal wealth, talent, educational assets, energy, and drive to our national economy. But the real secret sauce is the variety of experiences, language, and culture that recent immigrants bring to US companies. In a global economy, it is increasingly clear that the country with the most educated, diverse pool of qualified talent will win. The United States needs people with the ability to effectively connect markets around the world, and immigrants have precisely what it takes.

It's particularly important to the US economy that American companies compete successfully in foreign markets. Exports have been among the strongest components of US growth in recent years. Many of America's most profitable and important companies are heavily dependent on overseas revenue. Overall, about 40 percent of the revenues of Fortune 500 companies are derived from outside the United States.

Continuing and building on this track record of success is crucial. But American companies face huge obstacles in doing so. US companies have had some spectacular failures in Latin America, India, China, and other foreign markets where large and rapidly expanding middle-class populations offer tantalizing upside prospects for growth. Apple's smartphone market share has been surging in China, but it still lags Asian companies like Samsung and Lenovo and until recently trailed smaller firms like Coolpad and ZTE. The Home Depot failed in its attempt to bring American do-it-yourself approaches to China, where there was neither the need nor the interest, and eBay missed the mark in both China and India by misunderstanding the nature of the local relationship-driven business culture. Walmart and other American retailers have struggled to succeed in Latin America.

So how can US companies compete more effectively overseas?

It turns out that much of the insight and global perspective they need to be competitive around the world can be found on US college campuses. American elementary and secondary schools require reform, but our best institutions of higher education still lead the world and annually attract large numbers of foreign students who are eager to learn—and work—in the United States. In recent years, 70 percent of the graduate electrical engineering students in the United States have been foreign born, along with 63 percent of computer scientists and 60 percent of industrial engineers. This ready pool of highly educated, English-speaking professionals from all over the globe represents a resource that no other country can match...provided we create business and government policies that welcome them into our workforce.

Once hired, these diverse foreign students provide their employers with direct connections to other countries and cultures that cannot be replaced by commissioned studies and market research alone. Many large corporations are increasingly turning to these employees as sources of innovation, market strategies, and customer insights. From pharmaceuticals to media to telecom, US companies increasingly recognize that they must understand the cultures of the communities they hope to sell to if they want to succeed.

At one major American health-care business, a mid-level, Argentine-born manager was tapped by her peers in headquarters to boost the company's lagging Latin America sales. It was immediately obvious to her that the existing strategy left out local influencers in the academic field who would be critical to the sales process. Her Latin America–based colleagues had been requesting a more locally savvy strategy for years but to no avail. It turned out it took someone living in the United States and working day in and day out with US colleagues to make a difference. After months of coordination and collaboration with the New Jersey–based leadership team, the immigrant manager persuaded the company to adopt a totally different, locally relevant sales strategy for Latin America. It wasn't long before sales turned around and eventually soared.

The manager who made the difference had been lucky enough to get a green card after meeting her American husband at a prestigious US university a few years earlier. Had that not happened, she most certainly would have returned to Argentina and become a competitor rather than a collaborator.

Welcoming immigration policies assist the United States in other ways, too. Consider the role American colleges and universities play in enhancing the prospects for global democracy. A 2013 study by Marion Mercier of the Paris School of Economics analyzed the educational backgrounds of over nine hundred political leaders in the developing world since 1960. Mercier found that those who had studied abroad were more likely to lead their nations toward democracy (while those who'd served abroad in the military were more likely to endorse moves toward dictatorship). Another study by Antonio Spilimbergo of the International Monetary Fund found that countries with large numbers of citizens who'd studied in the United States and other democratic countries were more likely to embrace democratic forms of government.[16]

It seems evident that embracing foreign students is a powerful—and relatively inexpensive—way for the United States to spread the gospel of freedom abroad. Yet thanks to more restrictive immigration rules, the US share of overseas students fell from 23 percent to 18 percent between 2000 and 2009.[17] At a time when the message of democracy is more important than ever, we're voluntarily abandoning one of the most effective tools for disseminating it.

Managing Our Golden Gates

Most of America's biggest companies across sector and industry, from GE, ExxonMobil, JPMorgan Chase, Apple, and General Mills to Goldman Sachs, Google, Ernst & Young, and many others, find their businesses seriously hampered by the current broken immigration system, which has for years made hiring even the most skilled foreign workers difficult. Consider the H-1B visa program, which provides a way for skilled workers to enter the United States and work at for-profit companies for up to six years. Every year, the federal government is permitted to grant as many as eighty-five thousand H-1B visas. (A separate, uncapped H-1B program covers nonprofits and academic institutions.) But the number of H-1B visas requested every year is far greater than the number available. In fact, in 2013 and 2014, the number of requests was so vast that the government stopped accepting them after five days and held a lottery to choose the winners among the applications already received.[18] And that was before the Trump Executive Orders on immigration made the process even more difficult and confusing.

Restrictive immigration laws have left high-tech companies desperate for skilled foreign workers and compelled companies like Microsoft, Amazon, and Facebook to open labs in Vancouver, Canada, where foreign talent is welcome.[19]

At the same time, many of the best foreign students and professionals with the skills and insights to make a real difference inside US companies are forced to return to their countries with their newly minted American degrees. Tight quotas on green cards and a president openly hostile to immigrants mean that, as the House Republicans put it in the immigration reform principles document they issued in January 2014, "We end up exporting this labor and ingenuity to other countries."[20]

The US immigration system is extremely dysfunctional in myriad ways. Unrealistic limits on the number of immigrant visas issued, combined with the enormous difficulties of monitoring millions of visitors to the United States in order to enforce our complex residency rules, have resulted in a vast number of undocumented residents in the country—approximately eleven million people, or around 3 percent of the population.

This is not a new problem; there have been large numbers of "undocumented immigrants" in the United States for as long as there have been laws governing immigration. But the sheer scope of the problem is greater today than in the recent past, posing huge challenges for policy makers and for our society.

In fact, as Edward Alden, an expert on immigration and US policy at the Council on Foreign Relations, pointed out to me recently, the portion of the American population that is foreign-born today—around 13 percent—is very much in line with the percentage from most of our nation's history. (In census figures from 1860 to 1920, for example, the percentage of foreign-born residents never fell below 13.2 percent or rose above 14.8 percent.) But during the middle of the twentieth century, thanks to restrictive laws instituted during the preceding decades, immigration plummeted. The percentage of foreign-born Americans fell to an all-time low of 4.7 percent in 1970—around the time that many baby boomers were coming of age. Today those boomers include millions of America's most active voters. For them, the unusually low numbers of immigrants in their formative years seem somehow "normal"—which makes today's higher figures feel "unnatural" and even "dangerous," despite their historic normality.[21]

The election of Donald Trump has brought some of the most extreme and draconian "solutions" to national attention. Donald Trump has empowered the immigration enforcement service known as "ICE" to become a defacto "deportation force" to round up and expel immigrants living in the US illegally. Few sensible voices, even those at the extremes of the political spectrum, would go that far. For one thing, it would be incredibly expensive. Cost estimates vary from a low of $114 billion by the liberal Center for American Progress to a high of $420 to $620 billion by the conservative American Action Forum.[22] But setting aside costs, even if it were practical to round up millions of people, including those who have been living peacefully and productively among us for many years, to do so would be neither humane nor beneficial. Who would fill the gigantic gap in our economy that the millions of deportees would leave behind? Who would do the jobs they are doing? Who would pay the taxes and provide the services they are contributing? Deportation is ridiculous, inhumane, and exceptionally heartless.

Reform is essential. That is the one thing about immigration that everyone—from responsible leaders in academia, business, and the nonprofit sector to both major political parties—has long agreed on. Crafting and passing a comprehensive new law that would fix our broken system and make it possible for the United States to take advantage of the benefits created by immigration while addressing valid concerns over issues like security, social service costs, and cultural assimilation could not be more imperative.

And while it may seem impossible to find common ground and a meaningful solution in the current environment, recent history proves it's not. The evidence is S. 744, an ambitious immigration reform bill developed by a bipartisan group of eight US senators, known as the "Gang of Eight"—Charles Schumer (D-NY),

John McCain (R-AZ), Richard Durbin (D-IL), Lindsey Graham (R-SC), Robert Menendez (D-NJ), Marco Rubio (R-FL), Michael Bennet (D-CO), and Jeff Flake (R-AZ). After extensive debate and a lengthy amendment process—which resulted in ninety-two amendments being incorporated in the bill by voice vote—S. 744 was passed by the Senate on June 27, 2013, by a vote of 68 to 32.

S. 744 incorporated a wide range of provisions—some typically viewed as "conservative" in thrust, others as "liberal"—that, in combination, would have gone a long way toward solving our immigration dilemmas. It would have lifted the restrictive quotas on Indians and Chinese, increased the number of H-1B visas, allowed spouses of H-1B holders to work (no small matter), and offered new visas for entrepreneurs. It would have provided legal status for the eleven million undocumented residents in the United States and created an expedited path to citizenship for special subgroups, such as children of people who are in the United States without documentation and aspire to higher education (the same beneficiaries targeted by the so-called DREAM Act). It would also have provided measures and funding for securing the country's southern border while assuring due process protections for children, the mentally disabled, and other vulnerable immigrant groups.[23]

In short, S. 744 would have done a lot to enable the United States to take full advantage of the millions of diverse foreigners eager to contribute to American society and the economy but prevented from doing so by our damaged immigration system. And more than two-thirds of US senators voted to make it a reality.

Unfortunately, the corresponding bill (H.R. 15) never even made it to a vote in the House of Representatives. The House members who tried to forge an acceptable bipartisan compromise couldn't do so. In the years since then, further attempts to develop immigration reform packages have foundered on the shoals of partisan politics. Today, given the election of Trump, the promise of meaningful reform seems more distant than ever.

So immigration reform is neither impossibly complex nor hopelessly divisive. It would be possible for smart legislators from both sides of the aisle to agree on a good package of reforms that will largely fix our broken system. All that's missing is the leadership to make it happen.

In his inspiring 1869 speech "Our Composite Nationality," Frederick Douglass spoke about the destiny of the United States as a country that would embrace people of all kinds, from every land. "The outspread wings of the American eagle," Douglass declared optimistically, "are broad enough to shelter all who are likely to come."[24]

Today, Americans are struggling to determine whether they are ready to embrace Douglass's vision of an inclusive, open-hearted US democracy. Will the wings of the eagle still be outspread in welcome? Or will we surrender to fear and shut the golden gates through which so much of our national creativity and wealth have flowed? The decision is ours.

8. Of the People, by the People, for the People

If liberty and equality, as is thought by some, are chiefly to be found in democracy, they will be best attained when all persons alike share in the government to the utmost.

—*Aristotle*, Politics

On August 9, 2014, Michael Brown, an eighteen-year-old black man looking forward to his first year of college, was shot and killed by police officer Darren Wilson on the streets of Ferguson, Missouri, a suburb of St. Louis. Though Brown was unarmed and had been accosted by police merely for blocking traffic by walking in the street, a grand jury failed to indict the officer. The Justice Department subsequently declined to charge him with civil rights violations.

At the time, Brown's death seemed like just another tragic incident in the long history of uneasy, often violent interactions between black Americans and the mostly white police officers who patrol their communities. But within days of his death, the name Michael Brown and the word *Ferguson* became shorthand for racial injustice. And before the end of the year, the demonstrations and protests sparked by Brown's death triggered the Black Lives Matter movement and a national debate about the continuing quest for equity and empowerment by America's black community.

In Ferguson, the Michael Brown case had a deep and lasting impact. A US Justice Department investigation into the practices of the Ferguson police department confirmed what many black residents had experienced for years—a shocking history of racially motivated bias in policing. From 2012 to 2014, African Americans were disproportionately targeted for arrests, forcible detention, and tickets, though they committed crimes at the same rate as white citizens. The numbers were dramatic: 93 percent of the people arrested during the period were black, although blacks represent only about 67 percent of the population—and *every single person* charged with "resisting arrest" (a notoriously nebulous, subjective "crime") was black.[1]

Perhaps even more disturbing, the Justice Department found clear evidence that the local government deliberately manipulated policing policies to financially gouge black residents. With local officials drawing an ever-increasing portion of municipal budgets from fines, fees, and forfeitures, police were pressured by local officials to aggressively charge black citizens with minor crimes designed to yield maximum government revenues. For residents, the effects of the policy were devastating. One black woman who was ticketed for parking her car illegally a single time—and then failed to pay her fine on time—was arrested twice, jailed for six days, and forced to pay a $550 fee to a city court...after which she was told that she still owed the city $541 more.[2]

Michael Brown's death, and the spotlight it shed on government injustice in an otherwise unremarkable suburb of America's Midwest, created a new awareness of the persistence of discrimination in our nation's political system. The structure of Ferguson's local leadership helped explain the enormous gulf that had opened up between the governing and the governed. Ferguson's demographics had gradually shifted over the years to become almost 70 percent black. The demographics of the political representatives, however, had not followed suit. At the time of Brown's death, the city's mayor, James Knowles, was a white Republican; five of its six city council members were white; and of the fifty-three police officers working in the city, fifty were white.

One reason for this racial disparity: the unusual election system used in Ferguson. In accordance with the city's charter, local elections are held in odd-numbered years on the first Tuesday in April—dates when there are no state or national elections to draw media coverage or voter attention, virtually guaranteeing a low turnout. In the 2013 city election—the last one held before Michael Brown's death—just 11.7 percent of Ferguson's eligible voters went to the polls.[3] Low voter turnout made it easy for a few highly motivated citizens to be elected and shape the course of government, even where their views were unrepresentative of the majority.

The death of Michael Brown and the revelations about government misconduct from the Justice Department report spurred reform and activism in Ferguson. Black residents vowed to no longer passively accept their virtual disenfranchisement. A massive voter registration drive launched, with volunteers manning card-table sign-up booths all over the community, including one in the abandoned gas station that had been burned down by rioters during the unrest following Brown's killing.[4]

The efforts paid off. Thousands of new voters registered, and many of them came out to vote. On April 7, 2015, 30 percent of the eligible voters in Ferguson cast ballots—still a relatively low number but an increase of historic proportions. As a result, two new African American members were elected to the city council, making it, for the first time, 50 percent black.

Doyle McClellan, a white candidate who lost his bid for a city council seat in the election, expressed disappointment but urged Ferguson's citizens to stay engaged. Every time he knocked on a door to ask for support, he pointed out that becoming a powerful voice for change requires casting a vote not just once but in three consecutive elections. "You vote in a municipal, a congressional, and another municipal race," McClellan said, "and the politicians will notice, and they will come looking for your vote and want to hear what you have to say."[5]

Encouraged by their success in the 2015 municipal elections, the newly engaged citizens of Ferguson are vowing to continue the fight. But Ferguson still has a long way to go before it can claim a truly representative local government. The Ferguson-Florissant School District, which controls the local educational system, has a seven-member school board with five white members, though 77 percent of the students whose lives it governs are black. Voting rights advocates have mounted a lawsuit to force a change in an election system they say is biased against minority candidates.

The slowly shifting political structure in Ferguson offers reasons for hope. But a change in the racial makeup of the leaders in City Hall won't automatically lead to a more equitable distribution of power. It takes more than visible representation to overcome entrenched biases in government, policing, and policy. For evidence, you simply have to look at another troubled city, some 825 miles due east.

In April 2015, Freddie Gray, like Michael Brown, Eric Garner, Walter Scott, and Tamir Rice, became a household name after he died in police custody in Baltimore. Twenty-five-year-old Gray was arrested by Baltimore police, allegedly for possessing an illegal switchblade knife. (Evidence later suggested that the knife wasn't even discovered by police until *after* Gray had been arrested.)[6] The arrest, recorded on video, showed Gray screaming in pain as police officers dragged him, forced him to the ground, and pressed a knee into his neck. During the subsequent thirty-minute trip in a police van, Gray suffered severe spinal injuries. The Baltimore police commissioner later said that, contrary to department policy,

Gray had not been secured in the van, which may have contributed to further injuries. Gray fell into a coma and died a week later on April 19. On May 1, after a medical examiner's report ruled Gray's death a homicide, state prosecutors filed criminal charges ranging from false imprisonment to second-degree murder against six police officers involved in the incident.

Gray was arrested in a high-crime Baltimore neighborhood whose population is overwhelmingly poor—and black. His story fits the tragic nationwide pattern of young black men dying senseless deaths at the hands of police. But there's a strange, sad twist to his story that speaks to the complexity of race in America today. Unlike Michael Brown, Freddie Gray was not victimized by an overwhelmingly white political power structure. Baltimore inaugurated its first black mayor way back in 1987, and the city's black population—63 percent of the total as of 2010—is well represented in government.

Baltimore's mayor at the time, Stephanie Rawlings-Blake, is black. So was the president of the city council and nine of the council's fourteen members. So was the prosecutor handling the police misconduct case. And so was police commissioner Anthony W. Batts, who admitted that Gray hadn't been properly secured in the van. (Batts was fired for allegedly failing to respond aggressively enough during the unrest that erupted following Gray's death; his replacement, Kevin Davis, is white.) What's more, three of the six police officers charged in Gray's death were black, including the two officers who allegedly refused to call for a medic despite Gray's pleas for help. One of the black officers grew up in the same community as Gray.

How can this be? Shouldn't the visible, representative diversity in Baltimore government ensure better race relations and prevent racially charged incidents like these? You might think so—but simply changing the complexion of the police department and the civilian leadership that oversees it has not saved Baltimore from the same racial problems that Ferguson and so many other cities have experienced.

Does this mean that the efforts by people of color to gain fair representation in the government of Ferguson, Missouri—and similar efforts by minority-group members in cities and states across America—are irrelevant and pointless? No. Inclusion, representation, and power-sharing are essential *first steps* toward accountability and equity. But the story of Baltimore reflects the fact that managing diversity in government and policing isn't a simple matter, much less a racial numbers game. It's about the long, hard work of analyzing the systems and structures that perpetuate injustice and finding ways to uproot and reform them. This work requires the combined efforts of countless citizens of every background and from every walk of life, inside and outside the halls of government. Government must be representative in both numbers and actions.

The election of Barack Obama in 2008 was of course historic and marked a turning point for diversity in American politics. That a biracial man of modest means with Hussein as his middle name could rise to become president of the United States does speak volumes about how far we've come as a nation in our openness and tolerance of difference.

Obama's election was important not just because it was symbolic but because it inspired a generation of young people, especially from diverse backgrounds, to participate in the political process. The hallmark of Obama's exceptionally well-run campaign was his engagement of citizens through small-dollar donations, volunteerism, and voter turnout programs. But unfortunately, once he was in the Oval Office, much of the citizen engagement dissipated. There was no meaningful plan for harnessing the power and passion of the millions who had volunteered and campaigned for Obama. I'm even told that few of the many minority volunteers were offered jobs in the administration after the campaign ended, something many of them had been counting on. Aside from mobilizing them again in 2012, something the Obama campaign did quite successfully, much of the hope for change in citizen engagement wasn't realized.

Obama ran and won on a ticket promising hope and change. But after eight years of Obama and the election of Donald Trump, the quest for a fully inclusive and representative American government remains unrealized.

Advantage Women

Although most Americans see the United States as a model of democracy for the world, and in many ways we are, the poor representation of women in American government stands out as one of our biggest, most glaring failures.

Given that women are over 50 percent of the US population, most Americans would be stunned to learn that the United States lags behind countries such as South Africa, Rwanda, and Tunisia in the political participation of women. As of 2017, the eighty-three female members in the US House of Representatives and the twenty-one female senators make up just 20 percent of our Congress. As a result, the United States ranks seventy-fourth in the world in female representation in the national legislature.[7] Similarly, members of nonwhite minority groups, including blacks, Hispanics, Asians, and Native Americans, make up just 17 percent of Congress, although the population groups they represent amount to 38 percent of Americans.[8]

In the months after I left the Center for Talent Innovation, I spent a lot of time thinking about all the work left to do in advancing the political, economic, and social participation and empowerment of women. I vowed that I would not give up on this cause but do something even more meaningful and rewarding. I had spent four years striving to advance diversity in the corporate world. But despite all the effort, all the programs, and all the attention focused on the topic, from Sheryl Sandberg's book *Lean In* to the annual Most Powerful Women conference sponsored by *Fortune* magazine, something was still missing. And during my years working at the center with Sylvia Ann Hewlett, I'd learned how important it was for women to really support each other, not just talk about it.

In 1975, the year I was born, my mother was immersed in the women's movement, which was turning into a huge political and social force that would change the country forever. What women of her generation knew was that to achieve full and equal rights, women had to have power equal to men in every sphere. The women's movement of the 1960s and '70s focused on breaking down institutional barriers for women at home, at work, and in public life. They pushed for reforms in business and worked to overturn some of the most egregiously discriminatory legislation.

Into the 1970s, women couldn't open bank accounts without their husband's permission, help-wanted ads were segregated by gender, and fewer than 4 percent of jobs in corporate America were held by women. The women's movement mobilized millions of American women from all walks of life, every socioeconomic class, and both political parties to rally for equality. And they largely succeeded—for women my age and younger, the kind of institutional sexism that existed just forty years ago is unimaginable.

The mass mobilization of women in the 1960s and '70s motivated leaders at every level of government and from both political parties to take their issues seriously. Presidents Nixon, Ford, and Carter all made advancing women's equality a priority for their administrations. But forty years later, perhaps because we have come so far and achieved so much, the energy and passion women showed for political participation have significantly dissipated.

Women do vote—in fact, they overwhelmingly honor their civic duty and show up to the polls. As a result, women have turned every election since 1980. But across nearly every other measure of civic engagement, women are far behind. One of the biggest gaps: Women are far less likely than men to run for office or even consider running for office. This is especially true for younger women, who want to make a difference through other kinds of public service (such as working with nonprofits) but not through politics.[9] And when it comes to the type of active advocacy and engagement that can change laws and ensure lawmakers are accountable to the citizens that voted for them, women barely matter. They are less likely to speak at town hall meetings with candidates and elected officials, less likely ever to write or call their representative, and less likely to write op-ed articles promoting their views.[10]

Senator Kirsten Gillibrand of New York has been encouraging women to get more engaged in the political process for years. In her best-selling book *Off the Sidelines* and through her political action committee of the same name, she urges women to speak up and hold legislators accountable for serving female voters and advancing the issues that matter most to women. At the January 2014 launch of my nonprofit organization All In Together in Washington, DC, Gillibrand spoke about the importance of women's participation in the political process:

> *One of the reasons I wrote my book* Off the Sidelines *was because I wanted to create a conversation among women and through that conversation to make the point that their voices are really important and that their world view is different. It's perhaps so different that it's not being reflected here in Washington. There are so few women who are decision makers relative to men. There are only twenty women in the Senate, and only eighteen percent of the House is female.*

Gillibrand went on to talk about the issue of paid family leave, a cause many women support, yet one that has not progressed in Congress. She made the point that if women don't engage in the political process and demand attention to the issues that matter to them, progress will never be made. She said:

> *Our nature as women is often we want to be kind, often we want to be polite. Often we don't want to rock the boat. I'm asking you to please rock the boat. Be a pain in the ass. Our movement needs a call to action. We need to fight harder; we have to insist our views are heard. We have to be unafraid of making our peers uncomfortable, and we have to be willing to do everything we can.*

Senator Gillibrand sees firsthand all the ways female voters are not making the collective impact they could. A 2015 study by Nicholas Stephanopoulos of the University of Chicago Law School used polling data to compare the policy preferences of men and women on issues such as the minimum wage, health-care reform, and gun control. Stephanopoulos then analyzed the apparent impact of gender-based public opinion on the policies actually adopted at the state and federal levels. He found there is an inverse relationship between women's policy preferences and the policies adopted. As one journalist summarized the study, "In cases where there's major disagreement between men and women, the chance of a policy taking effect falls the more it's supported by women, and it falls dramatically: from 80 percent to about 10 percent."[11]

Perhaps even more surprising, Stephanopoulos also examined the impact of race and income on the power of public opinion, and he discovered that these characteristics have less effect on the influence of particular sets of policy preferences. In other words,

"Women are the most politically powerless group"—even more so than blacks, Hispanics, or the poor.[12]

Given that women are a majority of the US population, this kind of breakdown in representation is all the more frustrating. It was this frustration that led me to found All In Together with my exceptionally talented and passionate cofounder Courtney Emerson. Courtney and I had worked together at the Center for Talent Innovation, where I had hired her in her first job after she graduated from Princeton. Eleven years my junior, Courtney brings tremendous energy and insight into the specific challenges Millennial women face. With our partner Edda Coleman, she and I are working to inspire a generation of women to see political participation as an essential part of our full equality. In partnership with a group of visionary companies, we're holding a series of forums and training programs to encourage women to get involved and to take a greater role in politics. We're experimenting with a range of programs, from bringing women to Capitol Hill to meet and get to know members of Congress to holding in-depth forums for women to learn about the policy issues related to particular industries. And we've launched an online platform with critical information women need in order to advocate for issues that matter to them. Our goal is to inspire women and offer them the tools and resources to make a difference. If more women get involved in advocating for issues, engaging with their members of Congress, and ensuring their voices are heard and respected in the most important national debates, I believe we will be a stronger, more equitable, and more democratic nation.

There are many reasons why greater participation of women in politics is essential not just for women but for the nation. An overwhelming number of Americans view our political system as hopelessly broken. The gridlock in Congress over the last number of years has left our democracy badly wounded. But the one glimmer of hope might actually be women. In 2013, when Republicans forced a shutdown of the US government in a standoff over the budget, it was a bipartisan group of women senators who brokered the solution.

And that wasn't the only instance of women in Congress putting country ahead of ego and party. A recent study by Quorum found that female lawmakers in Congress are both more productive and more bipartisan. The average female senator introduced 96.31 bills in seven years compared to just 70.72 bills introduced by the average male senator in the same time period. And the average female senator cosponsored 171.08 bills with a member of the opposite party, whereas that figure was only 129.87 for the average male senator. It turns out that if you want a more productive, bipartisan government, you should send more women to Washington.[13]

In her book *Broad Influence, Time* magazine journalist Jay Newton-Small explores the positive impact female lawmakers have had on Washington. She found that female lawmakers took more time to build personal relationships with members of Congress on both sides of the aisle. These relationships made it possible to find common ground and overcome suspicion and rancorous political partisanship. And she discovered that women members worked harder to find consensus even where they might initially disagree. She argues compellingly that the presence of women in the House and Senate has had a measurable and exceedingly positive effect.

Obviously the subject of women in office was central to the 2016 presidential election. The historic run of Hillary Clinton, and perhaps especially her loss, energized many American women; her campaign was hugely propelled by the financial contributions of women supporters. On the Republican side, Carly Fiorina's presence and performance in the debates and as Ted Cruz's short-lived running mate was an important symbol for conservative women, who of course feel equally committed to women's advancement.

While Clinton lost, the potential to have a woman president is important and long overdue. But just as the historic election of Barack Obama did not substantively change the long-term engagement and participation of the black electorate, neither would have electing a woman president resolve all problems with female political empowerment. Having a president who looks like the electorate is absolutely imperative yet still not sufficient. We will need legions of citizens of all backgrounds to engage, vote, and run for office to ensure a truly representative democracy.

Vote and Voice

Overall voter participation and citizen engagement remain important challenges if we are to capitalize fully on the perspectives of all Americans in our democracy, across lines of race and culture. More than fifty years after the passage of the landmark Voting Rights Act, which sought to make the ballot available to every citizen regardless of race—participation in elections by *all* citizen groups remains a distant goal. In many cities and states, needless barriers remain, making it difficult for eligible voters to register and cast their ballots. These roadblocks are one of the most serious threats to the supremacy of American democracy and the inclusion of all our citizens so fundamental to the democratic ideal.

Barriers to voting are nothing new in America, and our history in regard to voting rights is checkered at best. The United States granted women the right to vote in 1920, later than many other nations. The full voting rights of black Americans weren't legally assured until 1965. Challenges to black voting persisted for years after and, some would argue, continue today. A recent spate of voter ID laws enacted across the country tend to disadvantage specific groups of voters—the poor, the elderly, the young, and people of color. (In Texas, for example, student and government-employee photo IDs are *not* acceptable proofs for voting, but concealed-handgun permits *are*.) A number of states have enacted restrictive voter registration rules that discourage participation and make registration drives by groups like the League of Women Voters practically impossible. Others have conducted highly partisan purges of registration rolls that arbitrarily eliminate thousands of eligible voters. Still others have imposed ever-increasing limitations on the times and places for voting, which erect obstacles that millions of working men and women can scarcely scale.

The barriers also include felon disenfranchisement laws that make it much harder for ex-felons to have a voice in the political process. They punish people of color who are incarcerated under discriminatory criminal laws and sentencing policies. According to one estimate, one African American in thirteen is barred from the right to vote by felon disenfranchisement laws.[14]

Many of the onerous voting restrictions now being established are unnecessary and arcane. A comparison of the US voting system—decentralized, subject to political manipulation, poorly funded, technologically archaic—with the systems used in other democracies around the world yields a shocking conclusion. A 2014 study by the independent investigative journalists at the Center for Public Integrity exhaustively analyzed voter restrictions, registration policies, and ID requirements from 234 countries. Their conclusion? "Although there is no single requirement in the US that is unique, the cumulative constraints in states with tougher ID and registration standards place these states among the most restrictive voting environments in the world."[15]

There's also evidence that our voter restriction rules are enforced in ways that redouble their discriminatory effect. For example, poll workers are more likely to ask minority voters to show identification before being allowed to vote—even in states that don't have voter identification laws! And when researchers sent out e-mails to local election officials asking for information about voting rules, the e-mails signed with Anglo-sounding names (like Greg Walsh) received more complete and helpful responses than those with Latino-sounding names (like Luis Rodriguez).[16]

These restrictions help to explain the embarrassing voter participation record of the United States. We regularly record lower voter turnouts than almost every other democratic nation, trailing such a wide array of countries as the UK, Japan, Germany, Portugal, Israel, Greece, and India. Our failure to make voting a universal rite of citizenship weakens our claim to be the standard-bearer of democracy for the world. And it plays a major role in our failure to create a government that takes full advantage of the talents and insights of our diverse population.

Consistently, the most restrictive voter ID laws have been initiated and passed by Republican governors and state legislatures. The Brennan Center for Justice at New York University School of Law maintains an authoritative database on legal and administrative changes that impact voting rights, either favorably or unfavorably. As of early 2016, the center lists twenty-one states that have enacted new voter restrictions since 2010. In sixteen cases, the restrictions were put in place by Republican-dominated legislatures; in Iowa, a Republican governor imposed the restrictions through executive order, and in Mississippi the state's voters passed the new rules through referendum. Only three Democratic-led states (Illinois, Rhode Island, and West Virginia) passed new laws limiting the right to vote, and those were generally less onerous than those enacted elsewhere.[17] As for current efforts to impose further restrictions, the center's 2015 roundup concludes, "Voter ID remains largely a partisan issue. Of the 52 restrictive ID bills introduced so far [in the 2015 legislative cycle], most have Republican-only sponsorship."[18]

Given that the minority voters most affected by voting restrictions tend to support Democratic candidates, it's hard not to conclude these efforts spearheaded mainly by Republican legislators are partisan political manipulations. It's an unfortunate, cynical, and shortsighted approach.

It's not a foregone conclusion that minorities will always vote Democratic. Republicans who have tried to attract minority votes have a history of success. In 2000 and 2004, George W. Bush won large numbers of Hispanic votes, including estimates ranging as high as 44 percent in his reelection victory. (Since voters naturally do not provide ethnicity data when casting their ballots, all such figures are estimates based on exit polls.) Subsequent Republican presidential candidates haven't fared so well. Senator John McCain's share of the Hispanic vote in 2008 was estimated at 31 percent, and former Massachusetts governor Mitt Romney's share was just 27 percent.[19]

As governor of Texas, Bush had learned a thing or two about how to connect with Latino voters. First of all, he knew Spanish and didn't hesitate to speak it on the campaign trail. But he also pushed an idea of "compassionate conservatism" that included a promise to reform immigration laws to offer a path to citizenship and a humane guest-worker program. Bush was able to walk a line with bona fide conservative credentials but also a more open and tolerant approach to Hispanic voters that worked for him on the presidential level—twice.

Sara Fagen is an expert on data analytics and technology who served as a senior aide and political director to President George

W. Bush. She observes that Bush's affinity for Hispanic voters was much more than a mere political ploy:

> *President Bush was the definition of a New England blue blood—born in Connecticut to a prominent Northeastern family. But after he moved to Texas, he developed a comfort level with Hispanic culture, learned to speak the language, and really felt connected to the community. As a very devout person, he respected the deep Catholic faith shared by many Hispanics. Their desire to make a better life for their families, and their concern over pocketbook issues affecting everyday Americans, are qualities they share with millions of conservatives. As President Bush often remarked, "Family values don't stop at the Rio Grande."*
>
> *The president also understood that the US immigration system was broken and sincerely wanted to fix it. He felt compassion for the desire of so many immigrants to find a better life for themselves and their children, and he felt it was a great injustice when their families were ripped apart. So for him, the personal and the political came together. His vision of the agenda he hoped to fulfill as president included the realization that a mature, responsible candidate doesn't try to win by destroying the possibility of collaboration in the future. He recognized his role in attracting Hispanics to the Republican coalition, and he was able to win many of their votes because of his authentic and sincere empathy for their concerns.*[20]

Today, sadly, few Republican political leaders are even trying to connect with Latino and minority voters. Their alienation of these important and growing groups is likely to haunt the party for years to come. By some estimates, given the changing demographics of the nation, even a candidate who won 60 percent of the white male vote could not win the presidency without meaningful support from women and minorities. Despite Trump's win, demographic changes mean that unless the Republican Party changes course and returns to the politically sound and morally decent tradition of inclusion that George W. Bush exemplified, their majorities may be short-lived.

Building the Biggest Tent

There are simple and complex solutions to creating a more accessible and inclusive democracy. Legislators, advocacy groups, and civil rights organizations are mounting efforts across the country to repeal laws and regulations that make registration and voting more difficult. The 1965 Voting Rights Act (VRA)—the single most effective measure of protection for voters of color in our nation's history—was passed by a wide majority of members of Congress from both major parties. Republican presidents Nixon and Ford renewed the act, and when Ronald Reagan reauthorized the VRA for twenty-five years in 1982, he strengthened the provisions barring discrimination based on race. Today, voting rights have become a highly partisan issue, and enormous challenges remain.

But there are some glimmers of hope. There is increasing bipartisan consensus that millions of Americans who have spent time in prison should not be excluded from the right to vote. In Virginia, a decades-long campaign by progressive groups and civil rights organizations persuaded Republican governor Bob McDonnell in May 2014 to issue an executive order that automatically restores the voting rights of nonviolent felons once they've paid their debt to society. And in November 2014, Steve Beshear, the outgoing Democratic governor of Kentucky, issued a similar order restoring voting rights to around 140,000 nonviolent felons. It was a small step toward making our system of government more inclusive of all our citizens—but a very big step, symbolically and practically, for the individuals involved. Unfortunately, Beshear's successor, Republican Matt Bevin, rescinded the order soon after taking office.[21]

Like the black citizens of Ferguson, minority Americans around the country are increasingly recognizing that political power grows directly from their active engagement in the electoral process—and as their numbers grow, so does their impact on the political direction of our nation.

The single largest ethnic minority in the United States are Latinos. Of course, this is a highly diverse group made up of people from many countries, with different languages and racial identities and widely varying political and cultural perspectives. But Latino leaders are striving to ensure that the voices of their communities will be heard at the ballot box—especially regarding issues that directly impact the American acceptance of diversity. The National Council of La Raza, the largest and most influential Latino advocacy organization, has issued a call to all eligible voters to "Defeat bigotry on the campaign trail—register and vote!" Clarissa Martínez de Castro, deputy vice president of La Raza, notes that the number of Latinos registered to vote rose from 11.6 million in 2008 to 13.7 million in 2012. The organization's goal for 2016: 16.7 million registered voters. If they succeed, it will make Latinos a huge and potentially game-changing political force.[22] In a time when hateful rhetoric targeting Latinos permeates political debate, this is an important development to which smart politicians on both sides of the aisle are paying close attention.

Sara Fagen, the former advisor to President George W. Bush, points out that issues like the economy, jobs, and education offer potential grounds for agreement between conservatives and

Latino voters. Clarissa Martínez de Castro agrees. "Latinos are not genetically programmed to vote Democratic!" she observes:

> Competition between the two parties for the votes of every group—including Latinos—is important. But the Republicans have been their own worst enemies when it comes to attracting Latino support. Most Latinos are in the US legally, and millions have been here for many years and are citizens and voters. But more than fifty percent know someone who is a recent immigrant. So they take the challenge of immigration reform personally, and they view it as a civil rights issue. When candidates exploit mistrust and fear of Latinos to score political points and to distract the voters from the sensible solutions that most Americans support, they hurt themselves and drive Latino voters away.[23]

On a more positive note, political leaders from both parties are encouraging more women and minorities to vote, run for office, and participate in the national political dialogue. The record numbers of women members in the 114th Congress are already having a positive impact on our political system and our country. But much more progress is needed. One of the most obvious and simple ways of improving democratic participation would be for every American to be automatically registered to vote when they turn eighteen. This would vastly simplify our outdated and burdensome system, but in the current highly polarized climate, there is little chance that Congress will pass such a sweeping reform.

It's a profound loss for our nation and for our democracy that we have left so many out of our political process. It's a reality that must change.

9. Unequal Justice

There may be times when we are powerless to prevent injustice,
but there must never be a time when we fail to protest.

—*Elie Wiesel*

Women in the World, Tina Brown's extraordinary annual gathering, brings together some of the most groundbreaking, visionary women from around the globe. In 2014, I had the privilege of attending the conference and hearing from the Russian protest band Pussy Riot, who spoke about their ordeal after challenging Russian president Vladimir Putin with public criticism. The women had been thrown into jail for a series of radical performances aimed at calling attention to Putin's oppression. What they said at Women in the World struck me as sadly relevant in our own country. After describing the deplorable conditions they endured, one of the singers said: "You can tell everything about the values of society by the way they treat their prisoners." Perhaps they were inspired by their great countryman, the novelist Fyodor Dostoyevsky, who wrote in *The House of the Dead*, "The degree of civilization in a society can be judged by entering its prisons."

If this is true, we Americans have reason to wonder what kind of country we really inhabit. The statistics about injustice in our criminal justice system are horrifying and completely out of whack with the values we espouse as a nation. Most of us view our justice system as a hallmark of our democracy, where justice is blind, and we have enshrined the notion of innocent until proven guilty. But Americans have increasingly been forced to reevaluate this view. From the laws on the books enforced by policing, to jury selection, plea deals, sentencing, and the death penalty, almost every dimension of our justice system needs serious and immediate reformation. Shocking statistics suggest the scope of bias plaguing our approach to criminal justice:

- The United States imprisons more people than any other country on earth. Americans make up less than 5 percent of world population, but the prisoners in our jails constitute almost one-quarter of all those imprisoned on earth.
- People of color make up around 30 percent of the US population but 60 percent of the prison population.
- During encounters with police, blacks are nearly twice as likely as whites to be arrested and four times as likely to experience the use of force.
- Black offenders are more likely than their white counterparts to be sentenced to prison, and blacks receive longer prison sentences than whites for the same crimes.[1]
- Black children are more likely than white children to be criminally prosecuted for minor offenses.

To really understand the scope and impact of our problems and the importance of this issue to our national diversity, it helps to examine where the problems begin. Some of our nation's laws have bias deeply entrenched in them and have led us to fill our prisons with minorities.

Law and Order

The nation's drug laws are now widely acknowledged to be the root of some of our worst racial injustices and are responsible for putting a large portion of Americans behind bars. It turns out that our drug laws have always been tinged with racial and ethnic prejudice. California's first law against opium use was passed in 1907 to give law enforcement officials a way to round up Chinese immigrants whose social and economic impact on Anglo society was widely feared. Similarly, a series of antimarijuana laws was enacted in the 1930s in reaction to the arrival of Mexican American immigrants who used the drug.[2]

Even tougher laws with similar racial overtones were passed during the 1980s as part of the "war on drugs" at a time when an epidemic of inner-city drug abuse was being blamed for societal breakdown, family collapse, economic woes, and a nationwide crime wave. I'll never forget the campaign led by then–first lady Nancy Reagan to "Just Say No." It was rolled out in the early 1980s when I was in elementary school. Mrs. Reagan, who was sincere and well-meaning in her efforts, helped draw attention to the drug epidemic and enlisted entertainers like La Toya Jackson to promote the campaign with her. But rather than inspiring lawmakers to invest in treatment and prevention, most of the response in the 1980s focused on getting tough and included an avalanche of anti-drug laws with strict minimum sentencing provisions.

Race was a major factor in how those drug laws were designed. Powder cocaine and crack cocaine are basically identical in their physical effects and social impact. In the 1980s, crack was more prevalent in inner-city black communities, and powder cocaine was more popular among white users. So federal laws were enacted that established minimum sentencing rules for use of crack cocaine that were one hundred times as severe as those for powder cocaine, producing an impact on black Americans that was way out of proportion to their contribution to the national drug problem. (The disproportion in sentencing rules has since been reduced but not eliminated; in the wake of a 2010 law, crack cocaine is now punished roughly eighteen times as harshly as powder cocaine.)[3]

One of the most significant laws of the past quarter century was the Violent Crime Control and Law Enforcement Act passed in 1994 and signed by President Clinton. It was the largest crime bill in history, with far-reaching implications for everything from eliminating the guarantee of Pell grants to inmates seeking an education to the so-called three-strikes law mandating life imprisonment for three-time criminal offenders. At the time, it was seen as an important step toward managing a crisis of crime that was sweeping the nation. But it also inspired state legislatures to pass their own "tough on crime" bills, to chilling effect. Though crime rates dropped, the national prison population has doubled since the law was passed. Today the bill is largely viewed as too aggressive and shortsighted.

Recently, President Clinton expressed regret at having signed and supported it. In a speech before the NAACP in July 2015, Clinton acknowledged the bill triggered mass incarceration across the country. "In that bill, there were longer sentences. And most of these people are in prison under state law, but the federal law set a trend. And that was overdone. We were wrong about that."[4]

Harsh laws like those in the 1994 Crime Bill are part of a panoply of statutes that have filled our nation's prisons with drug offenders, often guilty of relatively minor crimes. Most Americans favor tough treatment of major drug kingpins, but the impact of our drug laws extends far beyond that relatively small group. Of the more than 1.5 million drug arrests in the United States in 2014, more than 80 percent were for possession alone. On any given day, some five hundred thousand Americans are in prison for drug-law violations—a total ten times as great as in the year 1980.[5]

These vast numbers affect people of color disproportionately. Virtually all studies show that black Americans use drugs at around the same rates as other racial groups. But although blacks constitute less than 13 percent of the population, they make up 30 percent of drug arrests and 40 percent of drug-related incarcerations in state or federal prisons. Similarly, Latinos, who are around 17 percent of the population, suffer 47 percent of federal drug arrests and 37 percent of federal drug incarcerations.[6]

Statistics like these are important, but the real meaning of the numbers becomes much more vivid when you look closely at the individual lives they stand for.

Many middle-class Americans think of pot smoking as a harmless indulgence—a bad habit when carried to extremes but generally just one of the foolish experiments teenagers engage in. That's why politicians from Jeb Bush and Ted Cruz to Andrew Cuomo and (most notoriously) Bill Clinton have admitted using marijuana in their youths and suffered little or no damage to their reputations or careers.

It's not so easy for many young people of color. Though black and white Americans use marijuana at practically identical rates, blacks are 3.73 times more likely to be arrested for possession than whites.[7] In many cases, the impact is devastating.

DeMarcus Sanders was a young construction worker in Waterloo, Iowa, who was pulled over by police for having his car stereo blaring too loud. The officer said he smelled marijuana in Sanders's vehicle and proceeded to mount a search that yielded a single marijuana seed on the car floor. Sanders was arrested for possession, pleaded guilty, and ended up spending thirty days in jail.

Unfortunately, the jail sentence was just the start of Sanders's troubles. While behind bars, he was fired from his job and lost credit for the college courses he'd been taking part-time. State law mandated an automatic six-month suspension of his driver's license, making it almost impossible for Sanders to find and keep another job. And being unemployed prevented Sanders from paying off the court fees and fines he was hit with. Years later, he was still getting letters from the state demanding payment of some $2,346 he owes, including even room and board for his month in jail—and each letter included a threat of further jail time if the bill wasn't promptly paid.[8]

DeMarcus Sanders is no Jeb Bush or Bill Clinton, able to shrug off the incident as a youthful escapade. He is not even a young Barack Obama, another future politician who experimented with marijuana and escaped without paying a significant personal price—in his case, probably because he was sheltered by attending the most prestigious prep school in Honolulu as well as by having a mainly white family.

Most people of color aren't so lucky. For them, a misstep like using drugs, even casually as Sanders did, can have dire, lifelong consequences—a powerful illustration of what "white privilege" and its absence really mean in the lives of individual people.

The Conviction Gap

As we've seen, a number of US laws have been written in ways that produce unequal impact on people from differing backgrounds. Making matters worse, enforcement of the laws by prosecutors, judges, and juries is also often distorted by racial and other biases.

One form of legal discrimination that's particularly difficult to prove and prevent is the wholesale exclusion of blacks from juries in criminal cases. Many prosecutors are convinced that black jurors are overly sympathetic to defendants and consequently are too "soft on crime" to be trusted. The prosecutors' concern isn't completely unfounded. Many studies have shown that all-white juries are significantly more prone to convict black defendants than white defendants. Most fascinating, at least one study of more than seven hundred Florida cases found that this "conviction gap" disappeared when just a single black juror was included in the pool.[9] This research suggests that spending a few hours deliberating on a criminal case with a person of a different race can have a measurable impact on the fairness with which white jurors reach decisions of guilt or innocence.

Unfortunately, the response of too many prosecutors is to eliminate blacks from jury pools, hoping to create all-white juries more prone to convict. Many use "peremptory challenges" to reject jurors of color without having to justify their actions. The Supreme Court has found such racial discrimination in juror selection unconstitutional, but proving it is virtually impossible. After all, no intelligent prosecutor will ever admit he is rejecting a specific jury candidate because of his or her race. Instead, a justification is fabricated.

That's what happened in the 1989 case *Crittenden v. Chappell*, in which an all-white California jury convicted a black man named Steven Crittenden in the death of a wealthy white couple. Crittenden's lawyers appealed the conviction on the grounds of racial discrimination in jury selection, pointing out that the only potential black juror in the pool, a woman named Manzanita Casey, had been quickly eliminated from consideration. The prosecutor claimed she'd been challenged because of doubts that she expressed about the death penalty. But when the prosecutor's own notes were revealed in court, they showed he'd rated Casey "XXXX," his worst juror rating—while giving five white jurors who expressed similar doubts about capital punishment favorable ratings of "✓✓" or "✓✓✓."

Casey's color was the real reason for her exclusion. In October 2015, the Ninth Circuit Court of Appeals cited the prosecutor's notes in overturning Crittenden's conviction. But very few prosecutors who practice the same kind of discrimination keep written notes that expose their motivation. As a result, most get away with it, leading to markedly higher rates of conviction and imprisonment for black defendants than for whites.[10]

The racial disparities in our prisons have now become fairly well known, thanks to recent media coverage and powerful books like Michelle Alexander's acclaimed *The New Jim Crow*.[11] Less familiar is the fact that women are now the fastest-growing segment of the US prison population. Between 1980 and 2010, the number of women in prisons increased by 646 percent—nearly 1.5 times as fast as the rate of increase among men. Women of color suffer disproportionately: In 2010, black women were incarcerated at nearly three times the rate of white women, while Hispanic women were incarcerated at 1.6 times the rate of white women. Incarcerated women are mostly mothers who leave children behind when they go off to prison; 1 in 25 of those sent to state prisons are actually pregnant when they begin life behind bars. While in prison, women are more likely than men to be victims of sexual misconduct by correctional staff and to suffer from chronic or communicable diseases, such as HIV.[12]

The cumulative impact of mass incarceration is devastating, and every American should worry about its long-term consequences for the nation. Around 2.7 million children are growing up in American households in which one or both parents are incarcerated—including one in nine black children.[13] And the effects don't end when a prisoner finishes serving time. A criminal record impacts an ex-prisoner's life in many ways, from job opportunities to voting rights, public housing to student aid. Returning to normal life after time behind bars is incredibly difficult, and legal and social practices throughout society only serve to make it harder.

Thanks to these systems that multiply the impact of prejudice and discrimination, existing biases in criminal law, prosecutions, and sentencing practices have effectively landed a huge share of an entire generation of minorities in jail, undermining families, communities, and our country's potential in the process. The effects will be felt for generations to come. It's hard to imagine any challenge to our national commitment to diversity more pressing than this one.

Reform Across Divides

In recent years, there have been few instances of political leaders from opposite sides of the party spectrum advocating mutual goals. Yet the cause of criminal justice reform has united conservatives like Senator Rand Paul and businessman David Koch with liberals like Senator Cory Booker and civil rights activist Van Jones. Paul and Booker are an especially "odd couple" pairing—a conservative Republican of libertarian leanings and a liberal African American—with clashing views on many issues. But they've discovered common ground in collaborating to solve the huge, costly problems that our broken criminal justice system has caused.

While I don't know him personally, I'm struck that Rand Paul has a kind of acquired diversity that has led him to be a leader on this issue and to relate personally to it. He sees a thin line between abuses of minorities by our justice system and larger issues of freedom and the rights enshrined by the Constitution. He became especially passionate about the story of Kalief Browder, a black sixteen-year-old high school student from the Bronx. Accused of stealing a backpack—a charge Browder steadfastly denied—he was arrested and sent to New York's notorious prison on Rikers Island, where he spent almost two years in solitary confinement. Browder was subject to physical abuse and violence at the hands of his prison guards and fellow inmates. After three years, during which Browder missed both his junior and senior years of high school, his case was dismissed by prosecutors in March 2013.

When Paul heard about Browder's case, he was horrified. In a speech before the Conservative Political Action Conference, Paul detailed Browder's story: "He was never tried. He tried to commit suicide four times. If you ask Kalief Browder and you ask his mom or you ask anybody that lives around him in the Bronx whether or not the Bill of Rights is being defended, he lives in that other America that Martin Luther King talked about." Sadly, Browder's story has a tragic ending. He committed suicide at his home in June 2015 at the age of twenty-two.

Paul has now redoubled his efforts to reform the system that helped lead to Browder's needless death.[14] He and Cory Booker have teamed up to introduce what they call the REDEEM Act, which would provide incentives to states to keep young offenders under age eighteen out of adult courts, seal the criminal records of young people who commit nonviolent crimes before age fifteen, and make it easier for low-level drug offenders to get support after release from prison through programs like food stamps. Unfortunately, the proposal is currently on hold, being considered in slightly different versions by committees of the House and Senate.

After hearing Paul present his reform ideas in a speech at Howard University, one of America's leading historically black colleges, a writer for the online magazine *Salon* was moved to observe:

> *I never thought I would agree with Rand Paul on anything. I have always been very liberal, but I agree with the conservative junior senator from Kentucky when it comes to criminal justice issues. I'm just coming at the issue from a very different background: A few years ago, I served time in prison for a drug crime and after my release became a prison activist and journalist. Clearly, Paul has never been in prison, but he's won the begrudging respect of this liberal ex-con by addressing criminal justice reform with meaningful legislation.*[15]

Paul's commitment to reform and to what might easily be seen as a minority issue is especially important because of his conservative credentials and because he is a white man. Senator Booker is a highly respected, influential rising star in the Democratic Party and one of only two black senators in the current 114th Congress. (In fact, in the entire history of the Senate, there have been only nine black senators, including just four elected by the voters of their states.) But without the support of white, conservative senators like Paul, reform would have little chance of progress.

Driving policy change at the national level is a slow, arduous process, particularly in today's ultra-polarized political climate, but one sign that a seismic shift may be under way was the passage in October 2015, by committees in both the House of Representatives and the Senate, of major draft bills focused on criminal justice reform. Among other provisions, these bills are designed to reduce mandatory minimum sentences for drug offenders, which have played a large role in driving the phenomenon of mass incarceration. For example, the Senate version of the bill would make the provisions of the Fair Sentencing Act of 2010, which reduced the discrepancy in sentencing rules between crack and powder cocaine, retroactive, allowing thousands of nonviolent drug offenders—mostly black and Latino—to be freed from prison. Other elements in the proposed legislation are designed to improve policing practices, mitigate harsh rules regarding civil asset forfeiture for minor offenses, and make conditions in federal prisons less brutal.[16]

Democratic and Republican leaders are working together carefully to nurture the chances of these commonsense reforms. At a strategy conference convened by President Obama in December 2015, attendees included Senate Minority Whip Richard Durbin (D-IL), Senate Majority Whip John Cornyn (R-TX), and even the conservative antitax activist Grover Norquist, who supports criminal justice reform as part of his campaign to protect Americans from overreach by the IRS.

It's a tremendously hopeful sign when people from such different backgrounds as Rand Paul and Cory Booker, Richard Durbin and John Cornyn, and even Barack Obama and Grover Norquist can come together around an issue such as criminal justice reform. It's also an indicator of how vitally important it is for our nation to get this issue right. If America stands for anything, it must stand for equal justice under the law, and that means treating all citizens—no matter their race, ethnicity, or gender—with the respect, fairness, and dignity they deserve.

War on the Streets: Racial Conflicts over Policing

Of course, the racial problems that plague our justice system go beyond the laws themselves. The police, on a local and federal level, are responsible for enforcement of those laws. And as cases like those of Michael Brown and Eric Garner suggest, many police departments struggle with internal challenges regarding race and diversity.

Passed a few years after the beating of Rodney King by LA police, the 1994 Crime Bill empowered the civil rights division of the US Department of Justice to monitor local police departments around the nation and compel them—through a kind of forced collaboration called a consent decree or through legal action—to diversify if they demonstrated a "pattern and practice" of violating the civil rights of those they are tasked with protecting. Historically, police departments have not sufficiently invested in ensuring they reflect the communities they police, and in the worst cases, the departments themselves have become bastions of racism and exclusion. As of 2015, more than twenty police departments around the country operate under consent decrees, which essentially means they have failed in their efforts to diversify the department or have shown a pattern of violating the civil rights of people in their communities.[17]

Data increasingly confirms the biases in policing that many minority citizens have complained of for years. In 2014, independent journalism group ProPublica concluded that young black males run a risk of being shot dead by police that is twenty-one times greater than for their white counterparts. And of those killed when fleeing arrest (rather than threatening police with violence), 67 percent were black.[18]

Exacerbating these problems is the fact that minority communities are too often patrolled by white police officers, resembling the occupying foreign armies that control a conquered territory. In hundreds of cities around the country, the members of the police force are more than 30 percent whiter than the communities they serve.[19] The resulting cultural disconnect between the people and the officers who should serve them leads to needless tensions, misunderstandings, even violence—on both sides. In criminal justice, the lack of both inherent and acquired diversity can literally kill.

One of the most appalling examples of the pervasiveness and destructiveness of racial bias in policing comes from the city of Chicago. Following revelations that the Chicago Police Department (CPD) covered up the facts surrounding the 2015 death of Laquan McDonald at the hands of Officer Jason Van Dyke, Mayor Rahm Emanuel appointed a task force to investigate the department.

In April 2016, the task force released a twenty-two-page report on its findings, highlighting how dire the situation in Chicago truly is. It cited data that black or Hispanic citizens were the victims in 92 percent of police shootings between 2008 and 2015 (although these two groups made up just about 62 percent of the city's population in the 2010 census). Officers used Tasers disproportionately on blacks—76 percent of those tased by members of the department were black. Blacks were stopped on the street and pulled over in their cars disproportionately to whites. And when it comes to accountability for officers who engage in racist, sometimes illegal activity, the story is just as grim. Between 2008 and 2015, there were 1,300 officers with between ten and twenty civilian complaints against them, and 200 more with twenty to thirty complaints against them were allowed to continue working.

The report's authors were blunt in their assessment of the causes of these problems:

We arrived at this point in part because of racism.
We arrived at this point because of a mentality in CPD that the ends justify the means.
We arrived at this point because of a failure to make accountability a core value and imperative within CPD.
We arrived at this point because of a significant underinvestment in human capital.[20]

The task force recommended dozens of remedial actions, including a total overhaul and reinvestment in community/ police relationships, a structured reconciliation process, greater accountability and oversight, a focus on de-escalation training, and a clear policy requiring the early release of police video. Policies like these are probably needed at every police department, but policies alone won't fix the problem. It will take years of effort by committed officers, public officials, and the community to heal what's been so broken for so long.

It's not just local police forces that have work to do. The FBI also has a dismal record of diversity. Only 4.5 percent of FBI agents are African American, and just 6.8 percent are Hispanic. It's an issue that has the attention of leaders at the highest levels. FBI Director Comey was asked about this recently and made it clear where he stood. It's a "big challenge for the FBI. The FBI is overwhelmingly white and male...and I've got nothing against white males: I happen to be one."[21]

It's worth noting that the diversity gap between police departments and communities has been *improving* over time. The Bureau of Justice Statistics has been tracking the racial makeup of police departments since 1987. In its initial study, racial and ethnic minorities accounted for 15 percent of the members of local police forces. By 2007, minorities had increased to 25 percent, and in the most recent study, from 2013, they had increased a bit further to 27 percent. That means more than 120,000 black, Latino, Asian, and other ethnic minorities are part of local police forces around the country. The number of women officers has also increased—from a raw number of 27,000 in 1987 to 58,000 in 2013. However, women still constitute just around 12 percent of the nation's police forces.

Nevertheless, the slowly improving numbers of women and minorities in police departments don't mean that the problem is solved. While visible diversity matters, by itself it will not create both the perception and the reality of equal treatment of civilian populations. The Justice Department has acknowledged as much. Vanita Gupta, who heads the civil rights division at the department, said in a December 2015 speech:

No single solution, including a more diverse police force, will strengthen fragmented ties of community trust overnight or guarantee safe, effective, and constitutional policing. Yet greater diversity can increase trust between police officers and the communities they serve—trust essential to defusing tension, to solving crimes, and to creating a system where citizens view law enforcement as fair and just.[22]

Alex S. Vitale, a sociology professor at Brooklyn College who has studied the issue, found that black and white officers treat the public in much the same way. For example, disparate treatment of young people based on the color of their skin is demonstrated by both white and black police officers. "The overarching reality is that these [black] officers are part of an institution that has very clear expectations and demands and they respond to the demands in the way that white officers do."[23]

Is bringing more people of color into our police departments an important step toward creating the conditions that may lead to greater equity and justice? Absolutely. Is it sufficient in itself? No. As in every other field we have explored, for diversity in policing to make the intended impact, the entire police force must also embrace diversity and better community relations. Improved training and a major change in the culture of the criminal justice system are also required.

Thinning the Lines Between

Fortunately, communities around the country are beginning to respond to this complex problem. Many are taking steps to fix the diversity problems in their criminal justice systems, hoping to avoid becoming the next epicenter of racial tension or violence.

Some of the positive shifts in local criminal justice policy are occurring as a result of exposure of the more egregious practices that have routinely victimized diverse population groups. In chapter eight, we discussed the US Justice Department's finding that the St. Louis suburb of Ferguson, Missouri, routinely used bench warrants to arrest people of color for minor, nonviolent offenses (like traffic violations) as a way of generating huge fines and fees. Similar practices have been observed in other cities around the country.

In the wake of such reports, some local governments are abandoning these policies and adopting more humane and equitable ways of dealing with minor infractions of the law. Shortly after the revelations about Ferguson hit the news, officials in nearby St. Louis announced a plan to automatically "forgive" over two hundred thousand outstanding warrants that had been issued prior to October 1, 2014. Under this new program, nonviolent traffic offenders could set new court dates for hearings on charges against them without being subject to the onerous fees and fines they'd previously faced. "In light of Ferguson," said mayoral chief of staff Jeff Rainford, "we were thinking of how we can be more fair…This is a way for people to get this off their back and for us to get it off the books. But it also keeps people accountable for the underlying offenses."[24]

In many cases, communities around the country have been quietly, steadily forging alliances between local governments, police departments, and neighborhood organizations, seeking to break down the barriers of mistrust and hostility that may have built up over the years.

Richmond is a working-class town with a population of around 110,000 in California's Bay Area, eleven miles north of Oakland. A generation ago, like many cities with ethnic diversity and a challenging economic climate, Richmond struggled to deal with issues of crime and police misconduct. In a 1983 lawsuit, the families of two black men killed by police were awarded $3 million in damages, and Richmond was admonished for tolerating the brutality of a group of lawless police officers who called themselves "The Cowboys."

Today, the picture has been transformed. Richmond is still economically challenged and ethnically mixed—40 percent Latino, 27 percent black, 17 percent non-Latino white, and 13 percent Asian—but crime has fallen dramatically. Homicides in Richmond, which peaked at forty-seven in 2007, fell to eleven in 2014.

At the same time, relations between police and the community have become cooperative and mutually supportive. When cities across the country experienced confrontations between protestors and police in the wake of the Michael Brown killing, a very different scene unfolded in Richmond. Peaceful demonstrators gathered at a local community center to offer support to angry citizens in Ferguson and elsewhere. And when Richmond police chief Chris Magnus showed up at the event with several other officers, he was asked to hold up a sign with the slogan "Black Lives Matter." After a moment's hesitation, Magnus displayed the sign for photographers, and the image of a uniformed cop supporting the protestors soon went viral on the Internet.

Magnus took some flak from those who considered the protestors "anti-police," but he didn't back down. "I would do it again," he says.[25]

Magnus had led the Richmond police force for nine years,

playing a major role in transforming its culture from one of antagonism to partnership with the people of the town. He represents an important movement that has made a real difference in many cities, towns, and suburbs over the last three decades. Known as *community policing*, it's a system that promotes the use of partnerships and person-to-person interactions between police officers and civilians to address many of the problems that give rise to crime, such as poverty, joblessness, lack of educational opportunity, and mistrust of the police.

In effect, community policing is an organized effort to thin the dividing lines between two key population groups—police officers and the community members they serve. Providing opportunities for these two groups to get to know, trust, and work with one another is crucial to the long-term success of crime-reduction efforts.

A simple example of how community policing works is the story of a potentially dangerous confrontation that unfolded in Richmond on September 12, 2015. Police got word that a heavily armed man suspected of serious domestic violence had barricaded himself in a house. The local SWAT team was called into action. In some communities, the result would have been a firefight that might have hurt bystanders as well as the troubled offender. But one of the SWAT officers realized that he had previously befriended several neighborhood residents, including the mother of the armed man. He enlisted her assistance to persuade her son to come to the front door and discuss the situation with the officer. After a time, the man agreed to end the siege and surrender to police—all peaceably.

"It ends with no shooting and no deaths and no big drama," said Magnus. He attributed the outcome to the powerful line-crossing relationships that community policing builds.[26]

Success stories like Richmond have helped to spread the gospel of community policing. Columbia Heights is a suburb of Minneapolis where community policing has been credited in the years since 2008 with a dramatic improvement in both crime rates and community-police relationships. Under the leadership of police chief Scott Nadeau, officers have been trained to engage in between ten and forty hours of community policing practices every year—activities that range from mentoring schoolkids, running gym classes, and teaching recent immigrants to serving food at local church suppers and conducting Coffee with a Cop forums in which community members can raise their concerns and questions in a nonconfrontational setting. Youth outreach activities include a bullying prevention program led by local cops and—perhaps most popular—an annual visit when schoolkids get a chance to check out the inside of a real squad car.

Nadeau acknowledges that getting officers engaged in community policing wasn't easy. "It took months or years for some people to see the value... But I think even the officers we had that were more traditional saw the changes in the relationships between our police department and the community." Nadeau, who personally mentors a student once a week, describes how attitudes toward the police have changed in recent years. "Now when we walk down the hallways, the teachers smile, they're happy that you're there. I probably get about fifty to sixty high fives from some of the kids in the school."[27]

Community policing isn't just about creating a feel-good atmosphere between police and citizens—important though that is. Breaking down the barriers of distrust between largely minority communities and majority-white police forces produces concrete benefits in the battle to control crime. When community members view police as trustworthy individuals with their best interests at heart, they are less likely to harbor or protect criminals; they're more apt to cooperate with officers in solving crimes and play a proactive role in efforts to clean the streets of drug sellers, gang leaders, and gun dealers.

Gail Howard, a community leader in Redlands, California, has become an active supporter of her town's community policing program. After her own son survived a gang shooting, she was impressed by the thoroughness and honesty with which local police conducted the investigation, arrest, and conviction of the culprits. Now she helps run the town's Shop with a Cop program, which sends poor kids on holiday shopping trips with police officers. "Some of these kids," Howard says, "the only contact they have with police is seeing their parent be wrestled down to the ground and handcuffed, and we want them to know that there's good officers out there...I want kids not to be afraid to approach that police officer."[28]

Community policing takes a philosophical commitment by local leaders, long-term programs of training and counseling within police departments, and the investment of time and money to make nontraditional police activities routine. Federal funding to support community policing peaked in the late 1990s. Unfortunately, it declined in subsequent years, a result of many factors, from the intense focus on antiterrorism campaigns following 9/11 to the financial pressures on government budgets caused by the Great Recession of 2008–9. Today, however, due to the national impact of tragedies like Ferguson and the rise of the Black Lives Matter movement, renewed attention is being given to the importance of community policing.

Now New York, America's biggest city—and by some measure its most difficult to govern—is embarking on an ambitious effort to reform its own policing program. Having successfully reformed the Los Angeles Police Department, Bill Bratton was asked by Mayor de Blasio to return to the helm of the city's police department in 2013. Bratton in turn created a new post, that of deputy commissioner for collaborative policing, and appointed Susan Herman, an advocate for crime victims, to fill the job.

Herman is piloting a number of significant changes in how New York's criminal justice system operates. She works with prosecutors and judges to implement Project Reset, which channels nonviolent sixteen- and seventeen-year-old offenders away from the traditional justice system and into counseling programs run by the nonprofit Center for Court Innovation.

Herman has also been spearheading Operation Ceasefire, a violence-prevention program that has proven successful in a number of other cities, including Boston. Under Ceasefire, local gang members who have been identified as most likely to trigger violence in their communities are invited to meet with police officers and prosecutors. They're warned about the legal retribution they can expect from the criminal justice system if they participate in gun battles. Then community organizations step in to work with the gang members and others in the surrounding neighborhoods to change the lifestyles that precipitate violence.

In addition, Herman is helping the NYPD do more to aid crime victims. In her prior work as a victim advocate, Herman discovered that victims and criminals often come from the same population groups, have many of the same vulnerabilities, and share the same sense of alienation from the larger society—especially from the criminal justice system. Now she is working to install victim advocates in every police precinct, expedite notoriously slow victim compensation systems, and develop new procedures for dealing with victims and their families that are designed to minimize the psychological traumas they suffer. Herman's overarching goal is to create a greater sense of connection between the system and the people it serves, so the entire community will have a better chance to heal and grow together.

Herman says, "This is a fundamentally different way of policing. Instead of unfocused, massive enforcement efforts, you have a focused effort that attacks the real problem."[29]

If community policing can work in New York City, it should have a great chance of working practically anywhere in the United States.

10. The Customer Is King and Queen

We need to give each other the space to grow, to be ourselves, to exercise our diversity. We need to give each other space so that we may both give and receive such beautiful things as ideas, openness, dignity, joy, healing, and inclusion.

—*Max De Pree, Herman Miller, Inc.*

It must have seemed like a good idea at the time. In the fall of 2015, IBM launched an online video marketing campaign aimed at encouraging more women to pursue careers in science and technology. Using the Twitter hashtag #HackAHairDryer, the campaign was meant to build the company brand among female engineers and attract more women to work at the company. It featured a YouTube video challenging women to "hack a hair dryer" by inventing new ways to use the familiar styling appliance. As a female narrator recited statistics about the low numbers of women in the STEM fields of science, technology, engineering, and mathematics, hair dryers in pastel shades were shown being used in various cute, supposedly innovative ways—propelling Ping-Pong balls, blowing colorful streamers, producing musical notes by sending air flowing through harmonicas.

The campaign was launched at significant expense and with much fanfare—and soon collapsed in ridicule. Women scientists and engineers took to Twitter to mock the campaign's unconscious condescension and sexism. The news media reported some of the most scathing replies. Rocket scientist Stephanie Evans wrote, "That's ok @IBM, I'd rather build satellites instead, but good luck with that whole #HackAHairDryer thing." TOSH @amok_times wrote, "hey @IBM why do you think women are only interested in STEM when it involves beauty products?" And Stephanie Leary @sleary wrote, "How to get more women in STEM? Fire the bosses who think #HackAHairDryer is a good idea, replace them with women."

It seems unlikely that this was the kind of press IBM had been hoping for. Only a few weeks after the campaign launched, the company shut it down, issuing a statement that confessed, "It missed the mark for some and we apologize."[1]

IBM execs probably had good intentions. In an effort to reach female techies and present themselves to consumers as female friendly, they tried to appeal to women in ways they thought they'd relate to. But the ill-conceived program insulted women by relying on gendered assumptions based on stereotypes rather than real insights into the lives, talents, and values of female engineers.

Ironically, IBM is one of the few Fortune 500 companies with a female CEO—Virginia Marie "Ginni" Rometty has headed the firm since 2012. But as in other tech firms, its workforce lags when it comes to overall diversity. It seems likely that IBM could have avoided this embarrassing public failure if more women had been in the room when the program was developed.

Recognizing and Responding to the Changing American Consumer

There are endless examples of prestigious companies embarrassing themselves and tarnishing their own brands and reputations by missing critical insights into the customers they serve. It's a particularly common problem—and an urgent one—in an era when the diversity of American consumers is rapidly increasing, challenging business people to broaden their understanding of a wide array of cultures, values, tastes, and preferences.

One of my favorite examples of a completely ridiculous product failure—and one of the funniest—is Bic for Her pens. Launched in 2012, the pens came in pastel colors and were supposed to be designed to fit women's hands better than standard pens. One of the first commentators to ridicule this inane product was a writer at the online magazine *Jezebel*, whose scathing review was eventually picked up by multiple media outlets. As the story spread to the *Washington Post* and other media outlets, Ellen DeGeneres mocked the pens on her talk show in a hilarious monologue and a satirical "commercial" that's been viewed millions of times on YouTube. But best of all are the more than two thousand hilarious reviews on Amazon.com, featuring sarcastic comments like:

"I was disappointed to find that only one fifth of the pens I received were pink. Or, maybe more, I can't do maths."

"These pens fit perfect in my hands, but hubby feels they are unnecessary since he writes all the checks. I'd explain more but I have to go make him a sammich."

"Someone has answered my gentle prayers and FINALLY designed a pen that I can use all month long!...Since I've begun using these pens, men have found me more attractive and approachable. It has given me soft skin and manageable hair and it has really given me the self-esteem I needed to start a book club and flirt with the bag-boy at my local market. My drawings of kittens and ponies have improved, and now that I'm writing my last name hyphenated with...Robert Pattinson's last name, I really believe he may some day marry me! I'm positively giddy. Those smart men in marketing have come up with a pen that my lady parts can really identify with."

Given the demographics of the marketing world, it's possible that no women took part in the meetings where the Bic for Her debacle was planned. But the more likely scenario is that there were women in the room, yet their opinions went unheard, their concerns ignored. It happens every day in large and small ways in nearly every company. Even companies that have recruited a diverse employee base often fail to take advantage of the potential benefits because executives are unable or unwilling to pay attention to differing points of view.

It's a problem that has grown more serious in recent decades as the face of the American consumer has completely changed. Racial and ethnic minorities are increasing in number, and their buying power is growing even more quickly. LGBT Americans are coming out of the closet, establishing families, buying homes, and becoming a major segment of the consumer marketplace. Most significant of all, women are now the primary decision makers when it comes to purchasing consumer products, appliances, high-tech devices, cars, homes, health care, financial services, and countless other goods. Women also control roughly two-thirds of annual spending in the United States, a sum of about $12 trillion.[2]

When companies fail to fully embrace America's steadily increasing diversity, not only do they risk embarrassing themselves and alienating potential customers, as IBM and Bic did, they also risk provoking anger from consumer groups who feel significantly and painfully disrespected by them. When this happens, the backlash may be more than embarrassing; it may be truly costly, both in financial terms and in terms of company prestige and community relations.

Gap Inc. recently learned just how attuned consumers are to the diversity or lack thereof in advertising. A series of online ads for GapKids x ED children's line (ironically designed by Ellen DeGeneres, someone deeply and personally committed to diversity) sparked outrage on social media when the only black child in the ads was shown posing passively with a white child leaning on her, while white girls were seen doing gymnastics or using a telescope. The ad was captioned, "Meet the kids who are proving girls can do anything." Twitter followers erupted. One tweet read, "@GapKids, proving that girls can do anything, unless she's black. Then all she can do is bear the weight of White girls. #EpicFail." Another read, "Thanks for perfectly illustrating what 'passive racism' looks like in mainstream media. #DiversityFail She is not your armrest."

GapKids quickly removed the ad and apologized, but it was a truly unfortunate incident for a company that has worked very hard over the years to be a leader on diversity. Today, with more and more Americans willing to flex their collective buying power and their social media skills to put pressure on business, well-intentioned companies like Gap Inc. are being held to a higher standard than ever.

One group of consumers that has recently started to exercise economic clout in a powerful way is LGBT Americans. A 2015 study estimated the combined buying power of LGBT individuals in the United States at around $884 billion annually—roughly equivalent to the entire GDP of the state of Florida.[3] That's a lot of money… and when the people who control it are prepared to use it in the form of political influence, the power they command is considerable.

Many companies are making serious efforts to appeal to gay consumers and their families. During Pride month in June 2014, Honey Maid, AT&T, Levi's, and others launched successful ad campaigns targeted at the gay and ally community. Wells Fargo, Campbell's, and Amazon (Kindle) have all featured gay couples and families in ads. Now many companies ask their employees of diverse backgrounds to weigh in on their marketing and advertising campaigns, often turning to the employee resource or affinity groups for feedback. The strategy has largely succeeded, and these companies have mostly avoided the types of backlash that IBM and Bic faced.

Companies are right to work hard to prove their commitment to diverse communities, and many are taking that commitment very, very seriously. As of early 2016, Out Leadership, the first global LGBT business organization composed of senior leaders and companies committed to LGBT equality, boasts sixty-nine member companies on five continents; more than two hundred CEOs have spoken at Out Leadership summits held around the world.

The willingness of business leaders to stand up for inclusion and human rights is having a significant practical impact. In March 2015, when legislators in Indiana passed a so-called religious freedom law that many interpreted as protecting the right of businesses to discriminate against gays and lesbians, the uproar was quickly translated into economic terms. Business organizations and nonprofit groups that had been organizing conventions or meetings in Indiana threatened to cancel; popular entertainers crossed Indiana off the list of sites for their upcoming tours; and basketball fans even demanded that the annual Final Four college tournament be moved from its scheduled location in Indianapolis. The online service platform Angie's List announced that it would cancel a planned $40 million business expansion in the state, and a number of cities and states made plans to ban work-related travel to Indiana by government employees.

Indiana governor Mike Pence defended the law, claiming it was not intended to discriminate against anyone. But as the opposition continued to grow, state legislators hastily cobbled together a revision to the law that provided protections to LGBT consumers. The revised law was signed on April 2, 2015, quelling much of the furor.

In May 2015, within days of the passage of the revised law in

Indiana, a coalition of two hundred companies in Texas banded together to sign a pledge in support of diversity and gay rights. Their primary goal: to discourage Texas lawmakers from passing a bill similar to the one that got Indiana into hot water.

"Conventions, the Super Bowl, the Final Four—all those things would be at risk in Texas if this [religious freedom law] were to become part of our constitution," declared Bill Hammond, CEO of the Texas Association of Business. "We believe it would be bad for Texas business."

Another member of the pro-diversity coalition was Mark McKinnon, a former advisor to President George W. Bush. "It's like hanging a sign out front that says, 'Sorry, we're not a welcoming and hospitable state,'" McKinnon said. "We can't afford that negative image when it comes to recruiting top talent to come work in Texas, especially millennials who have no tolerance for anti-gay anything."[4] The fact that business executives in Texas—a reliably conservative group—have taken such a forceful stand on behalf of diversity is a testament to the ability of economic clout to influence political and social action. Unfortunately, lawmakers in a number of other states including North Carolina, Tennessee, Mississippi, and Georgia have been undeterred by the threat of economic backlash. They have passed or are considering bills limiting the civil rights of LGBT Americans, often under the guise of protecting the religious liberty of those who oppose gay rights.

Todd Sears, founder of Out Leadership, emphasizes that the battle for LGBT rights is far from over—in fact, it may simply have entered a new phase: "I think most of the recent laws trying to force LGBT people back into the closet are a response to the rising tide of marriage equality and other successes of the gay rights movement." He says:

It's sad to see antigay activists and legislators hiding behind religion in their efforts to find an excuse for discrimination. Now states like North Carolina are seizing on public anxiety about transgender people as another red herring to justify discrimination. That's the strategy behind laws like the one passed in March 2016 that requires people to use the public restrooms associated with the gender they were assigned at birth rather than the one they currently identify with. The excuse is that such laws are needed to protect "public safety"—yet there's never been a single case of assault or even a complaint linked to the use of a public restroom by a transgender person.

The North Carolina law is so obviously discriminatory that the backlash against it has been enormous. Companies like Bank of America, the state's largest employer, have attacked it publicly; performers like Bruce Springsteen and Ringo Starr have canceled plans to appear in the state; and even the state attorney general has said he won't defend the law in court. Still, as of now, the governor stands by the law, and eleven other states have similar laws currently under consideration or in the planning stages.

Over the long term, the tide of change is in our favor. But in the short term, the battles we face are intense.[5]

Other diverse groups are mobilizing their own economic power on behalf of their political and social rights. African Americans and their allies of other backgrounds who are angry over the deaths of young blacks at the hands of police officers launched a national boycott of stores during the height of the 2015 holiday shopping season. Promoted using the hashtag #NotOneDime, the campaign urged African Americans to refrain from shopping on Black Friday, the traditional start of the Christmas buying season, and to channel their retail spending during the entire month of December to black-owned businesses. The purpose of the boycott was to remind Americans—especially business leaders—about the size and importance of the black community. It's hard to measure exactly how effective the NotOneDime campaign was, but some in the movement believe it played a role in the reported nationwide decline of Black Friday retail sales by about a billion dollars between 2014 and 2015.[6]

As these two movements illustrate, for American businesses, accepting diversity isn't just about avoiding stupid mistakes that can cause a public relations nightmare. It's also about maintaining good relations with large, powerful, and growing segments of the population who care deeply about being treated with dignity and respect—and whose patronage should be an important part of any business's growth strategy.

Tapping the Opportunities

Of course many companies "get it," and there are numerous examples of the huge US business opportunities to be gained from embracing diversity. One that I have spent some time working on is the market for financial and wealth services for women. In two-thirds of American households, women are the main breadwinners or co-breadwinners, and more than half of married women with business degrees actually outearn their husbands. Women own 89 percent of American bank accounts and control 51 percent of all the personal wealth in the nation.[7] What's more, about 80 percent of American women will be solely responsible for their households' financial decisions at some point during their lives.[8]

These facts upend the outdated assumptions about family life that some people still hang on to—the ideas that men earn the lion's share of the income for their families and also make most of the important financial decisions. Yet many financial professionals—brokers, advisors, accountants, insurance agents—continue to treat female investors as an afterthought, partially because the profession has been male dominated for so long. Fewer than one third of financial advisors are female, and while there's no evidence that women prefer to have a female advisor, without women contributing their insights at major financial services firms, an important perspective is missing. Some financial advisors still operate as if in another era—they fail to solicit the opinions and preferences of women, omit female partners when sending out financial reports and e-mail notifications, and make inaccurate assumptions about what women investors want, especially by pushing products rather than getting to know their clients.

Even when there's no man in the picture, as when a woman is single, widowed, or divorced, many financial professionals have no idea how to work effectively with a female client. Women report significantly lower satisfaction ratings in regard to the treatment they receive from their financial advisors: They get less useful advice, less honest information, and less valuable assistance. This helps to explain why, after a husband's death, more than 70 percent of married women fire their financial professionals within a year. It's a natural reaction to being treated without respect, understanding, or sincerity—an all-too-common experience among women investors.[9]

Smart financial professionals and the firms they work for have begun to recognize the huge business opportunity that these underserved women investors represent. They are involving women in all financial planning decisions rather than thoughtlessly deferring to men. They are learning to *really* listen to female voices during group discussions and to question their own beliefs about women as investors (such as the flawed assumptions that women are always "risk averse" or uncomfortable with math). And they are identifying the hidden business potential in client groups that traditionally have been overlooked. For example, female same-sex couples, who may need more sophisticated financial tools to help them overcome the social and legal obstacles that still make life more difficult for them in some states of the Union.

Charles Schwab, one of the country's best-known brokerage firms, has long understood the value and importance of diverse customers. It has built a reputation for being one of the most thoughtful companies, able to connect and outreach to a wide range of customers, including women. Carrie Schwab-Pomerantz chairs the Charles Schwab Foundation and is the daughter of legendary pioneer and founder Charles Schwab. She has dedicated her career to helping Americans build greater financial literacy. Appointed to President Obama's Advisory Council on Financial Capability, she's a leading advocate for teaching financial skills more broadly to Americans, especially young people. She explains why the company has done well by reaching out to diverse customers who have been underserved by her industry:

We're not your traditional firm. A lot of it had to do with starting in San Francisco and not in the thick of Wall Street, but also my dad's vision. We've created what I might say is a feminine sensitivity.

My dad wasn't happy with how Wall Street treated individuals and everyday people. He wanted to democratize investing and open it up from what had traditionally just been something for the rich to something anyone could be a part of. In his time, investing was super expensive and an exclusive club. He saw a way to be different. He reduced commissions while his competitors increased them—that's how so-called discount brokerage was born. It enabled everyday people to invest. From there it sort of snowballed.

His strategy was inclusive. It brought people into investing that had been overlooked by others. He even changed the pay structure internally so that it discouraged any behavior that was not in the interest of the client.

Schwab-Pomerantz started working at the company at a very young age, when the company was just a couple years old. I asked her if she thought she had been an influence on her father and cited research that shows that men with daughters are more sensitive to women and underserved communities. "I'll take the credit," she said:

My dad knew I was very passionate about women and about economic parity, a living wage and equal opportunity for women. So when some women in the firm came to him and asked if we could start a women's initiative, he recommended I lead it. And I know, through our conversations and through his conversations with women friends, that my dad realizes our industry could be doing better for women. Would he say he understands that because he has a daughter? Maybe not, but he does understand it and supports our focus on supporting women as a firm.[10]

In recent years, companies in many other industries have also begun to recognize the huge untapped potential in America's increasingly diverse consumer base—and they've started to use their own organizational diversity as a way of tapping that potential.

Tracey Burton, former director of diversity at retail giant Target Corporation, observes: "I think the greatest benefit we have found is that diversity drives innovation. People from different backgrounds engaged in thoughtful debate leads to groundbreaking solutions. When you have a team that is engaged and reflective of your consumer base, you can better understand, anticipate, and meet the needs of your guests."[11]

Other firms have been learning and applying the same lesson. Insurance leader Liberty Mutual launched a number of ambitious enterprise-wide diversity and inclusion programs designed to address the changing internal and external talent demographics. In addition, Liberty Mutual is laser-focused on understanding the nuances of their ever-expanding, diverse customer base while also equipping the company's leaders with the cultural dexterity skills necessary to compete in a complicated, rapidly changing world in which innovation is more essential than ever. In the words of Francis Hyatt, the company's senior vice president for enterprise talent and human resource services:

> *Diversity isn't just about numbers. Yes, representation is a key part of the process, but it is also about creating an organizational environment and associated company policies that demonstrate that all employees can be their authentic selves and that the company values their contributions and supports their advancement. It is about having customers who recognize that the company respects and honors them and that their unique needs are valued and considered in our product and services offerings. It is about how we solve problems. We hold a diversity and inclusion lens when looking at everything we do.*[12]

Liberty Mutual's comprehensive approach to the challenge marks it as a company that really understands diversity and its important business value.

Plenty of individual businesspeople can attest to the value

of the outsider experience and the benefits it has brought to their careers. Bailey Dalton is an African American woman who dreamed as a girl about working for the FBI. Thinking that foreign-language proficiency might make her more valuable as a government sleuth, she studied Korean in college. She ended up spending several years in South Korea, working in jobs that ranged from liquor importer to radio disc jockey. The skills Dalton acquired by learning to "read" a culture wildly different from her own—and thrive in it—are proving highly relevant in her current career. Back in the United States, Dalton now works as a "social-behavioral analyst" for office furniture maker Turnstone, studying the ways customers think and behave and helping her firm anticipate their future needs.[13]

Going Global—Meeting the International Challenge

For generations, the vast continental geography and large population of the United States made it possible for companies to grow to an enormous scale based solely on domestic markets. But in today's era of globalization, that's no longer a practical reality. The fact is that the companies in the S&P 500—America's largest businesses—now glean more than 47 percent of their revenues from overseas markets. Many of the most successful do more than half of their business abroad. For Johnson & Johnson, foreign revenues are 53 percent of the company total; for Boeing, 58 percent; for Apple, 62 percent; for ExxonMobil, 67 percent; for Intel, 82 percent.[14]

The reality is that few companies can survive today without a sizeable global footprint, and that reality has compelled a deeper commitment to diversity. By definition, global business is all about diversity. In recent decades, markets with hundreds of millions of newly empowered middle-class customers have emerged in Asian countries such as China and India. A similar marketplace explosion is poised to occur in Africa in the next few decades. When *Business Insider* magazine compiled its 2015 list of fastest-growing economies based on World Bank forecasts, six of the thirteen countries listed—Rwanda, Tanzania, Mozambique, Côte d'Ivoire, the Democratic Republic of the Congo, and Ethiopia—were in Africa.[15]

And even as these developing marketplaces grow, they are undergoing radical cultural changes. For example, in many countries, women who were once socially and economically oppressed are joining the workforce, attaining political power, and achieving greater parity in the family and the community. In countries like China, India, Brazil, the United Arab Emirates, and Russia, women are pursuing college degrees at growing rates, even achieving more degrees, in some cases, than men.[16] Improved educational opportunities for women translate into better career options as well. A 2014 study found that women now control 27 percent of the world's total wealth, a share that is likely to continue to grow. And as the economic power of women increases, so do their expectations for just and equitable treatment. Case in point: When women in the United States are asked whether they support the idea of diversity in corporate leadership, 52 percent say yes—while in China, the number is 94 percent.[17]

As the world's most multicultural "nation of nations," the United States is uniquely positioned to understand and interact with rapidly evolving customer populations from every continent on earth. Yet for many American businesses, especially those that continue to neglect the importance of diversity or struggle to take full advantage of it, nothing is more difficult to get right than successful outreach to foreign markets.

The list of big, powerful US companies that have botched overseas expansion efforts due to cultural gaffes is impressive:

- Best Buy has been a popular US retailer of consumer electronics gear for decades and has even been named "Company of the Year" by *Forbes* magazine (2004). But it stumbled when it attempted to expand into markets in Europe, Turkey, and China, in part because it failed to understand overseas consumers' preferences for smaller, more conveniently located shops rather than the "big box" stores Americans love.[18]
- The Starbucks coffee chain is ubiquitous in the United States, but its popularity failed to translate when the company opened stores in such disparate countries as Australia and Israel. In both places, local people complained that Starbucks didn't understand the regional coffee culture and failed to create stores with the kind of homey ambience that local coffee drinkers appreciate.[19]
- The Home Depot assumed that the booming Chinese market represented a natural opportunity for its do-it-yourself products and opened twelve stores within a few years of entering the market in 2006. Too late, the company realized that the new Chinese middle class was flooding into vast apartment buildings that were too new to need renovation—and that Chinese people didn't understand the appeal of home remodeling projects as a hobby. The Home Depot shut its Chinese stores in 2012, having lost $160 million on the venture.[20]

In each of these cases, a highly successful American business assumed it could easily transplant a US model to a foreign market, failing to recognize that cultural, social, and economic differences would impact the preferences and choices of overseas consumers. Perhaps these costly mistakes might have been avoided if the decision-making teams had included a larger number of managers from diverse backgrounds with the ability to ask probing questions before the fateful blunders were committed.

Other US companies, however, have gotten the memo about the links between diversity and market success. The world's largest consumer products company, Procter & Gamble, has long understood that its future depends on reaching incredibly diverse markets, including rapidly expanding markets in Asia, Latin America, and Africa. Its longtime CEO, the legendary A. G. Lafley, was a pioneer in championing diversity as a vital tool for spurring innovation.

Lafley had significant personal experience with acquired diversity. He served in Japan with the US Army for several years, then managed P&G's operations there at a time when the global company was struggling to strengthen its foothold in Asian markets. His tour of duty in Japan—his own immersion in the outsider experience—gave Lafley a profound appreciation for the value of cross-cultural understanding. Upon returning to the United States as a top executive for P&G, he incorporated international travel time into his annual schedule. He constantly visited stores and homes in countries around the world, talking with consumers and observing local families as they shopped for, selected, and used products like those sold by P&G.

Lafley later explained the theory behind these exploratory journeys: "You develop a feel. You become more of an anthropologist, because you can't understand the language. Your power is observation and listening. Your ability to read nonverbal cues gets a lot better. Seeing the subtle things enhances your capability to read, understand, react."[21] Today, some corporations have hired "business anthropologists" in an effort to jump-start the acquisition of the kind of intuitive understanding that Lafley developed through personal curiosity.

Building on his sensitive awareness of the cultural variations among P&G's global customer bases, in 2006 Lafley launched P&G's Connect + Develop program to attract new business ideas from outside sources, including international partners, small businesses, aspiring entrepreneurs, and customers themselves. The company receives over four thousand new product ideas through this channel annually, and Connect + Develop is credited with creating more than half of P&G's new products over the past decade, ranging from Olay Regenerist skin therapy to Pulsonic toothbrushes. One recent example: Puffs Fresh Faces, a saline-infused wet-wipe product invented by entrepreneur Julie Pickens, who was discovered, recruited, and signed to a P&G contract through Connect + Develop. Pickens, a mother of three, had built her own small company by hiring stay-at-home moms in need of flexible, family-friendly work opportunities. Now she is bringing to P&G her intimate knowledge of the marketplace those women represent—a perfect example of how being open to new ideas from many sources can provide even giant firms with valuable infusions of creativity.[22]

One of the greatest advantages of companies with a diverse and open leadership team is deeper understanding of customer needs in a world of complex, fast-growing global markets. As we've seen, the marketplace is littered with missed opportunities and products that failed because diverse voices weren't in the room—or weren't listened to—when decisions were made. To avoid such perils and to maximize the innovation potential in any company, the combination of an inherently diverse workforce and leaders who prize difference and value every voice may just be the most transformative investment of all.

11. Running to Stand Still

Fellow males, get onboard. The closer that America comes to fully employing the talents of all its citizens, the greater its output of goods and services will be.

—*Warren Buffett*

In 2010, UK prime minister David Cameron tasked the minister of state for trade, investment and small business, Lord Davies of Abersoch, with commissioning a study examining gender diversity on UK executive boards. Following the financial crisis of 2008–9, Cameron and other leaders were concerned that the homogeneity at the top of the UK's most important companies put those institutions, and by extension the entire UK economy, at an unacceptably high risk. Across Europe, the subject of board diversity had reached a fevered pitch, with the European Union in Brussels seriously considering imposing EU-wide quotas for women in leadership. Cameron wanted the business community to understand that his administration considered good corporate governance fundamental to their agenda in securing the UK economy and that board diversity was part of good governance.

Davies's report, issued in February 2011, was extraordinarily direct in its assessment and directives. The largest companies in the UK belong to an exclusive club known as the Financial Times Stock Exchange 100—FTSE 100 or "Footsie," for short. At the time, only 12.5 percent of board members of the FTSE 100 were women, and the rate of increase in that number was glacially slow. In fact, as the report noted on the front cover, should the pace of female appointments continue at the same rate, it would take more than seventy years to achieve gender-balanced boards in the UK.[1] Lord Davies made it clear in the report that the Cameron coalition government would find that outcome unacceptable, and he issued a series of directives requiring UK companies to disclose their board representation and work aggressively to achieve greater diversity. The implication was obvious: UK companies needed to do better on board diversity or they would face legislation compelling them to do so.

Helena Morrissey, the young star CEO of Newton Investment Management, had already become a prominent spokesperson for corporate diversity. She felt strongly that quotas were not the answer, believing they would hopelessly undermine the perceived legitimacy of highly qualified women who achieve their success on merit. Convinced that progress could be made without quotas, Morrissey studied what experts in management, sociology, and neuroscience had discovered about team optimization, the dangers of groupthink, and the behavioral differences between men and women.

Morrissey reached a few simple but essential conclusions. First, having attended too many conferences on diversity in which women ended up talking only with other women, she realized that men and women needed to work *together* to solve the problem.

Second, she recognized the importance of reaching a threshold number of women in decision-making roles. "When I'm the only woman in the room," Morrissey says, "I'm conscious of the difference. When there are several women present—when we reach a critical mass—then women can be heard as voices with contributions to make, not merely as representatives of a female minority."[2]

This led Morrissey to support the notion of setting a measurable goal for inclusion of women and a time frame for achieving it—one that would prevent the effort from, in her words, "confusing talk with action and action with results."

The result was the 30% Club—an organization dedicated to ensuring that the FTSE 100 companies would have at least 30 percent women on their boards.

Morrissey enlisted two well-regarded male board chairs, Sir Roger Carr (then of energy giant Centrica) and Sir Win Bischoff (then of Lloyds Bank) to help her lead the charge. Together they recruited dozens of powerful board chairs who committed to faster progress. "Their leadership and evangelism," Morrissey recalls, "completely revolutionized the way this issue was perceived in the UK. It went from being viewed as 'special interest' to mainstream."

As membership in the 30% Club grew, the press took note. Helena Morrissey became a household name, widely and publicly calling for faster progress while working behind the scenes to help her partners achieve it. By the end of 2015, the number of women on FTSE 100 boards had grown to 26 percent, and Morrissey had set a new goal—to extend the 30 percent mark to all executive committee members of the FTSE 100 companies. Morrissey proved what many thought was impossible—that progress on diversity goals can be achieved when powerful forces are motivated, supported, and encouraged.

Diversifying Business Leadership—A Worldwide Movement

I first met Helena Morrissey in those early years and was privileged to attend and speak at many of the forums in London where she convened supporters. I was amazed by the passion and seriousness with which the male leaders took up the challenge she issued them and the resources and effort the member companies dedicated to the cause. Each one brought a sense of purpose and a sincere desire to succeed. It's most certainly a huge reason the effort has worked.

With the success of the 30% Club in the UK, Morrissey expanded her mission around the world. In the United States, she enlisted Bloomberg L.P. board chair Peter Grauer to take charge. In partnership with revered investor and Berkshire Hathaway board chair Warren Buffett, Grauer has been quietly recruiting the CEOs and board chairs of America's most venerable institutions to make a similar pledge to increase female representation on their corporate boards. Today forty-seven leaders of major US companies, including Muhtar Kent of Coca-Cola and Michael L. Corbat of Citigroup, have signed on, and the list is growing. Peter Grauer appeals to every CEO and chairman he knows. "The reactions," he told me, "run the gamut, but they have been overwhelmingly positive and even dramatically so.

"I raised the 30% Club to Macy's CEO Terry Lundgren when we were playing golf," Grauer recalls:

We were walking down the fairway and I started my pitch about why he should think about it and the importance of diversity to company boards and I got through about two sentences when he looked at me and said, "We're in!"

I said "Really?" He told me, "Look, Peter, sixty-five percent of my leadership team are women, half my board is already female, and remember my market is women, and so we get why this matters."

Grauer goes on to explain, "I am part of the Business Council of the United States, which includes 125 CEOs. I serially go to each of them to talk about this. The vast majority support what we're trying to do. Of course, there are a few who seem not to totally get it, but by and large I've been amazed at how important this is to most of them."[3]

Leaders like Peter Grauer are part of a growing group of prominent male business leaders in the United States who, while facing challenges and headwinds to progress, are promoting a meaningful commitment to diversity in their companies and beyond. And they're talking about it every chance they get. Peter has sponsored and led discussions on board diversity at the World Economic Forum in Davos and written a *Wall Street Journal* op-ed on the topic. For me, leaders like Peter have always been the most rewarding to work with, not just because of his sincere passion for progress but because of the power and influence he has to make change. Starting four years ago in partnership with his company's amazing human resources leaders Melinda Wolfe and Anne Erni, chief diversity officer Elana Weinstein, former CEO Dan Doctoroff, and now with Mike Bloomberg back in the CEO seat, Grauer has expanded his own horizons, learned from the insights of others, but most of all, leveraged his own bully pulpit as the chairman of one of the country's most prestigious companies to spur others to make progress. Chairmen like Grauer are part of a new and critically important group of champion white men whose leadership will be essential to furthering progress.

One firm that is tackling the issue of corporate boards that lack gender diversity is Biogen, a Cambridge, Massachusetts, biotechnology company that develops therapies for neurodegenerative and other diseases. According to Liftstream, a life sciences recruiting firm, the majority of US biotech companies don't have even a single woman on their board. This is especially shocking given the fact that highly qualified women have entered the life sciences industry in huge numbers over the past twenty years.

Biogen is proud of its many female executives who hold

advanced degrees in medicine, business, and science. Three members of the company's ten-person board are women, and their CEO has signed on to be part of the US 30% Club. Now, in an effort to spread this diversity to other firms in the industry, Biogen has launched a program called "Raising the Bar," which is designed to make women into highly attractive board candidates. The eleven Biogen managers in the inaugural class are attending specially designed three-day workshops at George Washington University on issues board members need to understand, from financial management to shareholder activism. Then they are linked to companies seeking female board candidates, not just in biotech but in other industries as well. Biogen's chief diversity officer Javier Barrientos fields inquiries from recruiters and companies seeking qualified women for their boards, and a number of Biogen women have been appointed to outside boards as a result.[4]

Biogen benefits because its rising executives are gaining valuable skills and knowledge, and the whole business community benefits from the increased creativity and breadth of insight that more diverse boards produce. Programs like this are a simple, tangible step toward diversifying corporate boards and strengthening industry.

In some ways, US businesses are setting an example on diversity that we should follow in other spheres. It's not easy, and the challenges are far from solved, but I'm optimistic about the direction. Business is a data-driven world, and in recent years the data linking better financial performance to diversity has piled up. Evidence ranges from analyses of big corporations on the Standard & Poor's 500 list, which consistently demonstrate that companies with more diverse boards perform better than companies that lack such diversity, to small-scale experiments led by a range of academics.

In 2015, MSCI, A US-based company that develops global market indices and other investing tools, released the results of a five-year study of more than 4,200 public companies. The researchers found that only 20.1 percent of the companies they surveyed have "strong female leadership" on their boards, defined by the presence of three or more women members. But those that had such female leadership enjoyed a return on equity 36.4 percent greater than otherwise similar businesses.[5]

A 2014 study by the National Academy of Sciences is one of the most interesting. It suggests that more diversity on Wall Street might help prevent market bubbles like those that precipitated the 2008 crash. In the study, 180 people with financial backgrounds were recruited to participate in mock stock-trading sessions. The subjects bought and sold imaginary shares, earning profits that were paid out in real cash, which created an incentive for them to take the trading sessions seriously. The twist: In some of the simulations, all the traders were of the same ethnicity, and in others, they were ethnically diverse.

The result: Simulated markets including diverse participants generated prices that became increasingly accurate relative to stock fundamentals as the trading sessions proceeded—while the prices in homogeneous markets became 33 percent *less* accurate. "In other words," as one journalist concluded, "when a bunch of white guys are trading among themselves, they are more likely to drive prices to irrational levels than when there is more diversity among their trading partners." The apparent reason: An excessive and unwarranted sense of trust among ethnically homogeneous traders leads them to accept inflated prices unjustified by logic.[6] This is exactly the kind of evidence that drove the UK government to see diversity as critical to avoiding financial crises like that of 2008, which brought the world economy to its knees. Many have concluded that more diversity on Wall Street and in the City of London might have prevented the crash.

The avalanche of data over the last decade linking diversity to financial performance has been noticed. Today there are few executive leaders who don't talk about or in some way focus on diversity as part of the overall business strategy. The results, though, vary widely, and I can't think of a single company CEO who would say he (or she) is satisfied with the progress they've made. There remains a lot of work to do.

Real Inclusion

When I left the Center for Talent Innovation, I thankfully had some choices about where to work next. I knew I wanted to start my nonprofit All In Together, but I also knew I wanted to continue working on broader diversity issues with large companies. I pitched an idea to two big firms: They could hire me part-time as an outside advisor to lead important conversations with CEOs and clients on diversity and leadership topics. To my delight, two wonderful organizations offered me a role. I picked Deloitte.

Deloitte LLP is one of the country's most prestigious and admired professional services firms, with seventy thousand employees and more than $16 billion in revenues. The firm's success over the last twenty years is due in no small part to its inclusive, talent-centric culture. I was extremely fortunate to have the opportunity to collaborate with the firm. Their growing human-capital consulting practice is consistently rated one of the best in the industry. But the real reason I chose to partner with Deloitte was because of how I felt in my conversations with them. From the first moment, it was apparent that the partners—particularly the male partners responsible for hiring me—understood my work in a personal way. To them, inclusion wasn't a buzzword or a compliance requirement; it was part of the DNA of their business and of its leadership culture. I didn't have to explain the importance of inclusion or why we should link our talent and innovation discussions with our clients. They already understood.

All the Deloitte leaders I've met or partnered with in my collaboration with the firm understand and support the importance of inclusion to their business, and that's no accident. Over the course of a twenty-year journey, beginning in 1992 with the recognition that the Deloitte partnership was losing women disproportionately, the firm has worked diligently to create an inclusive culture where everyone can succeed. In 2015, Deloitte became the first of the Big Four accounting firms to appoint a woman—Cathy Engelbert—as CEO, and it became the first major firm to have a woman—Janet Foutty—lead its consulting business as CEO. Their appointments were possible because of years of hard work and Deloitte's commitment to regarding inclusion as a core business and people imperative.

Since Deloitte's diversity work began more than two decades ago, its diversity strategy has grown to include a wide variety of programs designed to help women grow and succeed at the firm. Some focus on employee training, such as WINning New Business, which helps high-potential women develop skills in negotiating, relationship management, and personal brand-building. Others highlight the benefits of diversity, such as Women as Buyers, which organizes workshops to help Deloitte professionals, both men and women, do a better job of understanding and responding to the varied buying preferences and decision-making styles that male and female clients bring to the marketplace. And some programs can be career savers, such as the Mass Career Customization program that allows Deloitte professionals to "dial up" or "dial down" their workloads and travel schedules in response to stressful or demanding life circumstances, such as the adoption of a baby or a parent's illness.[7]

The Deloitte professionals I have come to know say that

the success of the firm's inclusion programs can be attributed to several factors. One is the fact that they are driven by clear, demonstrable business needs and that they evolve and adapt as those needs change. Everyone in the firm is focused on leveraging diversity as a driver of business success, and that makes a huge difference.

Another crucial element in Deloitte's success around diversity is its use of advanced analytics to measure and meet corporate needs. They look at every conceivable factor and make sure they understand exactly the challenges or opportunities they are solving for. This enables a laserlike focus on any areas that need extra attention and allows the firm to adjust its strategies and investments as needed. This approach has paid off. Two-thirds of Deloitte's new managers—the future leaders of the firm—are either female or multicultural.

Over the years, Deloitte's pioneering efforts on behalf of diversity and inclusion have won the company more than its share of awards, of which it is understandably proud. The firm's culture is the envy of many in the industry and beyond.

Diminishing Returns

The leader behavior I observed from my first interactions with Deloitte stood out because the inclusive culture of Deloitte and the visible leadership of a female CEO like Cathy Engelbert are unfortunately too rare.

Across the Fortune 500, there remains huge work to do in the visible representation of diversity in leadership and the culture that makes that reality even possible. Fewer than 5 percent of Fortune 500 CEOs are women—a number that has barely budged in the last decade. The pipeline of women is enormous and growing—women are obtaining 50 percent or more of the degrees in nearly every field and are entering the workforce in record numbers. But that rich pipeline is not translating to greater numbers at the top. Nearly every company I work with starts out with almost equal or even larger numbers of women in the junior ranks, but as you go up the corporate ladder, men become more and more dominant. By the time you reach senior leadership levels, the gap between men and women is cavernous. This gap remains the most stubborn diversity challenge in corporate America today. It's a glass ceiling nearly every woman is aware of yet very few have any idea how to break.

In a 2012 McKinsey study of sixty major corporations, women made up 53 percent of entry-level workers and 40 percent of front-line managers. But with each step up the leadership ladder, the participation of women declined. Women constituted 35 percent of directors, 27 percent of vice presidents, 24 percent of senior vice presidents, and just 19 percent of executives at the C-suite level.[8] The number of women CEOs has hardly moved in decades and seems stuck under 5 percent for the foreseeable future. On corporate boards, women make up 19 percent of board members in the S&P 500. The United States ranks tenth in the world for board diversity.[9]

Furthermore, the "best" jobs, as measured by specific, quantifiable criteria, are also still reserved for men. The nonprofit advocacy organization Catalyst looked at the types of work assignments given to 1,660 high-potential business-school graduates. On average, the men were given jobs with budgets twice as big and staffs three times as large as those given to the women. Over one-third of the men reported that their jobs gave them significant access to the top brass in the C-suite, while just about one-quarter of the women said the same.[10] So even when men and women are given comparable titles, the men get an edge in terms of what really matters—their path to the top of the corporate heap is subtly smoothed, and women are given a steeper and rockier road to climb.

As we explained in chapter two, women also suffer a well-publicized yet stubbornly persistent wage shortfall in comparison to white men. As of 2014, the gender pay gap, while slowly shrinking, was still significant, with women earning an average of 79 cents for every dollar earned by men.[11] And the gap is far worse for women of color. According to the National Women's Law Center, the typical African American woman earns 64 cents for every dollar paid to a white man; a Hispanic woman earns just 56 cents on the dollar.[12] Because the wage gap is based on an average of all wages, not a 1:1 comparison of similar jobs, the gap is attributable in part to the lower-wage occupations like teaching and administration that are still dominated by women. Another factor: The majority of minimum-wage workers are women, which contributes significantly to the 79 cents number often cited. Of course, that's not to dispute the fact that in every industry there are jobs where men and women are paid differently for the same work. It's a problem I believe every company in America should immediately rectify.

There is little correlation between the pipeline and the low numbers at the top. Countless hours and hundreds of studies have been devoted to answering the question why. Every study comes to nearly the same conclusion...many hours could be saved if we'd stop doing endless studies and actually start working on the problem! Sheryl Sandberg's best-selling book *Lean In* summarizes many of the key findings. I've read or written nearly every major study on the progression of women in corporate America, so let me save you the reading and summarize:

- Women are highly ambitious but often lack the same confidence as men so have to be asked over and over again to take stretch assignments.
- Men will go after jobs they are only partially qualified for, but women feel they need to be 110 percent qualified before they take the plunge.
- Women lack the mentors and sponsors they need to get ahead.
- The United States is poorly equipped to support working mothers because we have little family leave and flexible work is hard to come by.
- Senior executive leaders need to make women's advancement a greater priority.
- Women need networks of other women for moral and professional support.

If it sounds as if the challenges women face are partly of their own making, that's because many studies continue to confirm it. Women must be willing to go for top jobs and move beyond self-doubt to succeed. But—and it's a big but—the most overlooked barriers encountered by women and other groups poorly represented in the highest leadership levels of American companies are systemic. No amount of leaning in can change that. The biggest challenge to corporate diversity today is an institutional one.

Across the corporate world, after decades of extraordinary advancements by women and racial and ethnic minorities, progress toward taking full advantage of our country's diverse talent pool has dramatically slowed. Biases in recruitment, training, and promotion still favor white men. Bias is embedded in every step of the corporate ladder. And the higher the rung, the harder that bias is to prove and to upend.

In *Lean In*, Sandberg calls for a massive mentorship movement to help women overcome self-doubt and other personal challenges that she outlines in great detail. There is no downside to this, and many—especially young—women have benefited by participating in Lean In Circles or by finding a mentor. Unfortunately, for senior women waiting for promotion into top leadership, that strategy has limits.

In fact, what women (and minorities) need more than the advice and guidance of a mentor is the direct sponsorship support of men in power. Sponsorship creates the biggest difference because it offers an improved professional outcome. Sponsors forcefully advocate for the advancement of their protégés, and in return the protégés offer loyalty and incredibly hard work on behalf of their senior sponsors. It makes all the difference, because without sponsorship, promotions at senior levels simply don't happen.

This is not a new concept. No one becomes a senior leader in any company without the support of even more senior people. Yet we're only now beginning to appreciate the reality of it and how rarely women are sponsored compared to men. In the extensive research we conducted on the topic while I was at the Center for Talent Innovation, the conclusions were clear. Women are half as likely as men to be sponsored. Only one in five professionals of color have sponsors. Why? Sponsorship is vulnerable to unconscious (and conscious) bias because it requires trust and confidence. Sponsors most often invest in protégés that are like them, which in most cases means straight, white men.

The stubborn reality is that as long as the positions of power and influence are held by white men, they need to be the ones to sponsor and advance the women and minority employees junior to them. There are simply not enough women or minorities at the top of major companies to sponsor all the up-and-coming diverse talent with potential. Without direct support from the white men in power, little is likely to really change.

It's important to note that despite the depressing statistics, women have done far better in the corporate environment than minorities. Blacks and Latinos face even greater barriers to full participation in business. Many, concluding the odds are against them, opt out in favor of working in minority-owned or -led businesses. Even Asian Americans, often referred to as the "model minority" because of their high educational achievement levels and large numbers in corporate America, still encounter a thick "bamboo ceiling." In 2010, Asian Americans became a *majority* of the tech workforce in Silicon Valley for the first time—50.1 percent versus 40.7 percent for whites.[13] Yet very few ever make it into senior or executive leadership roles. They are often overlooked or seen as too passive or quiet. In the minds of many top executives, Asians somehow don't seem to fit the image of an American business leader.

Mark Feng fits the model-minority mold. An émigré from China, he has worked as an engineer and a consultant and has earned an MBA at the prestigious Harvard Business School. But when he read Sheryl Sandberg's *Lean In*, he recognized the cultural obstacles typically faced by women as powerful factors shaping his own career. Now Mark and several colleagues have formed a Lean In Circle for Asians, including four men and two women, where they are developing strategies for breaking the bamboo ceiling that keeps well-educated, ultra-talented Asian Americans from reaching upper management.[14]

It's a psychologically and socially difficult challenge. Though Asian Americans are a large, culturally varied group, many were raised in achievement-oriented families (often under the leadership of the proverbial "Tiger Moms") where the unspoken norms included hard work, self-reliance, modesty, and respect for authority. That's not a profile that attracts much attention in Silicon Valley or on Wall Street, where brash, outspoken, often iconoclastic self-promotion is the predominant style.

Feng and his colleagues have wrestled with the question of whether they need to change their personalities in order to succeed in American organizations. Or should they expect American managers to recognize and appreciate the very different leadership talents that Asian Americans bring to the workplace? Yi Chen, a member of Feng's Lean In Circle, likes to think he can rise in business without altering his persona. "That calm style of leadership," he says, "thought-process-focused leadership, can also be very valuable and be a balance."[15]

But Chen, like Feng, also acknowledges his need to learn to shine a brighter spotlight on his own achievements. That's why, even as the members of the circle have dispersed to careers around the country, they remain in touch via the Internet, encouraging one another in their battles to gain the recognition they deserve but so far have found elusive.

Of course, it's not just visibly diverse communities that have fought for a place in corporate America. Despite an ongoing revolution in social attitudes toward LGBT people and the advent of marriage equality, it's still legal in twenty-eight states to fire someone for being gay. Under the circumstances, perhaps it's not surprising that so far only one Fortune 500 CEO—Apple's Tim Cook—has come out as openly gay.

Clearing the Paths to Entrepreneurship

In the world of entrepreneurship, females and minorities experience disproportionate barriers. They have extraordinary difficulty getting funding from sources such as venture capital firms—only

7 percent of VC funding goes to firms run by women. Academic research has revealed that even crowdsourcing organizations such as Kickstarter skew largely toward projects run by white males. And a 2014 report by the Senate Committee on Small Business and Entrepreneurship found that women-owned businesses account for 30 percent of small companies but receive just 4.4 percent of total small-business loans.[16]

Deborah Jackson was one of a handful of pioneering women in the upper echelons of the financial services industry in the 1980s. Armed with a degree from Columbia University's school of business, she joined Goldman Sachs in 1980 and was heralded in *Institutional Investor* magazine as one of the new generation of female executives who would one day share leadership of the nation's eminent investment banks and brokerage firms.

But it never happened—and not because of lack of talent, effort, or accomplishment on her part. Instead, she concluded that there were other ways to have influence that would be more immediate and satisfying.

Jackson moved into the world of venture finance, where she hoped (among other things) to help channel investment money into the hands of some of the brilliant women entrepreneurs she'd encountered. She was appalled to discover the blindness among the otherwise highly perceptive venture capital investors (VCs) she worked with:

> *I've been on numerous competitive panels where I judge business plans alongside male VCs, and I've noticed a clear pattern. A male entrepreneur can get up and pitch his business, and I can just see that the guys are really comfortable. They sort of joke around together, and it's clear they understand one another.*
>
> *And then a woman entrepreneur comes up, and suddenly there's a little different feel in the room—a little more formality*

and a little less warmth. And if the woman is talking about a product that's important for the female consumer, the guys will all turn to me and ask, "What do you think, Deborah—is that a product that women will use?" In one way, it's a completely fair, honest question. But the fact that they have to ask it says to me that there's no way in hell they're going to fund that entrepreneur, because they don't get her product, her market, or her business idea.

And some VCs are outspoken about saying that they will only fund businesses that make products that they personally will use. Of course, that means you're going to cut out a huge slice of the population, since only a handful of VCs are women.[17]

No wonder Jackson reimagined her career to design a new approach to empowering women in business. In 2012, she founded Plum Alley, a crowdfunding site that raises money for ventures of all kinds run by women—for-profit companies, social businesses, creative and artistic projects. There are men who invest in Plum Alley ventures, but the majority of funders are women.

Creating a unique channel that shines a spotlight on some of the millions of women entrepreneurs in America today has enabled Jackson to break away from dependence on a traditional, male-dominated power structure whose gatekeepers generally lack the acquired diversity to see the opportunities in front of their noses.

As Deborah considered what else she could do to champion women entrepreneurs, she teamed up with Andrea Turner Moffitt, an expert in the field of women and investing. The two decided that to solve the problem of getting more money to the best women entrepreneurs, women investors had to be engaged and enabled to use their economic prowess to make a difference.

In 2015, they introduced Plum Alley Investments. It offers

a paid membership that gives members access to a short list of highly curated investment opportunities in companies that are founded by women entrepreneurs or have gender-balanced teams. Each Plum Alley company also boasts a strong financial structure, a business model designed to have a positive impact in the world, and an innovative technological profile.

In January 2016, Plum Alley Investments closed its first syndicate investment, which contributed part of a $7.5 million Series A funding round for Unitive, Inc. Founded by software engineer Laura Mather, Unitive develops enterprise software to help companies reduce the impact of unconscious bias on their recruitment, hiring, and promotion processes. Unitive's software should have broad implications for the future advancement of women and other underrepresented groups in our society.

The Myth of the (White) Boy Genius

America's high-tech industry—the network of companies that produce a large share of the world's computers, electronic gadgets, software, and information technology services, and that goes by the shorthand name of Silicon Valley—remains a visible representation of how much work is left to be done in American companies.

Silicon Valley has been a source of enormous creativity and profit over the past several decades. And there are a few well-known leaders from diverse backgrounds—women like Marissa Mayer, CEO of Yahoo, and Sheryl Sandberg, COO of Facebook; immigrants to the United States like Satya Nadella, the Indian-born CEO of Microsoft; and LGBT individuals like Tim Cook of Apple, one of the handful of top executives in American business who are openly gay. Yet beyond these headline-grabbing names, the number of diverse leaders with significant power and leadership in Silicon Valley is small. For all its technological creativity, the industry has been shockingly backward and insular when it comes to diversity. The geek culture remains mainly the domain of white men, and because some of the most successful tech entrepreneurs, like Steve Jobs, Mark Zuckerberg, Jack Dorsey, Bill Gates, and Reid Hoffman, are all white men, the perception of the tech boy wonder remains the norm.

Across Silicon Valley, a techie nerd culture dominated by white men has led to an often hostile and exclusionary environment for anyone who doesn't fit the mold, especially for women. Elissa Shevinsky, cofounder of the photo-sharing platform Glimpse, is one of the rare female entrepreneurs to have gained a foothold in high tech. But in the Valley she often felt she had to suppress her personality, values, and instincts in order to fit in. "I did my best to minimize the ways I would come across as other," Shevinsky says about her first job. "I just went along with the jokes. I didn't feel like I had the choice. There were just so many porn jokes. Even built into the code."[18]

At high-tech powerhouse firms, women constitute about 30 percent of the total workforce, but they are relatively absent from the significant technical roles. At Google, for example, just 17 percent of technical employees are female. The percentages are similar elsewhere: 15 percent at Facebook and Yahoo, 10 to 15 percent at most high-tech start-ups. As for other groups beyond the young-white-male stereotype, those numbers are startlingly low: Statistics from some leading Silicon Valley companies show Latino technical workers at 3 to 4 percent and black technical workers ranging between 2 percent and 4 percent.[19] It's a vicious cycle that must be broken. Few women choose technical majors such as computer science and engineering, because the fields are so male dominated, but without more women going into those fields, the culture in tech is unlikely to change.

At least the bigger, more established companies have begun to take the challenge seriously. They realize that greater innovation and growth require more diversity, and as they mature into publicly traded companies, they receive increased scrutiny from investors and the public at large. "Google is not where we want to be when it comes to diversity," says Laszlo Bock, the company's senior vice president for people operations. LinkedIn issued a public report on its demographics and admitted, "In terms of overall diversity, we have some work to do." Facebook uses similar language: "We have more work to do—a lot more."[20] And Intel recently announced a $300 million commitment to developing the next generation of diverse talent. Increasingly the industry funds and supports organizations like Girls Who Code and Black Girls Code that inspire and train more women to enter the field.

A few leaders from diverse backgrounds who have pushed their way toward the top of the high-tech heap are also making a difference. Julie Zhuo, a Shanghai-born computer scientist educated at Stanford, is director of product design at Facebook. She uses her position to promote more inclusive management and leadership approaches within the company. Zhuo leads a Lean In Circle that unites women from various departments at Facebook to share stories and challenges from their work and personal lives, and she strives to apply the same kind of openness to her job as chief designer of the Facebook user experience.[21]

Denise Young Smith, a black executive who heads the human resources at Apple, spearheads a similar spirit of change. "Apple has a history of being a very siloed organization," she notes. "It was incredibly effective for us, but as we become bigger and more complex, we are encouraging bringing people together." She created an internal website called In Your Voice where Apple employees are invited to share their own ideas and experiences in regard to the company's inclusion policy.[22]

Leaders like Zhuo and Smith represent the leading edge of the expansive racial and gender profile that Silicon Valley—like the rest of American industry—needs to develop if it hopes to remain relevant to global markets in an increasingly diverse world.

I could spend many pages and chapters listing every diversity program and initiative currently running in US companies. But despite all the efforts and the millions of dollars spent, I'm increasingly convinced that the numbers will not dramatically change until companies get serious about ensuring a company culture and environment that enables everyone to feel welcome and to succeed.

Do As I Do

The problem that American business has with diversity begins at the very top. Everywhere I go, well-intentioned, motivated leaders ask me what will work to ensure diversity at every level of corporate leadership. They have already realized that many of their efforts are not paying off. Even when they've set aggressive targets and goals and tried to hold leaders accountable, they often see little progress. But they rarely consider the very thing that's most likely hampering their efforts: leadership culture and behavior. They don't look closely enough at themselves.

Throughout this book I have argued that for diversity to bring considerable and lasting benefits to us economically and socially, we need to do more than just count how many of what kind of people we have at any given place or time. I have claimed that the real payoff will come when we all learn to cross dividing lines and connect with one another on a more meaningful level. The same principle is true for our businesses. For the paradigm in American companies to really shift, those in power—especially the white male leaders who overwhelmingly control the decision-making and set the tone for company culture—will have to focus much more seriously on their own behavior and insist on holding every leader beneath them in the hierarchy responsible for demonstrating inclusive, open leadership in everything they do.

The most important study I was part of while at the Center for Talent Innovation crystallized for me the kinds of differentiated investments companies should be making. In the 2013 study *Innovation, Diversity and Market Growth*, we wanted to understand the conditions required for diversity to drive innovation. We were really looking to prove the business case that there was a link, but the research confirmed something I had long suspected: The real payoff to the business and success in advancing diversity comes when diverse employees work in an inclusive, collaborative environment led by leaders with acquired diversity.

People with acquired diversity are able to connect with people different from themselves because they have had some type of outsider experience that allows them to appreciate the value that perspective brings. They don't look diverse or check the typical boxes, but they understand on a personal level why diversity matters. And they make an effort to connect with and encourage the full contributions of people different from them. This skill set turns out to be incredibly important in business today, not just because the workforce is so much more diverse than ever before but because the kind of open, collaborative mind-set demonstrated by people with acquired diversity is critical for innovation.

I often think of the white male chairman of a law firm I worked with over many years. He made diversifying the partnership a true priority and threw substantial resources behind the commitment. But on a personal level, he learned how to support and build trust with an up-and-coming black lawyer he was mentoring. He made himself vulnerable by confessing that he was uncomfortable dealing with the race issues. That in turn opened up an honest and much-needed dialogue between them. Ultimately, he related some of his own early career experiences to those of the young man and worked to help his young black mentee advance by giving him truthful feedback and creating a meaningful two-way dialogue. The relationship flourished, and both he and the younger lawyer learned a lot from the experience.

In business today, these kinds of small but significant connections are fundamental. They enable understanding and progress more profound in some cases than any big program. Were they to occur more frequently—if every CEO led by example and insisted that every white male leader make the effort to cross lines—we could indeed change the paradigm for the countless minority, female, and gay employees struggling to get ahead. To replicate at scale will take legions of leaders willing to try and an entire system of reward and recognition to ensure that becomes the norm.

Leaders with acquired diversity—leaders who are inclusive—help establish the "speak-up culture" that is critical to unleashing the full innovative capacity of each employee. They encourage the free flow of ideas, and they ensure everyone on the team contributes. For innovation to flourish, potential innovators must feel free to speak up and contribute their ideas, which is why leaders with acquired diversity are essential. And for diverse employees (including in this instance younger employees such as Millennials), working for leaders with acquired diversity can be a game changer. More open, inclusive leaders in tech might keep more women in technical fields and encourage more women to pick them. More inclusive, less hierarchical leadership in banking, insurance, Big Pharma, and other industries might make corporate America more appealing to the legions of Millennials who opt instead for start-ups where they think they can more fully contribute. And of course, more inclusive leadership might make it possible for companies to innovate more effectively for today's increasingly diverse marketplace.

Inclusive, collaborative leadership needs to be the model for the future of corporate America. Without it, we will lose both the innovation and talent wars. Unfortunately, only about 22 percent of professionals are fortunate enough to work at companies that are both diverse and truly inclusive. But those that do say they are far more likely to receive management support for their new ideas, to be heard and respected in meetings, to be empowered to make decisions, and to have their contributions recognized.

While this type of leadership is far from the norm, there are hopeful signs that the tide is turning. Jim Turley, the former CEO of Ernst & Young, has always been someone I admire. Under his leadership, EY's approach to diversity, with a strong focus on inclusion, has become one of the most admired in the industry. Even after his retirement in 2013, the legacy lives on. He tells a revealing story about a painful incident that taught him a valuable lesson about listening to diverse voices:

> *I like to facilitate our board discussions by getting right into the more contentious points, and we were having a discussion around a particular topic. Three women on the board made individual comments that were similar in direction, which I didn't respond to. Not long after they spoke, a fourth person, who happened to be a man, made a comment in line with what the women had been saying, and I picked up on his comment. I said, "I think Jeff's got it right," not even aware of what I had just done. To their great credit, the women didn't embarrass me publicly. They pulled me to the side, and they said, "Jim, we know you didn't mean for this to be the way it was received, but this is what happened." They played it back to me, and they said*

that that's what happens to women throughout their careers. It was a learning moment for me.[23]

It takes courage to exhibit the vulnerability Turley showed when he really listened to the complaint from his female board members—and even more courage to share the story publicly. But leaders who are willing to lower their guard, personally and professionally, and admit that they don't know all the answers and are eager to learn are leaders who are prepared to build successful worldwide organizations in the twenty-first century.

We need to systematically reward, promote, and encourage those who show this kind of leadership. At the end of the day, business culture turns on the accountability senior leaders insist on. Without visible, consistent, inclusive behavior demonstrated, reinforced, rewarded, and celebrated, there's little hope of real and lasting change.

12. The Myth of Meritocracy

> We conclude that in the field of public education the doctrine of "separate but equal" has no place. Separate educational facilities are inherently unequal.
>
> —*Earl Warren, Chief Justice of the United States*

Recently, I was riding through Washington, DC, in the back of a taxi when a story on the radio caught my attention. The District public schools announced student results from the most recent round of standardized testing. According to Schools Chancellor Kaya Henderson, the results were "sobering." Citywide scores were improving overall, but the racial divide in student achievement was cavernous. Seventy percent of white children in Washington public schools had tested at or above grade level in reading and English proficiency, compared with just 17 percent of minorities.

My heart sank. Sixty years after school segregation was declared unconstitutional in the landmark 1954 case of *Brown v. Board of Education*, how can we still be failing so many minority children so profoundly?

Central to our collective vision of the American dream is the idea that any one of us can, through education and hard work, rise from even the most adverse circumstances to achieve personal and professional success. And for millions of Americans, this vision has proven true. They've found the education system to be a pathway out of poverty, and over the past century some of the most prominent Americans have been products of public schools.

Of course, prior to *Brown*, this pathway to success was blocked for many African Americans. The segregated schools they were forced to attend offered few of the advantages that white students enjoyed. *Brown* promised change. Thanks to a unanimous Supreme Court decision, as well as the heroism of brave children like six-year-old Ruby Bridges in New Orleans, who crossed color lines under the protection of US marshals to claim her constitutionally guaranteed right to an equal education, millions of black children finally made their way through the same schoolhouse doors as their white counterparts.

But sadly, the ideal of equal educational opportunity embodied in *Brown* is far from achieved. Race, gender, and socioeconomic status all play a major role in determining the future potential of each young American.

The disparities begin in early childhood. Patterns of housing segregation historically maintained through government programs, banking policies, and discriminatory practices by real estate professionals and developers have led to public school districts that are often segregated by race and income. The common practice of basing school budgets on local real estate taxes—which ensures that wealthy neighborhoods have far more money to spend in their classrooms than poorer neighborhoods—exacerbates the discrepancies. Children of color tend to live in poorer neighborhoods where the schools are badly equipped, teachers are less well trained, classrooms are overcrowded, and local cultural facilities like libraries are few or nonexistent. They're also more likely to go to school short on supplies and with fewer learning tools like computers and books.

The problems continue in high school. High schools predominantly attended by white kids are far more likely to offer AP classes, courses in advanced science and math, and electives in art, music, and foreign languages than those attended by minority kids.

In the words of Catherine Lhamon, head of the civil rights office at the US Department of Education, "American schools are disturbingly racially segregated, period. We are reserving our expectations for our highest rigor level of courses, the courses we know our kids need to be able to be full and productive members of society, but we are reserving them for a class of kids who are white and who are wealthier."[1]

A typical pairing of suburban school districts, both in the St. Louis area, shows how the pattern plays out. The mostly white school district of Clayton spends an average of $17,851 per pupil. It pays an average teacher salary of over $71,000 and is able to ensure that 99 percent of core classes are taught by "highly qualified" teachers.

By contrast, the largely black school district of Normandy, just five miles away from Clayton, spends $15,096 per pupil. It pays the average teacher $59,560 and uses teachers who are *not* "highly qualified" in almost 40 percent of core classes.

The results are stark: Clayton boasts a four-year graduation rate of over 90 percent for all its students, *both black and white*, while Normandy's rate is just 61.4 percent. The average ACT college entrance exam score in Clayton is 25.7, compared with 16 in Normandy.[2]

We like to believe that America is the ultimate meritocracy—a country where no one is held back from accomplishment by race, ethnicity, religion, or gender. But the facts tell a different story. The black kids in Normandy start high school at a huge disadvantage compared to the white (and the few black) kids in the more diverse Clayton school. Then high school reinforces and magnifies the differences. It's a pattern that is unfortunately typical in communities across America.

How Diverse Classrooms Benefit *All* Americans

It's relatively easy to see how minority kids suffer when the schools they attend are poorly funded, overcrowded, and badly equipped and what they could gain from less segregated classrooms. This fact alone should make it clear that we have failed totally in fulfilling the ideals of *Brown*. But there are many powerful arguments for diversity in the classroom. The continued segregation of our schools shortchanges *all* students. Not only minority students but also white, majority students lose out when they attend schools that lack diversity.

Genevieve Siegel-Hawley is a professor of education at Virginia Commonwealth University who has dedicated her career to studying race and inequality in American schools. Here is how she summarizes the findings from hundreds of research studies, conducted over several decades, into the impact of school diversity on mainstream students: "Diverse schools benefit white students by providing far better learning outcomes. Enrollment in racially integrated schools is also associated with important social and psychological advantages that improve productivity in an increasingly diverse workplace." Among the specific findings identified by Siegel-Hawley:

- Classrooms with students of different racial and ethnic backgrounds foster "heightened dialogue and debate" that helps white students develop "complex, more flexible thinking" and "creative, high-quality solutions to problems."

- By facilitating contact between people from different backgrounds, classroom diversity "lowers intergroup prejudice" and fosters "stable friendships between white and black students, with white students experiencing the strongest effects."
- In later life, white students educated in diverse school settings "are more likely to report an increased sense of civic engagement" and "a concrete understanding of racial and social injustices, which in turn can help contribute to constructive civic engagement."[3]

Do these enhanced thinking, problem-solving, and social skills come with a price in terms of academic achievement? Evidently not. The issue has been studied many times, most recently—and exhaustively—by the National Center for Education Statistics. In a thorough 2015 analysis of the black-white educational achievement gap, the NCES concluded that, after controlling for socioeconomic status, "White student achievement in schools with the highest Black student density did not differ from White student achievement in schools with the lowest density."[4] In other words, white kids earn approximately the same test scores whether they go to schools that are mostly white, mostly black, or something in between.

It's a sad fact that, over the last several decades, countless white families, like those in Clayton, have launched massive public protests or pulled their kids out of public schools where minority students were bused in or where local demographics have changed. The evidence shows that fears of academic achievement dropping because minority students are in the school are unfounded—and that the social upheaval caused by generations of "white flight" and the de facto resegration of American public schools has been largely needless and avoidable. In places like Clayton, many white families chafe at the accusation that their protests are based on racial prejudice. Instead, they say they are simply seeking to defend the quality and safety of their schools. Yet given how unfounded their fears are, it's hard to see their protests as anything else.

"That's *My* Family!"—When School Is a Place for Everybody

I find the lack of inclusion at so many American schools particularly painful because my own life was profoundly shaped by the diversity of the schools I attended. It's heartbreaking to me that few Americans have a chance to enjoy these same benefits.

I recently spoke with Russell Shaw, the current head of Georgetown Day School (GDS), the wonderful independent school I was lucky enough to attend back in the late 1980s and early 1990s. Russell shared with me some of the ways GDS has continued to nurture and update its diversity commitment to meet the evolving challenges of the twenty-first century.

When GDS was founded in 1945, it was the first racially integrated school in the District of Columbia. At the time, Washington, DC, was governed not by an elected mayor but by a Senate committee. It was chaired by Theodore Bilbo, a Mississippi Democrat who was an active member of the Ku Klux Klan and had authored a virulently racist book titled *Take Your Choice: Separation or Mongrelization*. So it took courage for GDS to open its classroom doors to students of every race.

In the years since, GDS has remained at the forefront of the battle for inclusive education, often espousing perspectives considered controversial and challenging. In 1967, school director and board member Edith Nash penned a letter to GDS families in which she noted that GDS had been founded as a "color-blind" institution. But then she went on to observe that experience had shown the school's leaders that "we now must be color-conscious" in order to serve a diverse student body. This position wasn't universally popular—and it still isn't—but the school's leaders recognize its importance and continue to live up to it.

GDS takes the challenge of making diversity a living reality seriously. The school doesn't simply admit students from a range of backgrounds and then hope for the best. It offers educational and social programs, for students and faculty alike, designed to nurture a culture of true openness and inclusion, so that all can benefit from the presence of varied life perspectives and experiences. The school has a diversity office staffed by two full-time administrators with a mandate to shape curriculum offerings, school-wide activities, and professional development programs needed to support diversity. In 2015–16, the year-long training program in which all faculty participate is centered on the topic of implicit bias and how to overcome it. All GDS students take two full-year classes related to diversity—a course for sixth graders on social justice and one for ninth graders called "Diversity, Equity, and Inclusion."

Russell explained to me the philosophy behind GDS's diversity initiatives:

> We work hard to transcend the usual diversity approach, which uses a kind of "host and guest" model. The implied message in that model is, "This is our place, but we'll allow you to join us if you assimilate and fit in!" Instead, we're training our students to develop the capacity to create spaces where everyone can feel valued and empowered, without having to become like us. After all, if everyone who joins a group doesn't feel able to speak up

and share his or her ideas, experiences, and perspectives, we lose
most of the value that we hoped to gain by becoming diverse in
the first place.[5]

Taking diversity seriously requires GDS faculty and students to respond to shifting social, intellectual, and emotional currents on campus. One year, the high school seniors were caught up in the usual anxiety about college admissions, but with an unpleasant twist: Gossip flowed through the halls about which students of color were being admitted to prestigious universities, with the derisive implication that they'd been chosen solely because of their race. The talk stirred up jealousy, defensiveness, and resentment among the students.

One of the students disturbed by this turn of events was an aspiring writer named Joel Silverman. Joel had been talking about it in class one day when John Burghartd, a much-admired and loved member of the English faculty, posed a challenge to him. "Joel, instead of just complaining about it, why not do something? You're a writer. How about writing a play about what's happening? That could be a way of getting the problem on the table and forcing all of us to deal with it more openly."

Joel accepted the challenge. He wrote a play about the controversy, and it was performed before the whole student body that January, on Martin Luther King Jr. Day. Later in the day, students participated in facilitated discussions of the play and the issues it raised. The whole experience did a lot to detoxify the atmosphere of the school around the college admissions process and its unspoken racial component. It's a great illustration of how GDS has been able to rise to the challenges and conflicts that emerge whenever people from different backgrounds come together. Rather than sweeping issues under the rug, the GDS community tackles them head-on, with results that are healthy and enriching for everybody.

The kicker to this story is that Joel Silverman was inspired by his debut as playwright to pursue a career in Hollywood, where he is now a successful screenwriter, producer, and director.

Many of the activities around diversity at GDS are unrelated to conflict or tension and instead are expressions of pure joy. There are five major festivals linked to holidays that are celebrated with school-wide assemblies dedicated to appropriate themes, including the Harvest Assembly (gratitude), the Christmas Assembly (peace), the Passover Assembly (freedom), and the King Assembly (justice).

As hard as GDS has worked over the years to create an environment where students from every background can embrace each other and learn from one another, the school is not immune from the diversity challenges that every institution faces. In the spring of 2016, a number of incidents reflecting tension around race and gender erupted in the school, prompting administrators to suspend classes and devote time to working through the issues, much as they did back in 1989 during my own time at GDS. The reality is that there may never be a time or place where diversity and inclusion work perfectly. Schools must be ever vigilant in recognizing indications that difference is morphing into disagreement and then into disrespect and conflict, and they must support students in finding a positive way forward.

Affirmative Action: A Remedy Under Attack

Despite the positive, concrete educational benefits to students at all levels conferred by increased diversity, relatively few young Americans grow up in neighborhoods that are naturally diverse... which means that most public school classrooms at the primary and secondary level are more or less segregated by race, ethnicity, and class. Today, independent schools, which have strived for years to ensure greater diversity, are more diverse than public schools. So, for many young people, college offers the first opportunity for them to meet, live with, and learn alongside others whose backgrounds are very different from their own.

However, integration and inclusion don't happen automatically or easily at the college level. The same discriminatory systems that create barriers to achievement for millions of teenagers mean that many of those from diverse backgrounds are up against big obstacles when applying to college. Here is where programs of affirmative action, designed to give a small boost in the admissions process to candidates from varied backgrounds, are supposed to make up some of the difference. And affirmative action has helped. Over the last several decades, ethnic and racial minorities have earned college degrees in record numbers. And women—another once-disadvantaged group whose advancement was furthered by affirmative action—now actually outnumber men on campus.

But this is far from suggesting that the educational doors to social and economic equality have been flung wide open. Huge disparities in college graduation rates for minorities persist, driven by many factors: the weaker pre-college preparation many students from poorer neighborhoods receive; the economic difficulties they often experience, which force many to work part-time or even full-time jobs and skip semesters or drop out altogether when tuition bills become unaffordable; and the social isolation students may feel when they are among a handful of minority students on campus.

Today, making matters worse, the rollback of many affirmative action programs under legal, political, and social pressure threatens to close the doors to college for a generation of minority students. In a 2007 case focused on school busing, Supreme Court Justice John Roberts famously declared that "the way to stop discrimination on the basis of race is to stop discriminating on the basis of race," strongly implying that the time had come for an end to affirmative action. Roberts's words have been adopted as a rallying cry by opponents of affirmative action who demand "color-blind" admissions policies at colleges and universities. In effect, these opponents are untroubled by preferential treatment for particular students on the basis of countless other arbitrary factors, from geographic origin to "legacy" status for children of alumni; they object only when minority students get a small break in the admissions process.

The Roberts court has continued to chip away at the power of colleges and universities to pursue diversity in their student bodies. In *Schuette v. Coalition to Defend Affirmative Action*, a 2014 battle over admissions to public universities in Michigan, the Roberts court upheld a state constitutional ban on affirmative action, thereby clearing the way for other states to forbid the consideration of race in the college entrance process.

As a result, many colleges and university systems have been scrambling to devise other legally acceptable means of pursuing diversity goals. Some have been testing "place-based" admissions criteria, giving a helping hand to applicants from specific districts deemed underprivileged. Others have incorporated income and economic class data into admissions decisions. Still others, like the University of Texas, have experimented with plans that grant admission to a specified percentage of graduates from any high school (in the case of Texas, the top 10 percent of the graduating class); the idea is to give a subtle boost to smart students from otherwise underperforming school districts.

In the 2015–16 term, the Roberts court considered a legal challenge to the implementation of the Texas plan. Back in 2008, Abigail

Fisher applied to the University of Texas. Because she was not part of the top 10 percent of her high school class, Fisher was not granted automatic admission. Instead, she went through a separate admissions process in which race is considered along with many other factors. After being denied admission, she sued the university with the help of conservative legal groups that claim that *any* consideration of race should be excluded from the college admissions process.

In June 2016, the Supreme Court upheld the right of the University of Texas to use affirmative action in *Fisher v. University of Texas*. However, disturbing comments from the bench during oral arguments on the case had alarmed observers, including me. To audible gasps from the gallery, the late Justice Antonin Scalia questioned whether admitting African American students to public universities through the help of affirmative action might do a disservice to those minority students who would do better in "a slower-track school."[6] Scalia was alluding to the so-called mismatch theory, which holds that affirmative action harms minority students by pushing them into academic environments they aren't equipped to handle. It's a favored belief among conservative opponents of affirmative action, but the overwhelming bulk of scholarly evidence shows it's factually untrue.[7] The continuing popularity of the mismatch theory is an example of the "soft bigotry of low expectations" that has long plagued minority students.

At another point in the oral arguments, Chief Justice Roberts asked, "What unique perspective does a minority student bring to a physics class?" implying that for him the answer is "none." Unfortunately, attorney Greg Garre, representing the University of Texas, missed the opportunity to answer the question. There is value to diverse students learning together in *any* class, because their inherent differences trigger better thinking by everyone. And with hundreds of thousands of technical jobs going unfilled each year, the nation can hardly afford to exclude a critical future talent pool of diverse individuals from those physics classes! No wonder almost two thousand professional physicists signed a letter publicly rebuking both Scalia and Roberts for their remarks and defending the importance of diversity in science education.[8]

It was alarming to see such willful ignorance and continuing hostility to diversity on the part of some of America's most powerful jurists. Luckily, in upholding affirmative action in the case, Justice Kennedy, writing for the 4–3 majority said, "A university is in large part defined by those intangible 'qualities which are incapable of objective measurement but which make for greatness.' Considerable deference is owed to a university in defining those intangible characteristics, like student body diversity, that are central to its identity and educational mission."

Even though the Texas admissions system survived the court challenge, it remains to be seen whether any of the alternative systems aimed at encouraging diversity will be as effective as race-based affirmative action. If not, we run the risk of having our higher education system perpetuate rather than reduce racial, ethnic, and class barriers to full participation and advancement in our society. That's not the direction our nation should be heading.

Signs of Hope: Making the Benefits of Diversity Real

Of course, even when affirmative action or similar admissions programs succeed in ensuring a diverse student body, this alone is not enough to guarantee that the benefits of diversity will be enjoyed to the fullest. Simply having some black, Latino, and Asian faces on campus doesn't automatically translate into a richly rewarding multicultural learning experience.

At many colleges, observers report that students, both white and minority, tend to "self-segregate" into racially defined groups—sitting together in the cafeteria, socializing exclusively with one another, signing up for classes and joining clubs geared specifically to their own cultural issues and concerns. "When I walk around university campuses," says David Reingold, a dean at Purdue University in Indiana, "it feels like they haven't changed a whole lot in terms of self-segregation. Those tendencies are as pronounced as they were thirty years ago. And I don't think universities have figured out ways for students to build connectivity."[9]

The perpetuation on many campuses of the "Greek system" of fraternities and sororities reinforces the segregation at schools where the social structures revolve around them. Having joined a sorority myself in my first years of college, I appreciate why they are popular. But in the aggregate, the Greek system offers cover for exclusionary, sexist, and racist behavior that has no place on college campuses. It's hard not to see it as an enemy of progress.

The year 2015 may mark a turning point in the passion and activism of minority students across the country. Many are demanding that faculty and administrators give greater recognition to the students' particular experiences, values, and perspectives. During the fall of 2015, students at the University of Missouri were outraged over a series of racial affronts, ranging from the use of the N-word by a white student during homecoming week to a vandal's use of feces to scrawl a crude swastika on the wall of a dormitory bathroom. In response, hundreds of students took part in campus protests, culminating in a threatened strike by black players on Mizzou's football team. University president Timothy Wolfe seemed unable to quell the hostilities swirling across the campus; he resigned on November 9. In subsequent days, university officials announced a series of new diversity initiatives, but the issues raised by the student protestors remain troubling to many in the community, and the future of Mizzou is uncertain.

At other universities, issues of historical and cultural legacy have complicated the diversity challenge. At the same time as the Mizzou protests, members of the Black Justice League at Princeton University organized a sit-in at the office of president Christopher Eisgruber, demanding initiatives to help make the school a more welcoming place for minority students. The most controversial: a proposal to remove the name and image of Woodrow Wilson from a number of Princeton landmarks, including the university's schools of public and international affairs. Before becoming the nation's twenty-eighth president, Wilson served as both president of Princeton and governor of the state of New Jersey. And while his historical legacy includes such notable achievements as the successful negotiation of the Treaty of Versailles concluding the First World War, Wilson was also a virulent racist who imposed racial segregation of federal agencies and helped force the ouster of black professionals from many government jobs.[10]

Thanks to the student protests, many Americans became aware of Wilson's tarnished racial record for the first time. Newspapers around the country ran lengthy examinations of Wilson's legacy and place in American history. And on November 22, Eisgruber agreed to ask Princeton's board of trustees to develop a process for reevaluating Wilson's legacy and considering a more appropriate way to recognize his role in the university's history going forward—including both the positive and the negative elements of his legacy.[11] Ultimately, Princeton's board voted to keep the Wilson name. But the student protestors at Princeton had played a powerful educational role in forcing the university—and the nation—to confront an aspect of its racial history that many had chosen to ignore.

Issues like these remind us that diversity isn't just a numbers game. Merely having a certain percentage of black, Latino, or Asian students on campus doesn't mean that a college or university has succeeded in ensuring the kind of environment where diverse views are welcome and where all students benefit. Students with widely varying perspectives *all* need to be empowered to speak out vigorously on behalf of their unique viewpoints—even when the result is a cacophony of competing, sometimes clashing voices. Disagreement and even discomfort are the inevitable results. I would argue that clash is fundamental to education. Everyone in the college community—students, faculty, administrators, and concerned outside observers like alumni and family members—must learn to accept these discussions as signs of learning and growth. But this is easier said than done.

Journalist Eve Fairbanks has studied the kinds of culture clashes that can happen when a college supports diversity in a setting even more fraught with racial tension than the United States—post-apartheid South Africa. At the University of the Free State, where Fairbanks lived and worked for several years, the first black students were admitted in 1992, just two years before the end of apartheid.

Fairbanks observes that integration of the university has passed through two distinct phases. In the first phase, the relatively small numbers of black students were happy just to be there, and they accepted the norms and culture of college life without openly challenging them, though they often found them baffling and unfair. In the second phase, still being played out today, black students have become a majority—and as a result, they are increasingly vocal about changing campus traditions they find offensive, such as hazing, as well as about problems like the paucity of black professors. White students have pushed back against these demands for change, leading to significant clashes both on campus and off.

People throughout the university community are struggling

to deal with these battles. One South African professor summarizes the pattern this way: "People are fine with racial difference as long as there's no culture conflict."

Now the first black vice-chancellor at the University of the Free State, Jonathan D. Jansen, is tackling the problem by driving a series of institutional changes to accommodate the dramatically altered makeup of the student body. Perhaps most important, Jansen has initiated conversations between students of all races to forge a new, collaborative vision of what a truly inclusive campus culture would be like.[12]

The history of many US colleges, especially in formerly segregated parts of the country, isn't too dissimilar from the experience of South Africa. The lesson is that to take complete advantage of the potential benefits of educational diversity for *all* students, we may need to work through a process of reform and renewal similar to the one that South African universities are now experiencing.

Despite these challenges, it would be wrong to conclude that our educational system is hopelessly doomed or not making progress. A vivid example of how positive cultural change can transform an organization through the efforts of a few determined advocates is happening today at one of America's elite educational institutions—the business school of New York's prestigious Columbia University.

One of the key players in this story of change is my friend Dr. Katherine W. Phillips. Now a full professor and senior vice dean at Columbia Business School (CBS), Phillips has a long history of being a "first" in most of the positions she has held, dating back to when she was the first African American woman to earn a PhD from the Graduate School of Business of Stanford University. She has built a career around studying the impact of diversity in society, organizations, and work teams, having pioneered the field back in the 1990s when it was more generally known as "demography" and when most experts assumed that homogeneity was usually *beneficial* to well-run organizations.

Her mere presence in a leadership role at one of the world's greatest business schools makes Phillips an important inspirational figure. But she has also dedicated herself to conscious efforts to encourage cultural change around the issue of diversity in the field of business education. "I can't change the way leaders are trained at every business school," she acknowledges. "But when I walk into an environment like Columbia, I make a commitment to it. And when I make a commitment to a place, I want to bring my whole self to it—and if that means helping to change the way people view and treat one another, so be it."[13]

Phillips has been an advocate for diversity in the ways you might expect from a professor—for example, by creating and teaching an elective course on the subject. But she found that teaching the course was somewhat unsatisfying because it didn't reach *all* the MBA students at Columbia—and, in fact, the ones who could benefit the most from learning about diversity were often the ones who failed to sign up for the course. So now Phillips focuses her energies on change efforts that are more indirect yet, in the long run, more powerful.

"We're trying to make diversity part of the daily lives of Columbia students," she says. "Diversity is built into the cases and stories they study in their very first leadership course. We make sure diversity is reflected in the learning teams that students join and the workshops and presentations they attend. And we work hard to create safe spaces for student organizations that are dedicated to diversity."

The result has been a slow but unmistakable shift in the zeitgeist of CBS. "Now talking about diversity is *normal*," Phillips says. "People immediately understand that it's important, and they realize there is serious scholarship around it. We no longer have to struggle to make the case that diversity matters."

One of Phillips's proudest moments was when a group of women students at Columbia mounted a study of diversity practices at CBS itself. Prompted by a few trigger incidents—including the publication of a famous, highly critical *New York Times* article about sexism at Harvard Business School, and the lopsided, male-heavy list of 2012 winners in Columbia's prestigious Second-Year Fellows Program—a group of thirty-three students (a handful of supportive males among them) worked with faculty and administrators to research gender issues at CBS. They examined admissions practices, curriculum design, after-graduation career prospects, and even social matters like dating behavior among students. The result was a thoughtful, detailed report titled *CBS Reflects: Gender Equality* that spawned hundreds of conversations on campus and strengthened the impetus behind efforts to improve gender equality at the university.[14]

Now CBS Reflects is also the name of a grassroots student organization that monitors and encourages the implementation of many of the reforms recommended in the original report. The whole story reflects the way efforts by pioneers like Katherine Phillips can help to launch the transformation of entire institutions—first by influencing the attitudes and behaviors of a few individuals, then by encouraging honest conversations, serious self-reflection, and aspirations for change among an ever-widening circle of allies.

Cultural change can be difficult, scary—even painful. But it leads to new growth and to opportunities for achievement that are hard to imagine in the difficult moments before we dare to take the plunge. And educational reform that would make America's schools, colleges, and universities truly diverse institutions—where the backgrounds, experiences, values, personalities, and perspectives of *all* students are valued and respected—could go a long way toward making our dream of meritocracy more of a reality.

13. The Media Mirror

The goal is that everyone should get to turn on the TV and see someone who looks like them and loves like them. And just as important, everyone should turn on the TV and see someone who doesn't look like them and love like them. Because, perhaps then they will learn from them. Perhaps then they will not isolate them, marginalize them, erase them. Perhaps they will even come to recognize themselves in them. Perhaps they will even learn to love them.

—*Screenwriter, director, and producer Shonda Rhimes*

Like most little kids, I enjoyed dressing up when I was small. I had really only one "costume," if you could call it that—a set of Wonder Woman Underoos. I wore them with red cable-knit knee-high socks to look like boots, and I thought nothing of walking around the neighborhood ready to save the day in my state of virtual undress. Wonder Woman was everything. I let my friend Matthew wear his Superman Speedo when we went to the public pool together, but I knew Wonder Woman was the most important person in town.

I thought about this the other night when, flipping channels, I was stopped cold by the sight of Lynda Carter flying through the air. An old episode of *The New Original Wonder Woman* was playing on an obscure cable channel, and I had to watch!

As a forty-year-old, I noticed a lot about the show that I hadn't remembered. First of all, Wonder Woman was seriously sexy. The costume Lynda Carter squeezed into was skintight and skimpy. I have no idea how she was able to jump in her low-cut costume (and with the wonders of late-'70s special effects, her hair barely moved). When she roped a bad guy with her Lasso of Truth, I started laughing and didn't stop until the show was over. But all these years later, the overall takeaway was that Wonder Woman kicked ass. I totally get why my five-year-old self was obsessed with her. At some point I learned that Lynda Carter lived near us in DC. I routinely rode my bike down her block hoping to catch a glimpse, but I never did.

Wonder Woman was iconic for women of my generation and older. The original DC Comics character dates back to 1941, but the TV show, which aired from 1975 to 1979, was defining for women my age. She was strong, independent, and didn't need a man to help her take out the bad guys. Gloria Steinem put her picture on the cover of the first *Ms.* magazine and later wrote:

> *Wonder Woman symbolizes many of the values of the women's culture that feminists are now trying to introduce into the mainstream: strength and self-reliance for women; sisterhood and mutual support among women; peacefulness and esteem for human life; a diminishment both of "masculine" aggression and of the belief that violence is the only way of solving conflicts.*[1]

Wonder Woman was important because she reflected in entertainment a vision American women had for themselves. She was certainly part of my own feminist upbringing. Just watching her showed me, at an early age, what was possible.

Today my children are experiencing media in a way that has little in common with what I experienced as a kid. The single thirteen-inch TV set in our family room carried only four channels, and I was allowed to watch it for just thirty minutes a day. But though the content was limited, the impact was huge. Today the access and choices are nearly limitless, and the impact is even greater. Now more than ever, the movies and shows that get produced and flow in an unending stream throughout homes have a major impact on how all of us, children and adults alike, see the world.

Sadly, the entertainment industry, especially movies and TV, has hardly advanced since I was little. In fact, it now looks as though the *Wonder Woman* series may have been a high point for feminist TV! Despite the legacy of pioneers like the creators of *Wonder Woman*, the film industry, television, broadcast news, the print media, and the Internet have all fallen short of real inclusiveness, diversity, and equality. This failure to reflect the real America is affecting the national conversation about our future.

Thankfully, a new generation of actors, writers, journalists, filmmakers, and show runners from varied backgrounds is finally breaking down stereotypical thinking and capturing the true richness of the American social landscape. Women and minority voices in media and film are overcoming barriers, to critical and financial acclaim—though there is still plenty of progress left to be made.

Lack of Equality on the Big Screen

The year 2016 may very well mark a turning point in Hollywood's consciousness of and focus on the issue of diversity. After the Academy Award nominations were announced, an uproar ensued over the lack of diversity among the nominees. Famous faces from George Clooney to Spike Lee weighed in. A number of celebrities, including Will Smith and Jada Pinkett Smith, announced they would not attend the event in protest, and many called on host Chris Rock to do the same. On social media, the hashtag #OscarsSoWhite launched a torrent of passion about the lack of diversity among Oscar voters, the major Hollywood studios, and the nominees. The controversy became so widely discussed that when a blizzard threatened large swaths of the East Coast, the *New York Post* ran a cover with the headline, "This Weekend Will Be Whiter Than the Oscars."

The history of the Academy of Motion Picture Arts and Sciences, the body that nominates and selects winners of Hollywood's most prestigious prize, ignoring, snubbing, or leaving out actors, directors, and films focused on people of color is long and painful. The most glaring example in my lifetime was the total Oscar shutout of *The Color Purple*, one of the most exquisite and powerful films ever made. The film, directed by Steven Spielberg with an almost entirely black cast, including Whoopi Goldberg, Oprah Winfrey, and Danny Glover, was nominated for eleven Academy Awards in 1986, but it failed to win a single one and lost the Best Picture award to the decidedly mediocre *Out of Africa*. Even then, the complaints about bias among Academy voters were loud, yet little has changed since.

Over the last thirty years, Hollywood movies have made little progress in embracing, showcasing, and leveraging the talents of women and minorities. There are still huge, embarrassing gaps between the real America and the America depicted on movie screens—something the moviegoing public has begun to protest.

One of the most comprehensive recent studies of diversity in the movie business, a report titled *Inequality in 700 Popular Films*, analyzes the content of the one hundred highest-grossing pictures released every year from 2007 to 2014, including a grand total of 30,835 speaking or named roles in those pictures. The researchers found that, although racial minorities make up around 38 percent of the American population, they got fewer than 27 percent of the movie roles. Although something in the neighborhood of 3 to 4 percent of Americans identify as lesbian, gay, or bisexual, out of 4,610 speaking characters in the top 100 movies of 2014, only nineteen characters—not 19 percent but nineteen characters *in total*—were LGBT. (Not a single one was transgender.)

And although women—of course—represent slightly more than half of the human race, they had only 30.2 percent of the 30,835 speaking roles in those movies—and, of the top 100 films of 2014, only 21 had a woman in a lead role. (Sad to say, the percentage of women with speaking roles is almost exactly the same as the percentage who appear in films either fully or partially nude.) Throw age into the mix, and the treatment of women on-screen becomes even more warped: Only 25.7 percent of the female characters in 2014 movies appeared to be forty or older. In fact, not one of the high-grossing films of 2014 except a handful with ensemble casts featured a female character forty-five or older.[2] Maybe the Goldie Hawn character in *The First Wives Club* had it right when she quipped, "There are three ages for women in Hollywood: babe, D.A., and *Driving Miss Daisy*."[3]

The challenges for women in Hollywood are so significant that many talented women have opted to leave the studio system entirely. "The problem is systemic and sometimes the only way to change the system is to go out of the system and make change yourself," says Alysia Reiner, star of the Netflix hit series *Orange Is the New Black*. She and her business partner Sarah Megan Thomas launched their own production company, Broad Street Pictures, in 2014 to promote remarkable roles for women. Their first venture, the film *Equity*, starring a cast of women, was also produced, written, and directed by women. It premiered at the prestigious Sundance Film Festival in January 2016, and it was bought by Sony Pictures for wider distribution. Over the years,

Sundance has been an important outlet for female and minority filmmakers, as the festival has done what the Academy has failed to do—set an express goal of promoting and supporting women and minority filmmakers and follow through on those commitments (more on that in a moment).

Equally troubling is the scarcity of great characters and stories drawn from America's richly diverse culture and history for depiction on-screen. The number of big-budget, high-profile Hollywood pictures featuring African American lead characters is shockingly small. In the last twenty years or so, Edward Zwick's *Glory* (1989), Spike Lee's *Malcolm X* (1992), Steven Spielberg's *Amistad* (1997), John Singleton's *Rosewood* (1997), Steve McQueen's *12 Years a Slave* (2013), Ava DuVernay's *Selma* (2014), and F. Gary Gray's *Straight Outta Compton* (2015) are among the handful that come to mind. As for the Latino presence in film, once you get past the stereotypes of the Zorro movies and the sentimentality of *West Side Story* (1961), Hollywood has almost nothing to offer, with one or two exceptions, like Julie Taymor's artistic biopic *Frida* (2002).

Even when accomplished directors tackle stories drawn from American history, minority perspectives often get short shrift. Though African Americans, Latinos, and Asian Americans all played large roles in settling the American West, they're almost invisible in the vast array of classic pictures about life on the frontier. And when Spielberg examined the death of slavery in his epic *Lincoln* (2012), black characters existed only on the sidelines, despite the growing recognition among historians that African Americans played a major role in seizing their own freedom during the final chaotic months of the Confederacy. Even the famous activist and orator Frederick Douglass, who was a friend of Lincoln's, never appears in Spielberg's picture.

Adding insult to injury, Hollywood directors continue to cast white actors to play blacks, Latinos, Asians, and other minorities with shocking frequency. In 2015's *Aloha*, set in Hawaii, Cameron Crowe chose Emma Stone to play the Asian American character Allison Ng, a choice that prompted plenty of backlash from Asians and Hawaiians, including a scathing article by critic Jen Yamato titled "The Unbearable Whiteness of Cameron Crowe's 'Aloha.'" Similarly, the *Star Trek* character Khan, conceived to be of Indian Sikh descent, was played by white British actor Benedict Cumberbatch in *Star Trek Into Darkness* (2013), while Tony Mendez, a real-life CIA agent who was Mexican American, was played in the blockbuster *Argo* (2012) by the film's director, the white, California-born Ben Affleck. Casting choices like these seem to send a clear but unfortunate message to minority Americans: "Your story may be good enough to tell. But we don't think you're good enough to tell it."

Racial and ethnic minorities make up a huge share of the moviegoing public—and of course, half of movie fans are women. But you'd never know by looking at the content of the movies themselves.

Some Hollywood directors, producers, and studios do recognize the enormous opportunities in creating movies that reflect the diversity of the audience. This year's controversy is certainly not lost on Academy president Cheryl Boone Isaacs, herself African American, who stated in a post on Twitter a few days into the crisis that "we need to do more, and better, and quickly." Academy voters are 94 percent white, 76 percent male, and average sixty-three years in age. A few days later, in an unprecedented move, she announced a major commitment to radically diversify Academy membership. It's an important and visible call to action that so many, particularly African American and female stars, say is long overdue.

But it's not just the Academy that's taking diversity seriously.

Some of the movers and shakers in the business have been filling the diversity gap—and enjoying huge financial success as a result.

In 2015, Universal Studios set a new all-time record for movie revenues and achieved the feat with more than a third of the year to go, exceeding $5.53 billion by early August (and thereby passing the previous record, set by 20th Century Fox in 2014). More remarkably, Universal accomplished this through a "counter-programming strategy" built around diverse stars and stories. The studio's biggest and most lucrative hits included a musical biopic about an influential gangsta rap group (*Straight Outta Compton*), a movie about an all-female a cappella singing group (*Pitch Perfect 2*), and the latest installment in what has been called "the most racially diverse Hollywood franchise going" (*Furious* 7). As one industry commentator put it, "When everybody else in Hollywood is going after white guys in their 20s, Universal is going after everybody else."[4]

Will other studios follow Universal's lead? Hollywood has never been shy about imitating the successful formulas invented by others. Maybe Universal's record year will convince the rest of the industry to follow suit.

A New Burst of Color on the TV Screen

It's truly unbelievable, but when the Capitol Hill political drama *Scandal* made its debut in 2012, Kerry Washington became the first black female lead in a network TV drama in thirty-eight years. Washington's most recent predecessor was Teresa Graves, who starred as an undercover cop in the short-lived series *Get Christie Love!* way back in 1974. *Scandal* has proven to be a huge hit, helping to pave the way for a virtual explosion of TV shows featuring men and women in many shades of black and brown.

Shonda Rhimes's growing power and influence on network TV can't be underestimated in terms of what we see every night.

Among the many stars from diverse backgrounds now head-lining various network and cable shows are African Americans like Anthony Anderson and Tracee Ellis Ross of *Black-ish*, my all-time-favorite actress Viola Davis of *How to Get Away with Murder*, Terrence Howard and Taraji P. Henson of *Empire*, and Meagan Good of *Minority Report*. Black stars are even making inroads in the formerly all-white domain of talk show hosting, with South African Trevor Noah now occupying Jon Stewart's desk at *The Daily Show* and Larry Wilmore hosted *The Nightly Show*. People from a range of other ethnic and national back-grounds are finally claiming starring roles on television as well—Aziz Ansari (the US-born son of a Tamil Muslim family originally from India) of *Master of None*; Constance Wu and Hudson Yang (both US-born Chinese Americans) of *Fresh Off the Boat*; Gina Rodriguez (born in Chicago to Puerto Rican parents) of *Jane the Virgin*; and Mindy Kaling (born in the United States of Indian parents) of *The Mindy Project*.

It wasn't very long ago that the top-line stars of US television were almost exclusively white. Today they are just as American—but they are beginning to reflect the true makeup of American society, with roots in civilizations and cultures from around the world.

It would be wonderful if the current plethora of shows fea-turing the talents of minority men and women meant that the diversity battle on our TV screens has been won, once and for all. But the curious fact is that TV has experienced fleeting "golden ages" of diversity in the past—as I dimly sensed when Lynda Carter flashed across my screen when I was five. In the 1970s, the massive success of the miniseries *Roots* helped boost the careers of stars like LeVar Burton, Ben Vereen, and Louis

Gossett Jr. and launched a short-lived vogue for shows with black characters and stories. In the early 1990s, Bill Cosby became America's best-loved dad and ushered in a brief period when sitcoms featuring black families thrived. Around the same time, women enjoyed unprecedented success and power as creators of TV comedy series. In 1990, three of the five sitcoms nominated for Emmy awards were produced by and starred women: Susan Harris's *The Golden Girls*, Linda Bloodworth-Thomason's *Designing Women*, and Diane English's *Murphy Brown*. (English's show won the award.)[5]

But all these interludes when minorities and women seemed to be breaking through in the world of television quickly faded. White males reclaimed their dominance in practically every category of TV programming: dramas, sitcoms, news, talk shows. Only in the last few years have shows built around people of color (like those listed above) and comedies featuring female stars (like Tina Fey, Amy Schumer, Lena Dunham, and the aforementioned Mindy Kaling) made a major resurgence.

Will today's new "golden age" prove any more permanent than those of earlier eras? Demographic and cultural trends would seem to favor that outcome. As discussed throughout this book, the Millennial generation—now statistically the largest age cohort in US society—is both more diverse and more willing to embrace cultural diversity than any previous generation. Back in the 1950s, TV executives worried about whether audiences would accept and laugh with the Cuban husband and costar of the comedic heroine Lucille Ball; today there's little doubt that American audiences, especially those of Millennial vintage, are happy to watch and identify with performers from a wide range of backgrounds.

But programming decisions, today as always, are made by network and cable executives who are still overwhelmingly male and white. If they decide that on-screen diversity is just another fad—

like off-the-island reality programs and dramas about vampires or zombies—they may soon revert to business as usual. That means following the path of least resistance by buying shows created by people who look like them and tell stories centered on the same kinds of people—white males from Middle American backgrounds. How safe, how predictable, and how boring.

Behind the Camera: The Diversity Gap Among Media Industry Leaders

To this point, I've focused mainly on the faces we see on our television and movie screens—the characters depicted and the stories told. These are tremendously important because they shape the way we view ourselves, our society, and our world. A child who sees people like herself in the media comes to think of herself as important, interesting, and even potentially heroic—just like the characters in the stories that enthrall her.

But of course in the real world of Hollywood, the on-screen images are shaped by the people offscreen who make the big decisions about programming and content—the writers, directors, producers, studio heads, and corporate executives who craft the stories and sign off on all the major decisions. Whose story is worth telling? Which underdog group in society deserves to be immortalized on film? Which unrecognized source of talent should receive encouragement, guidance, and financial support? Which segment of the American population should we woo as the audience for our next big production? Business decisions like these are made in Hollywood office suites every day. And while they may seem to be merely matters of dollars and cents, they end up having an enormous impact on our national culture—and in the long run, on the way Americans see themselves.

Soledad O'Brien, the gifted television journalist, told me a story that vividly illustrates why the backgrounds of the people who mold America's stories are so important:

Back in 2005, I was in the studios of CNN during the horrific aftermath of Hurricane Katrina. Naturally our network was covering the events in New Orleans around the clock. At some point, I was standing next to a colleague, watching live images on a giant monitor of thousands of people—overwhelmingly poor black people—who had taken refuge in the New Orleans Superdome. They were waving desperately at the camera, holding up signs, and crying out to our reporters, saying "Somebody, please help us!" It was a heart-wrenching sight.

So imagine my shock when my coworker turned to me and remarked, "I can't believe that anybody could think this is about race!" At that exact same moment, the overwhelming reaction in my mind had been, "Oh my God, this is so about race!"[6]

The point of O'Brien's story isn't that her coworker is a bad person. The point is that it's almost inevitable that some see the world through a particular set of lenses...lenses that make issues of diversity, prejudice, and injustice practically invisible. Which is exactly why America's newsrooms—as well as its movie studios, TV network offices, newspaper editorial departments, book publishing headquarters, and every other media nerve center—are so desperately in need of greater diversity...not just of color, gender, and ethnicity but of thinking, perception, and understanding.

That's why controversies that may seem like "inside baseball," of interest only to Hollywood folk themselves, are actually important for American society as a whole. In September 2015, when Viola Davis became the first black woman ever to win an

Emmy as outstanding lead actress in a drama series, her speech quoting the great antislavery activist Harriet Tubman was poignant and relevant:

> *In my mind, I see a line. And over that line, I see green fields and lovely flowers and beautiful, white women with their arms stretched out to me over that line, but I can't seem to get there no how. I can't seem to get over that line.*

Davis went on to say, "The only thing that separates women of color from anyone else is opportunity. You cannot win an Emmy for roles that are simply not there."[7] It was bold and probably a bit risky for Davis to go public with her complaint about opportunity. But her comments led to increased scrutiny of the lack of offscreen diversity in Hollywood and its impact on the opportunities given to people of color, women, and other disenfranchised groups—issues that are overdue for attention.

In its 2015 report on diversity in Hollywood, the Ralph J. Bunche Center for African American Studies at UCLA examined the demographics of the "gatekeepers" and the "greenlighters" in movies and TV—that is, the people who make the decisions that shape our national culture. Among the findings:

- Film studio unit heads are 96 percent white and 61 percent male.
- Film studio senior management is 92 percent white and 83 percent male.
- Television network and studio heads are 96 percent white and 71 percent male.
- Television senior management is 93 percent white and 73 percent male.[8]

Similarly, in its 2015 report on the status of women in the US media, the Women's Media Center found that men accounted for 83 percent of directors, executive producers, producers, writers, cinematographers, and editors for the 250 most profitable films made in the United States during the previous year. None of 2013's top 100 films had a black female director.[9]

The problem with lack of diversity begins in the executive suites of the studios, but it reaches far deeper than that. Think about the writers' rooms where the stories and scripts for TV series are created. Despite the influx of new, more diverse on-screen talent that I described earlier in this chapter, the writers working behind the scenes to craft the stories remain overwhelmingly white and male. A 2015 report by the Writers Guild of America revealed that the numbers of people of color employed as TV writers actually *shrank* from 15.6 percent in 2011–12 (an all-time peak) to 13.7 percent in 2013–14. And women aren't doing much better. They represent fewer than a third of all TV writers, rather than the 50 percent or more that their numbers in the population would suggest.[10]

Lisa Garcia Quiroz, who leads the Time Warner Foundation, has been quietly trying to change this reality for years. Quiroz has helped guide Time Warner toward more fully embracing and investing in diversity as an important business strategy. In the late '90s while at Time Inc., Quiroz helped launch *People en Español*—only the second magazine targeted at the US female Hispanic market and the first to be published in Spanish by any major US publisher.

"I really saw the multicultural market juggernaut early on," Quiroz told me:

And when we launched the magazine, it was an opportunity to delve into the multicultural market more fully and to really spend time with big-name advertisers who were already begin-

ning to see the opportunity in this. Companies like Procter & Gamble and L'Oreal were already heavily investing in the multicultural market and saw this as an opportunity to expand their reach. People en Español *was successful because we understood that many Hispanics were born outside the US and were culturally tied to the Spanish language. They followed different stars and entertainers, and nothing to date had catered to their unique interests. They were underserved. It wasn't just the language but the complete lifestyle. To Time's credit, they totally got it and it became a huge success. There were pieces of the company that were already working to address the multicultural market but nobody looking at the overall demographic changes in the US and what that meant for the future. People didn't realize this would have profound repercussions for all of our audiences.*[11]

At Time Warner, the focus on expanding the business to better serve the multicultural market was championed across multiple fronts. Quiroz observes, "Clearly it helped that we had diverse leaders in the company who saw the opportunity, namely three Latinos and an African American. It was really because of them that we had businesses like AOL Latino and HBO Latino. And at Time Inc. we bought *Essence* magazine."

Quiroz's experience with *People en Español* inspired her to continue to find ways to meet the needs of the changing market:

When I came to head the Time Warner Foundation, there was a lot of interest from the CEO in refocusing our philanthropic efforts. We are a story-driven company, and what we heard from the creatives in the company was the importance of the written word. For me it seemed like a natural place to identify and really invest in finding a strong cadre of diverse storytellers.

But when we reached out to the existing incubators, they all were having the same problem finding diverse voices to nurture. We decided that was the right place to put our dollars. We realized we could use our money to encourage those organizations to work a little harder to find voices they might otherwise overlook. I like to think of what we do as a kind of angel investing. We reward those who come up with good ideas to make progress.

The strategy has especially paid off with organizations like the Sundance Film Festival, which thanks to Time Warner's support and encouragement has sought out and developed female and minority voices. The success of the female-centered Wall Street film *Equity*, which I mentioned earlier, is due in no small part to this strategy.

Over the years, Sundance has incubated a number of incredibly gifted diverse writers and directors who might never have otherwise had a chance. One such writer is Ryan Coogler, whose 2015 film *Creed* garnered both box office and critical success. Coogler's first feature-length film, *Fruitvale Station*, was incubated at Sundance when he was selected as a Time Warner/Sundance fellow. Quiroz comments, "It's unlikely that someone like Ryan, who was a young African American writer from USC, would have had a chance in Hollywood were it not for Sundance. They helped him develop his craft to ultimately become a huge star."

For Quiroz, the work continues. Her most recent effort, named OneFifty, is Time Warner's first-ever direct incubator for diverse writers and directors. The seventeen artists chosen for the inaugural class represent a broad range of perspectives and backgrounds, and Quiroz is optimistic it will bear fruit. "I see the change coming," she says. "It's coming slowly, but it's coming."

The Time Warner journey offers a bright spot in an otherwise disheartening landscape. But they are not alone in their efforts to bring more diversity to entertainment. As you might guess, in the world of television, Black Entertainment Television (BET) leads the way in employing writers from diverse backgrounds, with a staff that includes 55 percent female writers and 95 percent minorities. A handful of shows, including some of TV's biggest hits, are also exceptionally welcoming to minorities. *Grey's Anatomy*, *Scandal*, and *How to Get Away with Murder*—all three created under the auspices of the multitalented Shonda Rhimes—boast large percentages of female and minority writers.[12] And the hit evening soap opera *Empire* has one of the most diverse writing teams of all, more than half female and including a broad mix of ethnic backgrounds. The show's cocreator, Danny Strong, brags, "We've got African Americans, Latinos, white writers—it's this really cool blend of America."[13]

But the overall picture remains bleak. As one journalist put it:

> *Even as the hottest show on TV [Empire] boasts a majority-nonwhite writing staff, the work of vigorously recruiting non-white writing talent is still confined to a narrow pipeline: Diversity departments and fellowships help to fill one or two designated diversity slots on each staff. And that's just the start of the problem: As writer after writer revealed [in interviews], even when writers of color make it into that pipeline, the industry hasn't gotten much better at making them feel as though their voices matter.*[14]

Almost no one other than industry insiders knows or cares who writes the TV shows we watch. But the diversity of writer teams matters enormously to the quality of our media content. When a writers' room includes several people who have experienced life from a female, gay, or minority perspective, the stories Americans see, the characters they learn to identify with, and the perceptions of the world they share are all more likely to reflect the reality of our diverse, complex, vibrant society.

Reading America in Black and White

The visual media of movies and television aren't the only ones falling short on the diversity front. The book publishing industry—centered in liberal New York City and largely populated by progressive-minded graduates of Ivy League and other Northeastern colleges—has a disappointing track record when it comes to reflecting the varied backgrounds and stories that characterize twenty-first-century America.

Once again, numbers suggest the nature of the challenge. The biggest demographic survey of the publishing industry is the Diversity Baseline Survey (DBS), conducted in 2015 under the sponsorship of children's book publisher Lee & Low. The DBS tallied responses from more than three thousand professionals at thirty-four publishers and eight review journals. They reflected an industry that is 79 percent white. Other groups responding to the survey included those identifying as Asian (about 7 percent of the total), Hispanic (6 percent), African American (4 percent), and bi- or multiracial (3 percent). Among those in executive positions, where power in any business tends to be concentrated, the white share is even higher—86 percent.[15]

The annual salary survey conducted by *Publishers Weekly*—the magazine that plays about the same role in the book business as *Variety* in the entertainment industry—tells a similar story. Of the 425 publishing professionals who responded to *PW*'s 2015 survey, 89 percent identified as white, 5 percent as Asian, 3 percent as Hispanic, 2 percent as mixed race, and just 1 percent as African American.[16]

How important are the faces of the people who work at the big publishing companies like Simon & Schuster, Penguin Random House, HarperCollins, and Hachette? In one sense, not very important—after all, a smart editor or publisher should be capable of recognizing and encouraging a talented author no matter his or her color or ethnicity. But in practical terms, the lack of diversity in publishing creates a subtle barrier to understanding and acceptance that's very difficult for writers of color and other minorities to scale.

Novelist Daniel José Older, author of the acclaimed Bone Street Rumba urban fantasy series, is one of the relatively few minority writers who have broken through the barrier. (His series is published by Penguin, part of the giant Penguin Random House empire.) He talks about the ways creative people of color find their publishing dreams stymied. "A young writer that I mentor reached out to me last week," Older recalls:

> *"None of these agents look like me," she said, "and they don't represent anyone that looks like me." She's wrapping up a final draft of her first novel and I'd told her to research literary agencies to get a feel for what's out there. "What if they don't get what I'm doing?"*[17]

The sense that no one in the book business "gets" what people of color are doing leads many talented people to give up on the industry. The result: a self-perpetuating literary world in which minorities are almost invisible—where, for example, a study by the Cooperative Children's Book Center at the University of Wisconsin–Madison of 3,200 children's books published in 2013 found just ninety-three about black characters.[18]

Malaika Adero is an independent writer, editor, and consultant with a distinguished publishing career. She has worked at publishers large and small, from the acclaimed Amistad Press to giant Simon & Schuster, where she was vice president and senior editor of Atria Books. Adero points to a number of subtle ways in which the lack of minorities in key publishing roles impacts the entire book industry:

> Of course, publishers are leaving a lot of money on the table by making their book offerings so narrow. In a huge, diverse country like the US, it makes no business sense for publishers to do anything less than reach out to as wide an audience as possible.
>
> But the effects of this narrow publishing philosophy go a lot further. Because we aren't publishing enough books for the full spectrum of readers, specialized outlets like the black independent booksellers suffer. In recent years, the black bookselling community has dwindled to the point of being minuscule, largely because of a lack of great product from the big publishers to sell. With fewer sales channels, the marketing and publicity departments of the big publishers spend even less money on reaching out to the black community—so sales shrink further. The result of this self-fulfilling prophecy is that the supposedly weak market for African American books gets weakened further.
>
> Other industry practices make matters worse. Periodically, one or two of the big publishers decide they ought to become more diverse. So they set up an African American–oriented imprint, but they tend not to give the editor running it the staff, the support, and the autonomy needed to make it successful. And then after a few years, when the big house loses interest in sustaining the effort or when the economy takes a dip, they often shut down the dedicated imprint. The talented black professionals are now out, and the whole African American book community is adversely affected by having one or two more out of a job, especially since the numbers are so small from the start.[19]

The result is that African Americans, Asians, and Hispanics represent a vast potential book market that is significantly underserved, hurting readers and publishers alike. The fact that what Adero calls "superstars" from minority communities occasionally rise to prominence as authors tends to mask this reality. Ken Chen, poet and director of the Asian American Writers' Workshop, puts it this way:

> *I think there is a kind of cosmetic appearance of things changing with Junot Díaz and Jhumpa Lahiri being two of the central authors in American literature. But it would still be really difficult for someone [from a minority] to go to a bookstore and necessarily see themself.*

Chen notes that publishing professionals often claim that their failure to publish more works by people of color reflects the lack of a market for such books. That's bunk, Chen says:

> *Your ability to imagine that there is a market has to do with your ability to imagine that those people exist…And if [you] can't imagine that people of color actually exist and can buy books, then you can't imagine selling books to them. That's not just about a company corporate diversity policy; it's about actually knowing what's going on in communities of color.*[20]

Dispelling any doubt that people of color represent a strong book market, a Pew Research Center study found that the single demographic group in the United States most avidly dedicated to reading is black women.[21]

Given these realities, why does American publishing remain so stubbornly white? Racial bias in hiring probably plays a role. But equally powerful—perhaps more so—are rarely discussed industry practices that cause unintended racial impact. For example, the lowest rungs of book publishing—jobs like editorial assistant, in which recent graduates learn the craft of publishing and develop their first industry contacts—are relatively low-paid. And many aspiring publishers start at a rung even lower than this, serving internships that pay nothing at all. Economic reality means that these entry-level positions are virtually unaffordable to people from a poor or working-class background; they tend to be filled by bright young women and men whose affluent families can subsidize them for their first few years working in high-priced New York City.

Result: Every new generation of young publishers tends to be just as upper middle class, and just as overwhelmingly white, as the generation before it, regardless of the intentions of industry executives.

America's media businesses need to absorb and practice the same lesson other companies are already learning—the absolute necessity to create diverse teams at every level in order to reflect and leverage the creative strengths of our varied population. To achieve that, executives from the C-suite on down must examine the business practices, like unpaid internships, that unwittingly perpetuate patterns of discrimination. They must also look beyond mere hiring statistics to build companies that are genuinely welcoming to people with diverse backgrounds and perspectives.

"Publishers need to learn to truly value African American culture and communities in all of their diversity," Malaika Adero says. "And they need to create safe spaces for employees, including employees of color, where honest talk about grievances, concerns, and aspirations can happen. An employee affinity group may be just a social outlet. More valuable, in my judgment, are mentorship programs, formal and informal, that give young professionals a connection with a leader who will advise them, support them, and give them opportunities to shine."

Media executives must also break out of the stereotyped thinking in which too many corporate leaders are unwittingly trapped. As writer Annie Lowrey has observed:

> *There's a tendency for the media—indeed, for people in general—to see white dudes as "founders" or "entrepreneurs" or "bosses" or "disruptors" and to see women and people of color as anything else. The impulse is deep-seated. When you think of a leader, Jack Donaghy [the blowhard played by Alec Baldwin on the comedy* 30 Rock*] pops into your head rather than Oprah.*

Lowrey goes on to note the way media leaders who are *not* "white dudes" often get ignored or overlooked. For example, when *Vanity Fair* created its 2014 list of "media disruptors," it included Ezra Klein, one of the founders of the influential website Vox (who happens to be Lowrey's husband)—while omitting Klein's two equal partners, Melissa Bell and Matthew Yglesias.[22] Does the omission reflect conscious sexism and prejudice? Probably not—just a lazy, habitual way of thinking...the kind of thinking that needs to change.

Some media industry leaders are making a real effort to promote change. A few years after her eye-opening exchange with a news colleague about the Hurricane Katrina disaster, Soledad O'Brien was asked by CNN to craft a six-hour documentary series examining America's racial challenges forty years after the assassination of Dr. Martin Luther King Jr. *Black in America* earned rave reviews and drew more than thirteen million viewers, sparking impassioned conversations over dinner tables and around office watercoolers all over the country. But similar efforts to take a deep, honest look at our nation's diversity issues from a wide range of perspectives are unfortunately all too rare. That's one of the reasons O'Brien has started her own production company, Starfish Media Group, which is dedicated to telling the kinds of tough, challenging stories that too often go untold in America's mainstream media.

Getting the Message: Bringing Change to Hollywood

Thankfully, the highly visible success of diverse teams, talents, and projects in movies and television is finally grabbing the attention of the Hollywood powers that be. Examples of diversity-boasting films and series that have attracted huge, enthusiastic audiences include Universal's record-setting year of "counter-programming," the pioneering brilliance of performers and creators like Viola Davis and Shonda Rhimes, and other mold-breaking successes like Disney's girl-oriented animated megahit *Frozen* and Amazon's Emmy-winning series *Transparent*, starring Jeffrey Tambor as a funny, lovable transgender father.

Experience shows, however, that logic alone rarely leads to lasting change. Conscious, calculated efforts by leaders to push the envelope are also important. Now such leaders are popping up all over the media landscape. They include outspoken individuals like Davis, whose Emmy award speech I quoted earlier; filmmaker Spike Lee, who warned Hollywood leaders about the industry's lack of racial diversity when accepting an honorary Oscar in 2015, saying, "It's easier to be the president of the United States as a black person than to be the head of a studio"; and actress Patricia Arquette, who used her 2015 Oscar acceptance speech to call for wage equality in Hollywood, regardless of gender (evoking enthusiastic gestures of support from audience members like Meryl Streep and Jennifer Lopez).

As the number of people speaking out about these issues increases, the momentum for change snowballs. I was riveted by Jennifer Lawrence's scathing op-ed in Lena Dunham's online magazine *Lenny* in which she highlighted "how much less I was being paid than the lucky people with dicks." It made a huge impact. Her frequent costar Bradley Cooper applauded her courage and declared that in the future he would team up with his female colleagues, share information about his own salary, and apply joint pressure on studio executives to provide greater parity between male and female stars.[23] As more white male allies like Cooper emerge, the collective power behind efforts to improve fairness in the media business grows.

Are the problems of multimillionaire film stars like Jennifer Lawrence noteworthy by comparison with the challenges facing the average person of color or other disenfranchised individuals? Of course not—and Lawrence would probably be among the first to agree. But issues like pay equity in Hollywood have both practical and symbolic importance. When women and minorities get equal pay, it will mean they are getting equal power and an equal opportunity to have their voices heard. And that will mean we've taken a big step toward a world in which our culture more completely reflects the diversity of America...a change that will help transform attitudes and open doors at every level of society.

Thanks in part to the heightened awareness being driven by outspoken individuals, institutions in the media industry are beginning to respond. The Sundance Film Festival has long sought to highlight women directors and other forms of female talent in numbers beyond their representation in the rest of the industry. More recently, in partnership with Women in Film Los Angeles and other organizations, the Sundance Institute conducted a detailed study of barriers to female success in the movie business and launched programs to reduce those barriers. The

Sundance initiatives include a fellowship program that provides six talented young women with support, travel grants, mentorship, and professional coaching for a year; a "Financing Intensive" program that trains around one hundred female filmmakers in the process of finding funding and negotiating deals; and a series of industry conferences, consciousness-raising events, and networking sessions to provide women filmmakers with new opportunities to advance their careers.

It goes without saying that improving the lot of women, racial and ethnic minorities, LGBT Americans, and others who have been disenfranchised and disempowered in the real world is more important than improving the way these groups are depicted on TV or in movies. But there is a powerful synergistic relationship between the two that gives media portrayals of diversity a special importance. When *all* Americans can look in the media mirror and see faces that resemble their own, our ability to understand, appreciate, and love one another—and even ourselves—will be significantly enhanced.

14. Transcendence

Most people believe the mind to be a mirror, more or less reflecting the world outside them, not realizing on the contrary that the mind is itself the principal element of creation.

—*Rabindranath Tagore*

As human beings, we are more fulfilled by our relationships with others than by virtually anything else in our lives. We are bound by a common thread of humanity, and when we share and connect with others, we experience contentment and joy. Indeed, human bonds are life's deepest rewards. We seek love, acceptance, community, and connection throughout our lives, and when we find them, we feel complete.

And yet, as much as we seek love and acceptance, a human irony is that we also perpetually build endless barriers to finding them. We categorize everyone around us all the time. When we encounter someone new, within a matter of minutes, even seconds, we decide whether we have something in common and accept or reject him or her accordingly. We are naturally drawn to those most like us, and we feel more comfortable with those who share our backgrounds, religions, and experiences.

There is nothing wrong with this. It's human nature. But as our nation changes and we have more and more opportunities to be in contact with people different from ourselves, we must choose, in large and small ways, whether we will accept that reality or reject it. Increasingly, we will all be forced to examine the lines between us and decide to break them or strengthen them.

Throughout this book, I have spoken of experiences from my own life that have given me a deeper appreciation for the power of difference and the importance of crossing the many invisible but sometimes thick lines that divide. My early friendships with African American children, my gay friends, my French Catholic husband, and my biracial children have been the most profound and fulfilling connections I have ever made. Those relationships have fundamentally changed the way I see the world, I believe for the better. They have compelled me to open my heart and make a greater effort to confront my own biases and break them down. I am not a better person than anyone else—I struggle with my own biases, my fears of those different from myself. I like to think I have found ways to cross lines of race and gender and that I'm living a life in alignment with the principles I've laid out here, but I can always do better. We all can.

The challenges and opportunities our national diversity confers are vast. This tension between accepting and rejecting our diversity remains central to every dimension of our national life and likely will continue for generations. We may always fight over our personal and collective identities, insisting that we are one thing or another and refusing to recognize and embrace the extraordinary power of our complex, multifaceted American soul. I believe, though, that if we can better see how our diversity is at the very heart of our exceptionalism, we might make more progress. And I hope that by individually and collectively taking responsibility for doing better, we will.

Of course, in this highly polarized time, it's easy to lose heart. Will we ever make peace with ourselves? Can it really be as easy as building love and trust across our lines? I think it might be.

It's hard to imagine any conflict more intractable and divisive than that between Israeli Arabs and Jews. Since the founding of Israel in 1948, these two groups have been locked in a seemingly hopeless and endless battle. Politicians, diplomats, religious leaders, economists, and military experts have struggled to resolve the hostilities. Most of their efforts have come to naught.

It's all the more remarkable, then, that one of the most powerful programs attempting to break down the walls of anger and hatred separating these two peoples has been a simple summer camp program that takes place every year in rural Maine.

Since 1993, Seeds of Peace has brought together teenagers from various countries in the Middle East and other conflict-torn regions, including Israel, Jordan, Palestine, Afghanistan, and Egypt. They engage in many of the same activities found at any summer camp, from basketball and boating to arts and crafts and a talent show. Those who wish to do so take part in regular religious observances reflecting their own backgrounds and cultures. But the youngsters also engage in daily intergroup dialogue sessions to discuss the ongoing conflicts among their peoples and their personal experiences with those conflicts. Thanks to this blend of recreational, creative, spiritual, and social activities, many of the teenagers form strong personal bonds with one another. Some have forged lasting friendships crossing ethnic, racial, religious, and political lines.

Seeds of Peace is more than just a pleasant, feel-good story. It's also a model of how personal interactions can lead to acquired diversity, which in turn can help create opportunities to reduce intergroup suspicion, alleviate prejudice, and increase the possibility for peace.

For four years, behavioral scientists Juliana Schroeder and Jane L. Risen studied the young people who participated in Seeds of Peace. They were excited to track the impact of the program, since there have been few opportunities for scientists to conduct longitudinal (long-term) studies of the effects of interpersonal contacts between people from groups in conflict.

Schroeder and Risen found that the Israeli and Palestinian teenagers they studied felt "more positive toward, close with, similar to and trusting of the other side" after taking part in the Seeds of Peace programs. They also said that they felt "more optimistic about the likelihood of peace and more committed to working for peace," and declared "a greater intention to participate in other peace intervention programs." Even more significant, these newly positive feelings didn't disappear when the youngsters returned to their everyday lives. Follow-up surveys showed that the changed attitudes remained in place a year after camp had ended.[1]

If friendship can lessen the boundaries between two groups who have been raised to hate each other since infancy, could the simple act of reaching out, talking, and finding love and friendship be enough to help us resolve some of our biggest national challenges? I believe it can.

During the first week of October 2015, a grassroots organization called the Global Rally for Humanity posted messages on Facebook urging people to gather at thirty mosques and Islamic cultural centers around the country to protest the supposedly growing, sinister influence of Islam in America. One of those who saw the messages and felt moved to participate was a woman from Lancaster, Ohio, known only as Annie. (She has kept her last name confidential in order to protect her privacy.) At the appointed time the following Saturday, Annie showed up at the Noor Islamic Cultural Center in Columbus, dressed in a Green Bay Packers hat and carrying two anti-Islamic protest signs.

As shown on a fifty-minute video that later went viral on the Internet, Annie was in for a couple of surprises.

The first surprise was that she was the only protestor at the center. "Gee," she was heard to exclaim, "I can't believe these guys asked me to come and then didn't show up." (It later turned out that most of the protest rallies called for on Facebook had been canceled due to lack of interest.)

The second surprise came when Annie was engaged in friendly conversation by the leaders of the center.

Annie had assumed that Muslims would be evil, dangerous, and hateful people. She accused President Obama of being a secret Muslim, called Islam "a glorified death cult," and repeated prophecies she'd been taught, saying that Israel and Mecca would both soon be destroyed by nuclear weapons launched by Iran. Expecting the worst, she was startled when the center members who'd approached her responded calmly and politely to her accusations, told her they agreed with her worries about violence in the Middle East, and gently corrected some of her worst misconceptions.

"There's a lot of fear of Muslims wanting to spread Sharia law," one woman told Annie, "and that's, by the way, not at all the truth. The US Constitution is what we all follow, and the Constitution we all believe in."

As the conversation continued, Annie gradually relaxed. She finally agreed to accept a hug from Cynthia DeBoutinkhar, one of the center members, and to receive a personal tour of the center (although Annie jokingly wondered, as she headed toward the front door, "What if I catch on fire? I'll get kicked out of every Christian group I'm in today"). Ultimately, Annie took part in a friendly two-hour discussion about the Bible, the Torah, and the Koran, and departed carrying her own copy of an English-language Koran—a gift from the center. Her final words, according to DeBoutinkhar: "You were all really nice...I had no idea Muslims could be nice to me, even after I stood out there with those signs. Sorry."[2]

It might be easy to condescend to Annie—to consider her a silly, benighted individual who had fallen prey to foolish prejudices and superstitions. But on some level, in our own ways, we are all Annie. We all hold biases based on real and unreal beliefs, attitudes, and assumptions about others. And we could all do more to reach out, learn, and grow—as Annie did.

I certainly think of myself as open-minded and unbiased, but over this past year I realized that there was an entire group of people I was writing off—a segment of society that I had never taken time to get to know and had never really appreciated.

My childhood hometown of Washington, DC, was sharply segregated by race and class. But there was another form of segregation equally dramatic. Washington in my childhood was totally segregated by political party. Families in our neighborhood were nearly all Democrats. So growing up there—and then later, when I attended college and entered adulthood on the Upper West Side of New York City—I almost never came in contact with anyone who didn't generally share my own political views. I assumed that Republicans were money-driven, war-hungry, callous, and uncaring people, willing to let minorities and the poor suffer. I believed this simply because I didn't know any better.

Yet when I founded All In Together, I felt strongly that the group needed to be bipartisan. When I looked at the history of the women's movement, it was a bipartisan effort until the early 1980s. The landmark abortion case *Roe v Wade* (1973) began a process that led to the polarization of many women's organizations and the movement generally over the issue of abortion rights. I believe that women's political power nationally has been undermined by the highly partisan nature of that issue. This is not to say I'm not an unconditional and passionate advocate for abortion rights—I am! But for many American women, this issue has become a bright red dividing line separating us into warring camps. With All In Together, I wanted to find a way for women to unite to advance and lead, even without agreeing on every issue. The only way I could do that credibly was to establish All In Together as strictly nonpartisan.

While intellectually this idea seemed right to me, I knew almost no women who were Republicans or conservatives. I set out to change that and eventually met two amazing women who changed everything about the way I saw the political world, the parties, and myself.

Charity Wallace, senior adviser to First Lady Laura Bush and head of Global Women's Initiatives at the George W. Bush Presidential Center, was gracious enough to accept a lunch invitation from me at the suggestion of one of my board members. Looking back, I can't believe how awkward I made that first lunch. I honestly wasn't sure what to say or how to relate to Charity. I was sure we would have little in common. After all, we came from very different worlds. I suspect she was equally uneasy. Many Republicans feel that women's organizations tend to advocate exclusively liberal priorities, which makes them understandably uncomfortable.

Over lunch, I explained the work we were doing at All In Together, and I asked Charity some questions about her work with Mrs. Bush. She patiently explained their efforts to promote democracy around the world. Mrs. Bush had been engaging with women in conflict zones like Iraq and Afghanistan and teaching them how to lead their communities and stand for elective office. She had also offered years of public and private support to Aung San Suu Kyi, president of the National League for Democracy in Burma, and had built a program to help first ladies around the world use their positions for positive change.

I was dumbfounded. I'd had no idea that Mrs. Bush was such a champion of women—it wasn't widely reported during her husband's presidency. I'd also had no idea how much important work she had been doing since leaving the White House. Charity was incredibly kind, and if I offended her, she managed not to show it. In any case, it turned out that Charity and I had many shared passions and beliefs about women, feminism, and the work left to do for equal rights. She immediately offered to support All In Together, and we pledged to spend more time together.

I left the lunch with many of my most deeply held assumptions shaken. How could I have been so wrong? How could I have painted so many people with the same brush? How could I have carried so many biases about people based on their political party alone? I vowed I'd never do it again. But before long, I realized how entrenched my biases really were.

Much to my surprise, my relationships with Republican women have become some of the most rewarding in my life. When I think of the women who have changed me most and expanded my view of the world, Laura Cox Kaplan, who oversees regulatory affairs and public policy at PricewaterhouseCoopers, tops the list. She has made a transformational impact on me and become one of my most treasured friends. Laura and her husband, Joel Kaplan, held senior roles in the George W. Bush administration. Born and raised in a small Texas town, she's a Republican through and through. But contrary to what I assumed before knowing her, she's a passionate feminist (though she might not use the word to describe herself). She has devoted herself to advancing women in everything she does and has used her leadership position on the executive committee at PwC to increase the company's commitment to women in business and politics.

When Laura and I first met for breakfast at the posh Hay-Adams hotel in Washington, we couldn't stop talking. I found her incredibly smart, chic, energetic, and charming. And since the day we met, she has been nothing but supportive of our work and of me personally. She has patiently and thoughtfully helped us navigate the complex world of Capitol Hill and build trust with Republican lawmakers and influencers. And on a personal level, she has totally blown up all the assumptions I had about women with her profile. Laura and I disagree on many things, but these differences have never once overshadowed our mutual respect, love, and admiration. And we have found common ground in our shared values and passion for advancing women.

Laura introduced me to wonderful, feminist, Republican members of Congress like Elise Stefanik from New York's 21st District, who in 2014 became the youngest woman ever elected to Congress, and Barbara Comstock of Virginia's 10th District, who regularly brings groups of young women to Capitol Hill to encourage them to get involved in the political process. I really can't overstate the impact of Laura's friendship and sage guidance on my life and worldview. It's been a truly beautiful thing.

I still find that some biases are hard to shed. In October 2015, Charity invited me to her annual women's leadership forum. From the moment I got off the plane in Dallas, I felt as if I had stepped into another world—almost enemy territory. Here I was, a staunch, lifelong left-leaning liberal Democrat who had passionately opposed President Bush's election and most of his actions as president, heading to the Bush presidential library to meet the man himself. As I rode in the car to the event, I braced myself, trying to imagine what I would say or feel. Looking back, it seems ridiculous. What did I think would happen? Would there be a Democrat detector at the door with an automatic ejector? I was being completely absurd.

When Charity met me at the library, I made an awkward joke about how she'd ever managed to get me to Dallas. She looked at me as if I had five heads. I sat down and shut up.

I can't quite explain what happened that day when I met the president and first lady. It was very brief—a handshake and a picture—but I understood instantly why President Bush had been elected. His charisma was electric: He was warm and personable and funny. Although I was just one of innumerable meet-and-greets he had done that day, he made me feel important. It was extraordinary and unforgettable.

But more than his warmth, the president's remarks struck me. Both he and Mrs. Bush spoke about the importance of women's empowerment, of the investments he had pushed for to advance women's rights and health around the world during his years as president and since leaving office. I was astonished to realize that President Bush and I have shared values. I was reminded that he'd called for immigration reform and authorized unprecedented resources to fight AIDS in sub-Saharan Africa, both actions I supported.

There are still plenty of areas of disagreement between myself and President Bush; the Iraq war and the response to Katrina are just two examples. But rather than seeing him in polarized terms as I did before meeting him, I now have a deeper appreciation for him as a human being. I was changed that day—a change that was begun by my friendships with Charity and Laura and confirmed in Dallas.

What really changed? Was it my politics? No, I remain a committed Democrat and always will be. But I learned that when we listen and build trust, even with people we disagree with, our hearts and minds open and expand in meaningful ways. I see Republicans differently now. I can listen with openness to those with differing views in ways I could not before. I have come to recoil at the most divisive political messages from both parties. I chafe at tweets from Democrats insisting that all Republicans are "bad for women," just as I cringe when I hear Republicans say that Democrats "hate freedom."

Both of these oversimplified perspectives are wrong. Are there extreme elements in our political parties? Of course—we've talked at length about them. But what kind of country will we become if we are unable to even listen to one another? What can we accomplish if we regard everyone who's different from us with suspicion? What opportunities will we miss to find new friends, learn new things, and develop great ideas? I have been guilty of shutting out opposing voices. But as I've made the effort to get to know people with different views, my own horizons have expanded in ways I wish we were all open to.

My friendships with Charity and Laura have enabled me to move past biases and stereotypes I've held most of my life. I like to think that I've equally changed them. The point is, how much more united and powerful would we be as a nation if we all made a greater effort to cross the many lines that not only divide but bind us? It may seem silly to compare biases regarding political parties to the entrenched blights of racism or sexism. But I suspect that the political lines that divide us are nearly as thick as the lines of race, gender, religion, ethnicity, and sexual orientation that have caused so much heartache for centuries.

The experience of crossing lines is so powerful and transformational that we should all strive to cross as many of them as we can, as often as we can, in every way that we can.

It is my sincere hope for the nation that each of us, through actions large and small, will work harder to use friendship, empathy, understanding, and shared values to break the lines that divide us.

I hope police officers will invest more effort in building community bonds than in firing their guns.

I hope judges and prosecutors will stop locking up minorities disproportionately and instead work with communities to find ways to reduce crime and the factors that cause it.

I hope political leaders will strive to represent all Americans, from both inside and outside their districts and parties, and work to forge trust with one another.

I hope educators will push for more diverse classrooms and help students in those classes understand the many challenges and opportunities diversity presents.

I hope parents of all races and backgrounds will talk without judgment to their children about diversity and the differences between us.

I hope business leaders will hold themselves and their colleagues accountable for guaranteeing the success of the women and minorities who work for them.

I hope Hollywood will greenlight more stories that speak to all Americans with actors who reflect the full range of our population.

I hope all citizens will step up and engage with our political process to ensure their voices are heard.

I hope we will come to see our differences as our greatest strength, not a weakness, and that our leaders will work to inspire us to unite rather than divide.

I hope we will reject those who seek to build walls and boundaries between us.

But most of all, I hope each and every one of us will look deeply within ourselves and ask how we can build trust and understanding with someone we might otherwise avoid or overlook. Isn't that who we really are as Americans? I know it is! No other nation on earth has shown more propensity for welcoming difference, even with all our challenges and conflicts.

Our diversity remains and always will be our greatest, most unique, and special strength. May all Americans come to believe and embrace that powerful truth. I hope.

Acknowledgments

I could not be more grateful for the incredible support and encouragement of many wonderful friends and family during the process of creating this book. Philippe Chivée has been an unfailing rock, and for everything I achieve or accomplish he is there to support me unconditionally. Pretty great. Thank you, P.

This book would not have been possible were it not for the tireless support, energy, work, research, contribution, counsel, and persistence of the amazing and gifted Karl Weber. I am eternally grateful for the long hours he dedicated to bringing my thoughts fully to life. It's not possible to overstate the importance of his contribution and guidance. The only word I have to describe Karl is: *exceptional*.

My parents, Shelah and Stefan Leader, taught me that making a difference is more important than making money and that social justice is the responsibility of each of us. Their example, especially my mother's, has always been one I have tried to follow. Thank you both for making sacrifices so that I could attend extraordinary schools. I'm hugely grateful for all the doors of understanding that have been opened to me as a result.

I would also like to thank my entire extended family for their support and enthusiasm for everything I do. And of course Stella and Serena, who are the lights of my life. I'm sorry there are no pictures in this book, but one day you'll read it and I hope you'll be proud. I love you!

I must also acknowledge and thank the true believers—my agents Denise Marcil and Anne Marie O'Farrell and my editor Kate Hartson, who saw the potential of this book when no one else did. Thank you, Margaret Reilly King and the WME team, for your support.

I also owe a huge debt of gratitude to Courtney Emerson, cofounder of All In Together and my longtime collaborator. I regularly depend on her wisdom, which is always way beyond her years, and I'm eternally grateful for her friendship, partnership, and encouragement. Thank you, Courtney, for putting up with my perpetually divided attention.

Thank you to Laurye Blackford and Katherine Urbon for helping me see the big picture, and to Annie Pace and her amazing team at Pace PR for bringing my work to wider audiences. Thank you to Edda Collins Coleman for her dedication to our work at All In Together and for her friendship, creativity, and support. Thank you to Sarah Weller and LeAnna Weller Smith for beautifully illustrating my vision on the cover and with my website.

I would also like to acknowledge my dearest and most loyal friends and confidants, especially Vanessa Kaster, Beth Lusko and Jeff Gunderman, Karen Sumberg, Jennifer Mendelson and Hal Shaftel, Alysia Reiner and David Basche, Lucy and David Coke, Ari and Wendy Pelto, Laura Cox-Kaplan, Victoria Meakin and Dave Feldman, Tonya Williams, Rachel Pearson, and Farrell Redwine.

Thank you also to Sandra Grossman, Ted Alden, Susan Esper, Katherine Philipps, Russell Shaw, Helena Morrissey, Lisa Garcia Quiroz, Clarissa Martinez, Francis Hyatt, Todd Sears, Sara Fagen, Deborah Jackson, Soledad O'Brien, Peter Grauer, and Malaika Adero for the wonderful interviews and contributions. Thank you to Bernard Coleman for the feedback on the book manuscript. Thank you to everyone at Georgetown Day School for their commitment to transformational learning, which I was the beneficiary of. And thank you to all my GDS 1993 classmates who have made and continue to make a lasting impression on my life.

I must also thank every one of the founding board members of All In Together, especially Karyn Twaronite of Ernst & Young, who was the first person to support All In Together financially and made everything possible. I'd also like to thank Roslyn Brooks, Laura Cox-Kaplan, Jocelyn Cunningham, Anne Fulenwider, Michelle Gadsden-Williams, Deborah Gillis, Holly Gordon, Hannah Grove, Julie Haskell, Kathy Horgan, Jake Jones, Gayle Lemmon, Victoria Meakin, Angela Moskow, Susannah Samet, Sabrina Spitaletta, and Charity Wallace for their support and guidance.

I am also grateful beyond words for the support of my colleagues at Deloitte, especially Jason Geller, Marc Kaplan, Jocelyn Cunningham, Susannah Samet, Christie Smith, Deb DeHaas, Brent Bachus, Cathy Engelbert, Josh Haims, Diane Sinti, and everyone in Human Capital.

Last, but certainly not least, I'd like to extend an extra special thank-you to Brian Donovan and Sean Cunniff, who sparked the inspiration for the title and shape of the book.

Lauren Leader-Chivée
New York, New York
April 2016

Notes

Chapter 2   The Diversity Dividend

1. Annie Lowrey, "How Working Women Help the Economy," *New York Times*, April 15, 2014.

2. "Highlights of women's earnings in 2014," *BLS Reports*, US Department of Labor, Bureau of Labor Statistics, November 2015, http://www.bls.gov /opub/reports/cps/highlights-of-womens-earnings-in-2014.pdf.

3. Joanna Barsh and Lareina Yee, "Unlocking the full potential of women in the U.S. economy," McKinsey & Company, April 2011, http://www.mckinsey .com/client_service/organization/latest_thinking/unlocking_the_full_potential.

4. US Department of Labor, Bureau of Labor Statistics, *Monthly Labor Review*, December 2013, http://www.bls.gov/opub/mlr/2013/article/labor-force -projections-to-2022-the-labor-force-participation-rate-continues-to-fall.htm.

5. "Characteristics of Minimum Wage Workers, 2013," *BLS Reports*, US Department of Labor, Bureau of Labor Statistics, March 2014, http://www .bls.gov/cps/minwage2013.pdf.

6. David Gelles, "Salesforce Makes Strides Toward Gender Equality in Silicon Valley," *New York Times*, July 25, 2015, http://www.nytimes .com/2015/07/26/business/salesforce-makes-strides-toward-gender-equality -in-silicon-valley.html.

7. "The Economic Impact of Women-Owned Businesses in the United States," National Women's Business Council, October 2009, https://www .nwbc.gov/research/economic-impact-women-owned-businesses-united-states.

8. Daniel Costa, David Cooper, and Heidi Shierholz, "Facts About Immigration and the U.S. Economy: Answers to Frequently Asked Questions," Economic Policy Institute, August 12, 2014, http://www.epi.org/publication /immigration-facts/.

9. Thomas Barta, Markus Kleiner, and Tito Neumann, "Is there a pay-off from top-team diversity?" *McKinsey Quarterly*, April 2012, http://www .mckinsey.com/business-functions/organization/our-insights/is-there-a-payoff -from-top-team-diversity.

10. Dorothee Enskog, "Women's Positive Impact on Corporate Performance," September 23, 2014, credit-suisse.com.

11. James Surowiecki, *The Wisdom of Crowds: Why the Many Are Smarter Than the Few and How Collective Wisdom Shapes Business, Economies, Societies and Nations* (New York: Doubleday, 2004).

12. US Census Bureau, 2012 National Population Projections: Summary Tables, http://www.census.gov/population/projections/data/national/2012/summarytables.html.

13. "Section 3: Political Polarization and Personal Life," in *Political Polarization in the American Public*, Pew Research Center, June 12, 2014, http://www.people-press.org/2014/06/12/section-3-political-polarization-and-personal-life/.

14. "Growth in Urban Population Outpaces Rest of Nation, Census Bureau Reports," US Census Bureau, March 26, 2012, http://www.census.gov/newsroom/releases/archives/2010_census/cb12-50.html.

15. "Analysis: Race and Americans' Social Networks," Public Religion Research Institute, August 28, 2014, http://publicreligion.org/research/2014/08/analysis-social-network/.

16. Ann Friedman, "The Importance of Friendship Diversity," *The Cut, New York*, September 26, 2014, http://nymag.com/thecut/2014/09/importance-of-friendship-diversity.html.

17. See, for example, Shaila Dewan, "Discrimination in Housing Against Nonwhites Persists Quietly, U.S. Study Finds," *New York Times*, June 11, 2013, http://www.nytimes.com/2013/06/12/business/economy/discrimination-in-housing-against-nonwhites-persists-quietly-us-study-finds.html.

18. Sue Sturgis, "How slavery continues to shape Southern politics," Institute for Southern Studies, September 23, 2013, http://www.southernstudies.org/2013/09/how-slavery-continues-to-shape-southern-politics.html.

19. Andy Kiersz, "RANKED: The economies of all 50 US states and DC from worst to best," *Business Insider*, August 3, 2015, http://www.businessinsider.com.au/state-economy-ranking-july-2015-2015-7#/#49-alabama-3.

20. Emily Badger, "Why Segregation Is Bad for Everyone," *The Atlantic CityLab*, May 3, 2013, http://www.citylab.com/work/2013/05/why-segregation-bad-everyone/5476/.

21. Eric Jaffe, "More Immigration Means Higher Wages for All Workers," *The Atlantic CityLab*, July 7, 2015, http://www.citylab.com/work/2015/07/more-immigration-means-higher-wages-for-all-workers/397766/.

22. David Lubell, "US cities race to attract immigrants," *Aljazeera America*, December 25, 2013, http://america.aljazeera.com/opinions/2013/12/us-cities-in-a-racetoattractimmigrants.html; Paul McDaniel, "How States And Local Economies Benefit From Immigrants," *Immigration Impact*,

American Immigration Council, July 26, 2013, http://immigrationimpact
.com/2013/07/26/how-states-and-local-economies-benefit-from-immigrants/;
Encarnacion Pyle, "Cities that welcome immigrants reap benefits, national
official says," *Columbus Dispatch*, July 10, 2015, http://www.dispatch.com
/content/stories/local/2015/07/09/new-immigration-policy-discussed.html.

Chapter 3   *Love Across the Lines*

1. Interview with the author.

2. Interview with the author.

3. Interview with the author.

4. "Innovation, Diversity, and Market Growth," Center for Talent Innovation, September 2013, http://www.talentinnovation.org/publication
.cfm?publication=1400.

5. Joseph P. Ryan, *Samuel Stouffer and the GI Survey: Sociologists and Soldiers during the Second World War* (Knoxville: University of Tennessee Press, 2013).

6. Gordon W. Allport, *The Nature of Prejudice* (New York: Basic Books, 1954), page 281.

7. Quoted in "Black Soldiers," Mr. Lincoln and Freedom website, Lehrman Institute, http://www.mrlincolnandfreedom.org/inside.asp?ID=50.

8. Jim Garamone, "Former Chairman Discusses Truman's 1948 Integration Order," US Department of Defense website, July 28, 2008, http://archive
.defense.gov/news/NewsArticle.aspx?ID=50623.

9. Gary Langer, "Racial Discrimination: An Army Survey," ABC News, January 6, 2009, http://blogs.abcnews.com/thenumbers/2009/01/racial-relation
.html; Deepti Hajela, "Asian American soldier's suicide called a 'wake-up call' for the military," *Washington Post*, February 21, 2012, http://www.washington
post.com/politics/asian-american-soldiers-suicide-called-a-wake-up-call-for
-the-military/2012/02/19/gIQA7Ke4QR_story.html.

10. Kimberly Hefling, "Female soldiers raise alarm on sexual assaults," Associated Press, July 21, 2008, http://www.nbcnews.com/id/25784465
/ns/us_news-military/t/female-soldiers-raise-alarm-sexual-assaults
/#.VEbSR0vuSQ0.

11. Courtney Kube and Jim Miklaszewski, "Pentagon's annual report on sexual assault shows alarming rise," NBC News, May 6, 2013, http://usnews
.nbcnews.com/_news/2013/05/06/18090415-pentagons-annual-report-on
-sexual-assault-shows-alarming-rise?lite; Helene Cooper, "Pentagon Study Finds 50% Increase in Reports of Military Sexual Assaults," *New York Times*, May 1, 2014, http://www.nytimes.com/2014/05/02/us/military-sex-assault-report.html.

12. "Statement by Secretary of Defense Ash Carter on DOD Transgender Policy," US Department of Defense, July 13, 2015.

13. US Census, American Community Survey, cited in William H. Frey, "The Major Demographic Shift That's Upending How We Think About Race," *New Republic*, November 28, 2014, https://newrepublic.com/article/120387 /people-identifying-white-and-black-are-future-america.

14. "Fact Sheet," *Off and Running, POV* documentary, PBS, September 7, 2010, http://www.pbs.org/pov/offandrunning/fact-sheet/.

15. Michael Quintanilla, "Honoring the Family Name," *Los Angeles Times*, July 31, 1991, http://articles.latimes.com/1991-07-31/news/vw-321_1_columba -bush.

16. Eli J. Finkel, "Explaining Jeb Bush's 'Hispanic' Error," *New York Times*, April 9, 2015, http://www.nytimes.com/2015/04/09/opinion/explaining-jeb -bushs-error.html.

17. Adam Clymer, "Jack Kemp, Star on Field and in Politics, Dies at 73," *New York Times*, May 2, 2009, http://www.nytimes.com/2009/05/03/us/03kemp .html.

18. Stephanie Capparell, *The Real Pepsi Challenge* (New York: Free Press, 2007).

19. David Madland and Ruy Teixeira, "New Progressive America: The Millennial Generation," Center for American Progress, May 2009, http://cdn .americanprogress.org/wp-content/uploads/issues/2009/05/pdf/millennial _generation.pdf.

20. "Big demands and high expectations: The Deloitte Millennial Survey," Deloitte Touche Tohmatsu Limited, January 2014, https://www2.deloitte .com/content/dam/Deloitte/global/Documents/About-Deloitte/gx-dttl-2014 -millennial-survey-report.pdf.

21. Dr. Rochelle L. Ford, Joanna Jenkins, and Sheryl Oliver, "A Millennial Perspective on Diversity & Multiculturalism," American Advertising Federation, Howard University, 2011–12, http://aaftl.com/wp-content /uploads/2012/04/Millennial-White-Paper.pdf.

22. "A Shifting Landscape: A Decade of Change in American Attitudes about Same-Sex Marriage and LGBT Issues," Public Religion Research Institute, February 26, 2014, http://publicreligion.org/research/2014/02/2014-lgbt -survey/.

23. Interview with the author.

24. Quoted in Adam Liptak, "Another Factor Said to Sway Judges to Rule for Women's Rights: A Daughter," *New York Times*, June 16, 2014, http://www.nytimes.com/2014/06/17/us/judges-with-daughters-more-often -rule-in-favor-of-womens-rights.html.

25. Sam Palmisano, quoted in Ira Sager, "Sam Palmisano on Improving Business Education," *BloombergBusiness*, May 1, 2014, http://www.bloomberg

.com/news/articles/2014-05-01/center-for-global-enterprises-sam-palmisano
-on-improving-b-school.

26. The outline of the story that follows comes from the article "A Baseball Story," by sportswriter Joe Posnanski on his *JoeBlog*, March 28, 2015, http://joeposnanski.com/a-baseball-story/.

27. Ibid.

Chapter 4   Past as Prologue

1. Sue Halpern and Bill McKibben, "How Manchester's Burgeoning Bhutanese Population Is Pursuing the American Dream," *Smithsonian*, April 2014, http://www.smithsonianmag.com/travel/how-manchesters-burgeoning-bhutanese-population-pursuing-american-dream-180950187/?no-ist.

2. Nick Gass, "Poll: 6 in 10 GOP voters back Trump's Muslim ban," *Politico*, December 14, 2015, http://www.politico.com/story/2015/12/poll-muslim-ban-support-216748; Lisa Hagen, "Poll: Majority of Republicans support Trump's Muslim ban," *The Hill*, December 9, 2015, http://thehill.com/blogs/ballot-box/presidential-races/262656-poll-majority-of-republicans-supports-trumps-muslim-ban.

3. "De-Romanticizing Our Immigrant Past: Why Claiming 'My Family Came Legally' Is Often a Myth," American Immigration Council, November 25, 2008, http://www.immigrationpolicy.org/just-facts/de-romanticizing-our-immigrant-past-why-claiming-my-family-came-legally-often-myth.

4. "Thinking About a Majority-Minority Shift Leads to More Conservative Views," Association for Psychological Science, April 8, 2014, http://www.psychologicalscience.org/index.php/news/releases/thinking-about-a-majority-minority-shift-leads-to-more-conservative-views.html.

5. Sara Kehaulani Goo, "What Americans want to do about illegal immigration," Pew Research Center, August 24, 2015, http://www.pewresearch.org/fact-tank/2015/08/24/what-americans-want-to-do-about-illegal-immigration/.

6. Actually, there is some controversy in scholarly circles over exactly how prevalent those "No Irish Need Apply" signs were. See Richard Jensen, "'No Irish Need Apply': A Myth of Victimization," *Journal of Social History*, Vol. 36, No. 2, revised December 22, 2004, http://rjensen.people.uic.edu/no-irish.htm. However, there's no doubt that Irish immigrants to America were in fact subjected to prejudice and discrimination.

7. Vincent J. Cannato, "How America became Italian," *Washington Post*, October 9, 2015, https://www.washingtonpost.com/opinions/how-america-became-italian/2015/10/09/4c93b1be-6ddd-11e5-9bfe-e59f5e244f92_story.html.

8. Ibid.

Chapter 5 Demographic Destiny

1. Brian Bremner, "Japan's Incredible Shrinking Empire," *Bloomberg Businessweek*, June 5, 2014, http://www.bloomberg.com/news/articles/2014-06-05/japan-must-open-up-to-foreign-labor-for-economic-boost.

2. Jared Diamond, "Three Reasons Japan's Economic Pain Is Getting Worse," *Bloomberg View*, April 25, 2012, http://www.bloombergview.com/articles/2012-04-25/three-reasons-japan-s-economic-pain-is-getting-worse.

3. "Japanese women and work: Holding back half the nation," *The Economist*, March 29, 2014, http://www.economist.com/news/briefing/21599763-womens-lowly-status-japanese-workplace-has-barely-improved-decades-and-country.

4. Nikhita Mendis, "Employing Japan's Women," *Brown Political Review*, April 17, 2014, http://www.brownpoliticalreview.org/2014/04/employing-japans-baby-making-machines/.

5. Ibid.

6. Jason Clenfield, "How to Become an Activist: Start as a Japanese Part-Timer," *Bloomberg Business*, May 29, 2014, http://www.bloomberg.com/news/articles/2014-05-29/how-to-become-an-activist-start-as-a-japanese-part-timer.

7. "Japan's Incredible Shrinking Empire."

8. Ibid.

9. "Employing Japan's Women."

10. Thomas Wilson, "As Europe opens its doors, Japan considers clamping down harder on asylum seekers," Reuters, September 9, 2015, http://in.reuters.com/article/2015/09/09/europe-migrants-japan-idINKCN0R91AH20150909.

11. "Employing Japan's Women."

12. William H. Frey, "The Major Demographic Shift That's Upending How We Think About Race," *New Republic*, November 28, 2014, https://newrepublic.com/article/120387/people-identifying-white-and-black-are-future-america.

13. Jack Losh, "Are you intersex?" *The Sun*, February 14, 2014, http://www.thesun.co.uk/sol/homepage/news/5444757/Facebook-to-allow-users-to-customise-their-gender.html.

14. "Current World Population," One World Nations Online, http://www.nationsonline.org/oneworld/world_population.htm.

15. Rick Perlstein, "Exclusive: Lee Atwater's Infamous 1981 Interview on the Southern Strategy," *The Nation*, November 13, 2012, http://www.thenation.com/article/exclusive-lee-atwaters-infamous-1981-interview-southern-strategy/.

16. Beth Schwartzapfel and Bill Keller, "Willie Horton Revisited," The Marshall Project, May 13, 2015, https://www.themarshallproject.org/2015/05/13/willie-horton-revisited.

17. Lee Fang, "RNC Adviser Alex Castellanos Admits That His Infamous Jesse Helms Ad Hurt Race Relations," *ThinkProgress*, December 4, 2009, http://thinkprogress.org/politics/2009/12/04/72291/castellanos-hands-admit/.

18. Katharine Q. Seelye, "Gov. Paul LePage of Maine Says Racial Comment Was a 'Slip-Up,'" *New York Times*, January 8, 2016, http://www.nytimes.com /politics/first-draft/2016/01/08/gov-paul-lepage-of-maine-denies-making -racist-remarks/.

19. Eli Stokols, "Jeb: Trump using racial 'dog whistle,'" *Politico*, September 3, 2015, http://www.politico.com/story/2015/09/bush-trump-dog-whistle -213334.

20. David Freedlander, "Dante de Blasio's Killer Ad May Have Won NYC Primary for His Dad," *Daily Beast*, September 14, 2013, http://www.thedaily beast.com/articles/2013/09/14/dante-de-blasio-s-killer-ad-may-have-won -nyc-primary-for-his-dad.html.

21. Nikita Stewart, "After a Sleepover With Mayor de Blasio, a Friendship Formed," *New York Times*, March 20, 2015, http://www.nytimes .com/2015/03/22/nyregion/after-a-sleepover-with-mayor-de-blasio-a-friend ship-formed.html.

22. Leon Neyfakh, "Bill de Blasio's Bad Bet," *Slate*, January 13, 2015, http:// www.slate.com/articles/news_and_politics/crime/2015/01/nypd_and_bill_de _blasio_why_new_york_s_mayor_was_wrong_to_count_on_police.html.

23. Neil Munro, "Jeb Bush Spanish-Language Ad Touts Obama-Like Diversity Instead of Patriotism," Breitbart website, September 15, 2015, http://www.breitbart.com/big-government/2015/09/15/jeb-bush-spanish -language-ad-touts-obama-like-diversity-instead-patriotism/.

24. Lizette Alvarez and Manny Fernandez, "Marco Rubio and Ted Cruz Diverge in Approach to Their Hispanic Identity," *New York Times*, December 16, 2015, http://www.nytimes.com/2015/12/17/us/marco-rubio-and-ted-cruz -diverge-in-approach-to-their-hispanic-identity.html.

25. Jessica Mendoza, "Why Bernie Sanders is vowing to stand against Islamophobia, racism," *Diversity Now*, October 30, 2015, http://diversity nowbygloballearning.blogspot.com/2015/10/why-bernie-sanders-is -vowing-to-stand.html.

26. Aaron Morrison, "Nikki Haley Black Lives Matter Race Speech: South Carolina Governor Future Of More Diverse GOP?" *International Business Times*, September 2, 2015, http://www.ibtimes.com/nikki-haley-black-lives -matter-race-speech-south-carolina-governor-future-more-2080014.

27. "The Brennan Center's judicial diversity event features Senator Elizabeth Warren," NYU Law website, February 7, 2014, http://www.law.nyu.edu /news/brennan-center-broadening-the-bench.

28. Jorge Ramos and Brett LoGiurato, "Cory Booker: 'I don't want to live

in a post-racial society,'" *Fusion*, May 4, 2015, http://fusion.net/video/130174 /cory-booker-i-dont-want-to-live-in-a-post-racial-society/.

29. The profiles of Erica, David, and Ali are drawn from *The Race Card Project* by journalist Michelle Norris and can be explored, along with many others, at the website, http://theracecardproject.com.

Chapter 6   Bias Blindness

1. "Trump Supporters Think Obama is A Muslim Born in Another Country," Public Policy Polling, September 1, 2015, http://www.publicpolicy polling.com/main/2015/08/trump-supporters-think-obama-is-a-muslim -born-in-another-country.html.

2. Eduardo Porter, "Racial Identity, and Its Hostilities, Are on the Rise in American Politics," *New York Times*, January 5, 2016, http://www.nytimes .com/2016/01/06/business/economy/racial-identity-and-its-hostilities -return-to-american-politics.html.

3. Lindsey Bever, "Sam's Club CEO called 'racist' for remarks on diversity," *Washington Post*, December 15, 2015, https://www.washing tonpost.com/news/morning-mix/wp/2015/12/15/sams-club-ceo-called-racist -for-remarks-on-diversity/.

4. John Logan and Brian Stults, "Separate and Unequal," US2010, http:// www.s4.brown.edu/us2010/projects/authors_su.htm.

5. Rakesh Kochhar, Richard Fry, and Paul Taylor, "Wealth Gaps Rise to Record Highs Between Whites, Blacks, Hispanics," Pew Research Center, July 25, 2011, http://www.pewsocialtrends.org/2011/07/26/wealth-gaps -rise-to-record-highs-between-whites-blacks-hispanics/.

6. Jenna Johnson and Mary Jordan, "Trump on rally protestor: 'Maybe he should have been roughed up,'" *Washington Post*, November 22, 2015, https:// www.washingtonpost.com/news/post-politics/wp/2015/11/22/black-activist -punched-at-donald-trump-rally-in-birmingham/.

7. Brentin Mock, "Busting the Myth of 'The Ferguson Effect,'" *The Atlantic CityLab*, June 17, 2015, http://www.citylab.com/crime/2015/06/busting-the -myth-of-the-ferguson-effect/396068/.

8. "Stark Racial Divisions in Reactions to Ferguson Police Shooting," Pew Research Center, August 18, 2014, http://www.people-press.org/2014/08/18 /stark-racial-divisions-in-reactions-to-ferguson-police-shooting/.

9. Bruce Drake, "The Civil Rights Act at 50: Racial divides persist on how much progress has been made," Pew Research Center, April 9, 2014, http:// www.pewresearch.org/fact-tank/2014/04/09/the-civil-rights-act-at-50-racial -divides-persist-on-how-much-progress-has-been-made/.

10. Christian de Looper, "Microsoft's Nardella remains under fire for controversial pay raise comments," *Tech Times*, October 14, 2014, http://www

.techtimes.com/articles/17877/20141014/microsoft-chief-remains-under-fire
-controversial-comments.htm.

11. Georgia Wells, "Facebook, Microsoft Say They Offer Equal Pay to
Women, Men," *Wall Street Journal*, April 12, 2016, http://www.wsj.com
/articles/facebook-microsoft-say-they-offer-equal-pay-to-women-men
-1460466005.

12. Noah Kulwin, "Venerated VC Michael Moritz Opens Mouth, Inserts
Foot on Question About Hiring Women," *Re/code*, December 3, 2015, http://
recode.net/2015/12/03/venerated-vc-michael-moritz-opens-mouth-inserts
-foot-on-question-about-hiring-women/.

13. Monnica T. Williams, "Colorblind Ideology Is a Form of Racism," *Psychology Today*, December 27, 2011, https://www.psychologytoday.com/blog
/culturally-speaking/201112/colorblind-ideology-is-form-racism.

14. James Hamblin, "Medicine's Unrelenting Race Gap," *The Atlantic*,
December 10, 2014, http://www.theatlantic.com/health/archive/2014/12/the
-race-problem-in-medicine-race/383613/.

15. Jerome D. Williams, "A Message to Ponder on For Barney's, Macy's, and
the NYPD: Shoplifting Comes in All Sizes, Shapes, and Colors," *Huffington
Post*, November 21, 2013, updated January 25, 2014, http://www.huffington
post.com/jerome-d-williams/barneys-shoplifting-racial-profiling_b_4318452
.html.

16. David R. Francis, "Employers' Replies to Racial Names," National
Bureau of Economic Research, http://www.nber.org/digest/sep03/w9873
.html, accessed December 25, 2015.

17. Chris Mooney, "Across America, whites are biased and they don't even
know it," *Washington Post*, December 8, 2014, https://www.washingtonpost
.com/news/wonk/wp/2014/12/08/across-america-whites-are-biased-and-they
-dont-even-know-it/.

18. https://implicit.harvard.edu/implicit/.

19. Katie Koch, "Peering into our blind spots," *Harvard Gazette*, February 26, 2013, http://news.harvard.edu/gazette/story/2013/02/peering-into-our
-blind-spots/.

20. "Colorblind Ideology Is a Form of Racism."

21. Po Bronson and Ashley Merryman, *NurtureShock: New Thinking About
Children* (New York: Twelve, 2009), chapter 3.

Chapter 7 Outspread Wings

1. "The Expanding Web of Connections Among the Paris Attackers,"
New York Times, November 23, 2015, updated December 9, 2015, http://
www.nytimes.com/interactive/2015/11/15/world/europe/manhunt-for-paris
-attackers.html.

2. Amber Phillips, "Virginia mayor cites Japanese internment camps (favorably) in making case for halting Syrian refugees. Really," *Washington Post*, November 18, 2015, https://www.washingtonpost.com/news/the-fix/wp/2015/11/18/the-mayor-of-roanoke-va-cited-japanese-internment-camps-favorably-in-make-case-for-halting-syrian-refugees-really/.

3. "Ronald Reagan on Redress Act," August 10, 1988, http://faculty.history.wisc.edu/archdeacon/404tja/redress.html.

4. All quotations from Sandra Grossman are from an interview with the author.

5. Wil S. Hylton, "The Shame of America's Family Detention Camps," *New York Times*, February 4, 2015, http://www.nytimes.com/2015/02/08/magazine/the-shame-of-americas-family-detention-camps.html.

6. "Statement by Secretary of Homeland Security Jeh Johnson Before the Senate Committee on Appropriations," Department of Homeland Security, July 10, 2014, https://www.dhs.gov/news/2014/07/10/statement-secretary-homeland-security-jeh-johnson-senate-committee-appropriations.

7. David McCabe, "Administration to close immigration detention center at month's end," *The Hill*, November 18, 2014, http://thehill.com/news/administration/224626-administration-to-close-immigrant-detention-center.

8. Edward Alden, interview with the author, November 24, 2015.

9. "Text of Republicans' Principles on Immigration," *New York Times*, January 30, 2014, http://www.nytimes.com/2014/01/31/us/politics/text-of-republicans-principles-on-immigration.html.

10. "President Barack Obama's State of the Union Address," Office of the Press Secretary, White House, January 28, 2014, https://www.whitehouse.gov/the-press-office/2014/01/28/president-barack-obamas-state-union-address.

11. Daniel Costa, David Cooper, and Heidi Shierholz, "Facts About Immigration and the U.S. Economy," Economic Policy Institute, August 12, 2014, http://www.epi.org/publication/immigration-facts/.

12. Ibid.

13. Jeremy Quittner, "Not Made in America: Where U.S. Innovation Really Comes From," *Inc.*, April 10, 2014, http://www.inc.com/jeremy-quittner/foreign-patents-and-united-states-innovation.html.

14. Cited by Yatin Mundkur, "Immigrant Entrepreneurs: Vital for American Innovation," *Techonomy*, January 23, 2014, http://www.forbes.com/sites/techonomy/2014/01/23/immigrant-entrepreneurs-vital-for-american-innovation/.

15. Jennifer Alsever, "Immigrants: America's job creators," *Fortune*, June 2, 2014, http://fortune.com/2014/06/02/fortune-500-immigrants/.

16. Charles Kenny, "Foreign Students in the U.S.: A Good, Cheap Way to Spread Democracy," *Bloomberg Businessweek*, March 20, 2014, http://www

.bloomberg.com/news/articles/2014-03-20/foreign-students-in-the-u-dot-s-dot
-are-good-way-to-spread-democracy.

17. Ibid.

18. Neil G. Ruiz, Jill H. Wilson, and Shyamali Choudhury, "The Search for Skills: Demand for H-1B Immigrant Workers in U.S. Metropolitan Areas," Brookings Institution, July 18, 2012, http://www.brookings.edu/research /reports/2012/07/18-h1b-visas-labor-immigration#overview; Costa, Cooper, and Shierholz, "Facts About Immigration and the U.S. Economy."

19. Karen Weise, "Vancouver, the New Tech Hub," *Bloomberg Businessweek*, May 27, 2014, http://www.bloomberg.com/bw/articles/2014-05-22/vancouver -welcomes-tech-companies-hampered-by-u-dot-s-dot-work-visa-caps.

20. "Text of Republicans' Principles on Immigration."

21. Edward Alden interview with the author; Fred Dews, "What Percentage of U.S. Population Is Foreign Born?" *Brookings Now*, October 3, 2013, http://www.brookings.edu/blogs/brookings-now/posts/2013/09/what -percentage-us-population-foreign-born.

22. Philip E. Wolgin, "How Much Would It Cost to Deport All Undocumented Immigrants?" *Newsweek*, August 19, 2015, http://www.newsweek.com /how-much-would-it-cost-deport-all-undocumented-immigrants-364316.

23. "A Guide to S.744: Understanding the 2013 Senate Immigration Bill," American Immigration Council, July 10, 2013, http://www.immigrationpolicy .org/special-reports/guide-s744-understanding-2013-senate-immigration -bill.

24. Frederick Douglass, "Our Composite Nationality," address delivered in Boston, Massachusetts, December 7, 1869, TeachingAmericanHistory .org, http://teachingamericanhistory.org/library/document/our-composite -nationality/.

Chapter 8   Of the People, by the People, for the People

1. Mark Berman and Wesley Lowery, "The 12 key highlights from the DOJ's scathing Ferguson report," *Washington Post*, March 4, 2015, https://www .washingtonpost.com/news/post-nation/wp/2015/03/04/the-12-key-highlights -from-the-dojs-scathing-ferguson-report/.

2. Wilson Andrews, Alicia Desantis, and Josh Keller, "Justice Department's Report on the Ferguson Police Department," *New York Times*, March 4, 2015, http://www.nytimes.com/interactive/2015/03/04/us/ferguson-police-racial -discrimination.html.

3. Ian Millhiser, "This Is The Most Important Reform Ferguson Can Enact To Give Its Black Residents A Voice," *ThinkProgress*, August 18, 2014, http:// thinkprogress.org/justice/2014/08/18/3472278/this-is-the-most-important -reform-ferguson-can-enact-to-prevent-another-standoff/.

4. Aamer Madhani, "Voices: Ferguson voter turnout disheartening," *USA Today*, April 9, 2015, http://www.usatoday.com/story/news/2015/04/09/voter -turnout-ferguson-chicago/25527397/.

5. Ibid.

6. Scott Calvert, "Baltimore Prosecutors Say Freddie Gray Arrest Was Illegal Before Finding Knife," *Wall Street Journal*, May 19, 2015, http://www .wsj.com/articles/baltimore-prosecutors-say-freddie-gray-arrest-was-illegal -before-finding-knife-1432076045.

7. "Women in national parliaments," Inter-Parliamentary Union, http:// www.ipu.org/wmn-e/classif.htm, accessed April 8, 2016.

8. Jens Manuel Krogstad, "114th Congress is most diverse ever," Pew Research Center, January 12, 2015, http://www.pewresearch.org/fact -tank/2015/01/12/114th-congress-is-most-diverse-ever/.

9. Jennifer L. Lawless and Richard L. Fox, "Girls Just Wanna Not Run: The Gender Gap in Young Americans' Political Ambition," American University School of Public Affairs, March 2013, https://www.american.edu/spa /wpi/upload/Girls-Just-Wanna-Not-Run_Policy-Report.pdf.

10. Frank M. Bryan, *Real Democracy: The New England Town Meeting and How It Works* (Chicago: University of Chicago Press, 2004); David E. Campbell and Christina Wolbrecht, "See Jane Run: Women Politicians as Role Models for Adolescents," *Journal of Politics*, May 2006, Vol. 68, No. 2, pages 233–47.

11. Quoted in Tez Clark, "These graphs show the veto power of white men in politics," Vox, June 13, 2015, http://www.vox.com/2015/6/13/8768773 /white-men-politics-influence.

12. Ibid.

13. Mariel Klein, "Working Together and Across the Aisle, Female Senators Pass More Legislation Than Male Colleagues," Quorum, February 19, 2015, https://www.quorum.us/blog/women-work-together-pass-more-legislation/.

14. "Felony Disenfranchisement: A Primer," Sentencing Project, http:// sentencingproject.org/doc/publications/fd_Felony%20Disenfranchise ment%20Primer.pdf.

15. Sasha Chavkin, "Your Country, Your Vote—A Rough Guide to Global Voter Restrictions," International Consortium of Investigative Journalists, Center for Public Integrity, May 5, 2014, http://www.icij.org/blog/2014/05 /your-country-your-vote-rough-guide-global-voter-restrictions.

16. Ariel White, Noah Nathan, and Julie Faller, "New evidence shows election officials are biased against Latino voters," *Washington Post*, February 18, 2015, https://www.washingtonpost.com/blogs/monkey-cage/wp/2015/02/18/new -evidence-shows-election-officials-are-biased-against-latino-voters/.

17. "States With New Voting Restrictions Since the 2010 Election," Bren-

nan Center for Justice, http://www.brennancenter.org/new-voting-restrictions-2010-election, accessed January 8, 2016.

18. "Voting Laws Roundup 2015," Brennan Center for Justice, June 3, 2015, https://www.brennancenter.org/analysis/voting-laws-roundup-2015.

19. Julio Ricardo Varela, "The Latino Vote in Presidential Races: 1980–2012," *Latino USA*, October 29, 2015, http://latinousa.org/2015/10/29/the-latino-vote-in-presidential-races/.

20. Interview with the author.

21. David Weigel, "Kentucky's new governor reverses executive order that restored voting rights for felons," *Washington Post*, December 23, 2015, https://www.washingtonpost.com/news/post-politics/wp/2015/12/23/kentuckys-new-governor-reverses-executive-order-that-restored-voting-rights-for-felons/.

22. Caroline May, "La Raza Projects: 16.7 Million Latinos Registered to Vote by 2016," Breitbart website, September 23, 2015, http://www.breitbart.com/big-government/2015/09/23/la-raza-projects-16-7-million-latinos-registered-vote-2016/.

23. Interview with the author.

Chapter 9 Unequal Justice

1. Sophia Kerby, "The Top Ten Most Startling Facts About People of Color and Criminal Justice in the United States," Center for American Progress, March 13, 2012, https://www.americanprogress.org/issues/race/news/2012/03/13/11351/the-top-10-most-startling-facts-about-people-of-color-and-criminal-justice-in-the-united-states/.

2. Erin Fuchs, "Historian: Anti-Drug Laws Have Always Been About Race," *Business Insider*, August 19, 2013, http://www.businessinsider.com/richard-miller-on-anti-drug-laws-2013-8.

3. "Race and the Drug War," Drug Policy Alliance website, http://www.drugpolicy.org/race-and-drug-war, accessed December 7, 2015.

4. Dan Merica, "Bill Clinton says he made mass incarceration issue worse," CNN Politics, July 15, 2015, http://www.cnn.com/2015/07/15/politics/bill-clinton-1994-crime-bill/.

5. "The Drug War, Mass Incarceration and Race," Drug Policy Alliance website, June 12, 2015, http://www.drugpolicy.org/resource/drug-war-mass-incarceration-and-race, accessed December 7, 2015.

6. Ibid.

7. "The War on Marijuana in Black and White," American Civil Liberties Union, June 2013, https://www.aclu.org/files/assets/aclu-thewaronmarijuana-rel2.pdf.

8. Ibid.

9. Steve Hartsoe, "Study: All-White Jury Pools Convict Black Defendants

16 Percent More Often Than Whites," *Duke Today*, April 17, 2012, https://today.duke.edu/2012/04/jurystudy.

10. Mark Joseph Stern, "How Prejudiced Prosecutors Create All-White Juries," *Slate*, October 30, 2015, http://www.slate.com/articles/news_and_politics/jurisprudence/2015/10/crittenden_and_foster_all_white_juries_are_unconstitutional.html.

11. Michelle Alexander, *The New Jim Crow: Mass Incarceration in the Age of Colorblindness* (New York: New Press, 2010).

12. "Incarcerated Women," Sentencing Project, revised September 2012, http://www.sentencingproject.org/doc/publications/cc_Incarcerated_Women_Factsheet_Sep24sp.pdf, accessed December 8, 2015.

13. "The Drug War, Mass Incarceration and Race."

14. Anthony Terrell, "Man cited by Rand Paul in press for criminal justice reform dies," MSNBC, June 8, 2015, http://www.msnbc.com/msnbc/man-cited-rand-paul-press-criminal-justice-reform-dies.

15. Keri Blakinger, "Rand Paul is playing with fire: The shockingly reasonable ideas that could doom him with Republicans," *Salon*, April 20, 2015, http://www.salon.com/2015/04/20/rand_paul_returns_to_the_scene_of_the_crime_drug_war_crusade_takes_him_back_to_howard_university/.

16. Seung Min Kim, "Senate Judiciary approves criminal justice overhaul," *Politico*, October 22, 2015, http://www.politico.com/story/2015/10/criminal-justice-overhaul-senate-judiciary-approves-215064.

17. Goldie Taylor, "More Than 20 U.S. Cities Are Currently Under a DOJ Consent Decree, But Do They Really Work?" *Blue Nation Review*, May 27, 2015, http://bluenationreview.com/more-than-20-u-s-cities-are-currently-under-a-doj-consent-decree-but-do-they-really-work/.

18. Ryan Gabrielson, Ryann Grochowski Jones, and Eric Sagara, "Deadly Force, in Black and White," ProPublica, October 10, 2014, http://www.propublica.org/article/deadly-force-in-black-and-white.

19. Jeremy Ashkenas and Haeyoun Park, "The Race Gap in America's Police Departments," *New York Times*, updated April 8, 2015, http://www.nytimes.com/interactive/2014/09/03/us/the-race-gap-in-americas-police-departments.html.

20. Chicago Police Accountability Task Force, *Recommendations for Reform*, April 2016, https://chicagopatf.org/wp-content/uploads/2016/04/PATF_Final_Report_4_13_16-1.pdf.

21. Sari Horwitz, "As U.S. pushes police to diversify, FBI struggles to get minorities in the door," *Washington Post*, March 12, 2015, https://www.washingtonpost.com/world/national-security/as-us-pushes-police-to-diversify-fbi-struggles-to-get-minorities-in-the-door/2015/03/12/01bd5806-c753-11e4-b2a1-bed1aaea2816_story.html.

22. "Head of the Civil Rights Division Vanita Gupta Delivers Remarks at Announcement to Advance Diversity in Law Enforcement," US Department of Justice, December 11, 2015, http://www.justice.gov/opa/speech/head-civil-rights-division-vanita-gupta-delivers-remarks-announcement-advance-diversity.

23. Victoria Bekiempis, "The New Racial Makeup of U.S. Police Departments," *Newsweek*, May 14, 2015, http://www.newsweek.com/racial-makeup-police-departments-331130.

24. Nicholas J. C. Pistor, "St. Louis to forgive about 220,000 warrants for nonviolent municipal offenses," *St. Louis Post-Dispatch*, October 1, 2014, http://www.stltoday.com/news/local/crime-and-courts/st-louis-to-forgive-about-warrants-for-nonviolent-municipal-offenses/article_7f9dbef3-7409-5e81-ae28-3c79faa8b147.html.

25. Elizabeth Weise, "'All lives matter' a creed for Richmond, Calif. police," *USA Today*, September 24, 2015, http://www.usatoday.com/story/news/nation/2015/09/23/richmond-community-policing/72563038/.

26. Ibid.

27. Kate Abbey-Lambertz and Joseph Erbentraut, "The Simple Strategies That Could Fundamentally Change How Communities View Their Police," *Huffington Post*, updated February 17, 2015, http://www.huffingtonpost.com/2015/02/17/community-policing-police-trust_n_6607766.html.

28. Ibid.

29. Mark Obbie, "'This Is a Fundamentally Different Way of Policing,'" *Slate*, September 3, 2015, http://www.slate.com/articles/news_and_politics/crime/2015/09/meet_susan_herman_the_woman_bill_bratton_has_tasked_with_repairing_the_nypd.html.

Chapter 10   The Customer Is King and Queen

1. Emily Peck, "IBM Apologizes For Telling Women Engineers To 'Hack A Hair Dryer,'" *Huffington Post*, updated December 7, 2015, http://www.huffingtonpost.com/entry/ibm-apology-hack-a-hair-dryer_us_5665a739e4b08e945ff004c9; Liz Dwyer, "Women Scientists Burn IBM Over 'Hack A Hair Dryer' Campaign," *TakePart*, December 7, 2015, http://www.takepart.com/article/2015/12/07/women-scientists-burn-ibm-hack-hair-dryer; Christina Passariello, "IBM, Seared by Hair Dryer Hacks, Pulls Plug on Campaign," *Wall Street Journal*, December 7, 2015, http://blogs.wsj.com/digits/2015/12/07/ibm-seared-by-hair-dryer-hacks-pulls-plug/.

2. "Women Are Not a 'Niche' Market. They Are a Significant Business Opportunity," report by Pershing LLC, https://www.pershing.com/our-thinking/thought-leadership/women-are-not-a-niche-market.

3. "America's LGBT 2014 Buying Power Estimated at $884 Billion," Witeck

Communications press release, June 10, 2015, http://www.witeck.com/press releases/americas-lgbt-2014-buying-power-estimated-at-884-billion/.

4. Mitchell Schnurman, "How big business in Texas is rallying to defend gay rights," *Dallas Morning News*, May 4, 2015, http://www.dallasnews.com/business/columnists/mitchell-schnurman/20150504-schnurman-texas-business-rallies-to-defend-gay-rights.ece.

5. Interview with the author.

6. "#NotOneDime on Black Friday...Or At Least, $1 Billion Less," *Sojourners*, December 1, 2015, https://sojo.net/articles/notonedime-black-friday-or-least-1-billion-less.

7. Jessica Bennett and Jesse Ellison, "Women Will Rule the World," *Newsweek*, July 5, 2010, http://www.newsweek.com/women-will-rule-world-74603.

8. "Women Are Not a 'Niche' Market."

9. Ibid.

10. Interview with the author.

11. Quoted in Alison Kenney Paul, Thom McElroy, and Tonie Leatherberry, "Diversity as an Engine of Innovation," *Deloitte Review*, No. 8, 2011, http://dupress.com/wp-content/uploads/2011/01/US_deloittereview_Diversity_as_an_Engine_of_Innovation_Jan11.pdf.

12. Interview with the author.

13. Patricia R. Olsen, "A Sociologist of the Sale," *New York Times*, June 22, 2014, page BU8, version at http://www.nytimes.com/2014/06/22/jobs/in-digital-marketing-the-sociology-of-the-sale.html.

14. Matt Krantz, "10 U.S. companies take the most foreign money," *USA Today*, July 15, 2015, http://americasmarkets.usatoday.com/2015/07/15/10-u-s-companies-take-the-most-foreign-money/.

15. Elena Holodny, "The 13 fastest-growing economies in the world," *Business Insider*, June 12, 2015, http://www.businessinsider.com/world-bank-fast-growing-global-economies-2015-6.

16. Bennett and Ellison, "Women Will Rule the World."

17. "Power of Purse Highlights Women's Wealth Leadership," report by Morgan Stanley, January 23, 2015, http://www.morganstanley.com/articles/power-of-purse.

18. "10 Successful American Businesses That Have Failed Overseas," International Business Degree Guide, September 12, 2013, http://www.internationalbusinessguide.org/10-successful-american-businesses-that-have-failed-overseas/.

19. Ibid.

20. Paul Gallant, "10 biggest overseas blunders: Mistakes international businesses can learn from," HSBC Global Connections, April 10, 2014, https://globalconnections.hsbc.com/brazil/en/articles/10-biggest-overseas-blunders-en.

21. Quoted in Hal Gregersen, "A.G. Lafley's Innovation Skills Will Weather P&G's Storm," *Bloomberg Business*, June 3, 2013, http://www.bloomberg .com/news/articles/2013-06-03/a-dot-g-dot-lafley-s-innovation-skills-will -weather-p-and-g-s-storm.

22. Lydia Dishman, "How Outsiders Get Their Products To The Innovation Big League At Procter & Gamble," *Fast Company*, July 13, 2012, http://www .fastcompany.com/1842577/how-outsiders-get-their-products-innovation-big -league-proctor-gamble.

Chapter 11   Running to Stand Still

1. "Women on boards," February 2011, https://www.gov.uk/government /uploads/system/uploads/attachment_data/file/31480/11-745-women-on-boards .pdf.

2. Interview with the author.

3. Interview with the author.

4. Shirley Leung, "For Women, Business As Unusual at Biotech," *Boston Globe*, April 17, 2015, https://www.bostonglobe.com/business/2015/04/16 /not-enough-that-biogen-has-women-its-board-wants-help-others -same/6LvJ02lDHvS9mrTReC8OQM/story.html.

5. Christina Cauterucci, "Companies with Women on Their Boards Do Better—And Not Just Because They Know Shampoo," *Slate*, December 8, 2015, http://www.slate.com/blogs/xx_factor/2015/12/08/companies_with _women_on_their_boards_do_better_and_not_just_because_they.html.

6. Neil Irwin, "Why More Diversity on Wall Street Might Fight Bubbles," *New York Times*, November 17, 2014, http://www.nytimes.com/2014/11/18 /upshot/why-more-diversity-on-wall-street-might-fight-bubbles.html.

7. Susan Adams, "Making A Female-Friendly Workplace," *Forbes*, April 8, 2010, http://www.forbes.com/forbes/2010/0426/human-capital-deloitte -antoinette-leatherberry-womens-initiative-work.html.

8. Joanna Barsh and Lareina Yee, "Unlocking the Full Potential of Women at Work," McKinsey & Company, 2012, cited in "Women in the Workplace: A Research Roundup," *Harvard Business Review*, September 2013, https://hbr .org/2013/09/women-in-the-workplace-a-research-roundup.

9. "2014 Catalyst Census: Women Board Directors," Catalyst, http://www .catalyst.org/knowledge/2014-catalyst-census-women-board-directors.

10. Christine Silva, Nancy M. Carter, and Anna Beninger, "Good Intentions, Imperfect Execution? Women Get Fewer Of The 'Hot Jobs' Needed To Advance," Catalyst, November 2012, cited in "Women in the Workplace."

11. "Pay Equity & Discrimination," Institute for Women's Policy Research, http://www.iwpr.org/initiatives/pay-equity-and-discrimination, accessed November 17, 2015.

12. "Closing the Wage Gap is Crucial for Women of Color and Their Families," National Women's Law Center, November 2013, http://www.nwlc .org/sites/default/files/pdfs/2013.11.13_closing_the_wage_gap_is_crucial_for _woc_and_their_families.pdf.

13. Dan Nakaso, "Asian workers now dominate Silicon Valley tech jobs," *San Jose Mercury News*, November 30, 2012, http://www.mercurynews.com /ci_22094415/asian-workers-now-dominate-silicon-valley-tech-jobs.

14. Liza Mundy, "Cracking the Bamboo Ceiling," *The Atlantic*, November 2014, http://www.theatlantic.com/magazine/archive/2014/11/cracking-the -bamboo-ceiling/380800/.

15. Ibid.

16. "Big gender gap in small-business loans, report says," *Crain's Chicago Business*, July 23, 2014, http://www.chicagobusiness.com/article/20140723 /NEWS07/140729922/big-gender-gap-in-small-business-loans-report-says.

17. Interview with the author.

18. Joel Stein, "Arrogance Is Good: In Defense of Silicon Valley," *Bloomberg Business*, August 7, 2014, http://www.bloomberg.com/bw/articles/2014-08-07 /silicon-valley-tech-entrepreneurs-behind-the-stereotype.

19. Claire Cain Miller, "If You Work in Silicon Valley, Odds Are You're a Man," *New York Times*, May 28, 2014, http://www.nytimes.com/2014/05/29 /upshot/if-you-work-in-silicon-valley-odds-are-youre-a-white-man.html; Alison Griswold, "When It Comes to Diversity in Tech, Companies Find Safety in Numbers," *Slate*, June 27, 2014, http://www.slate.com/blogs/money box/2014/06/27/tech_diversity_data_facebook_follows_google_yahoo_in _releasing_the_stats.html; Cristina Rouvalis, "I am woman, hear me code," *Hemispheres* magazine, July 2014, page 60, and at http://www.hemispheres magazine.com/2014/07/01/woman-hear-code/.

20. Griswold, "When It Comes to Diversity in Tech, Companies Find Safety in Numbers."

21. Chanelle Bessette, "She's not just pushing pixels," *Fortune*, June 2, 2014, http://fortune.com/2014/06/02/tech-star-julie-zhuo/.

22. Michal Lev-Ram, "Apple's new voice," *Fortune*, September 18, 2014, http://fortune.com/2014/09/18/denise-young-smith-apples-new-voice/.

23. Boris Groysberg and Katherine Connolly, "Great Leaders Who Make the Mix Work," *Harvard Business Review*, September 2013, https://hbr .org/2013/09/great-leaders-who-make-the-mix-work.

Chapter 12 The Myth of Meritocracy

1. Quoted in Nikole Hannah-Jones, "School Segregation, the Continuing Tragedy of Ferguson," ProPublica, December 19, 2014, https://www.pro publica.org/article/ferguson-school-segregation.

2. Data from Missouri Department of Elementary and Secondary Education, cited in Hannah-Jones, "School Segregation."

3. Genevieve Siegel-Hawley, "How Non-Minority Students Also Benefit from Racially Diverse Schools," Research Brief No. 8, National Coalition on School Diversity, October 2012, http://www.school-diversity.org/pdf/Diversity ResearchBriefNo8.pdf.

4. "School Composition and the Black-White Achievement Gap," National Center for Education Statistics, June 2015, https://nces.ed.gov/nationsreport card/subject/studies/pdf/school_composition_and_the_bw_achievement _gap_2015.pdf.

5. Interview with the author.

6. Anemona Hartocollis, "With Remarks in Affirmative Action Case, Scalia Steps Into 'Mismatch' Debate," *New York Times*, December 10, 2015, http:// www.nytimes.com/2015/12/11/us/with-remarks-in-affirmative-action-case -scalia-steps-into-mismatch-debate.html.

7. Libby Nelson, "Why Justice Scalia thinks affirmative action hurts black students, and why he's wrong," Vox, December 10, 2015, http://www .vox.com/policy-and-politics/2015/12/10/9885594/scalia-affirmative-action -mismatch.

8. Letter to SCOTUS from physicists, Google Docs, https://docs.google.com /document/d/1OzQiHgplpHpqltEMXHxhwwr-hZqDAUH2zyTv2R4hksw /edit.

9. Quoted in Frank Bruni, "The Lie About College Diversity," *New York Times*, December 12, 2015, http://www.nytimes.com/2015/12/13/opinion/sun day/the-lie-about-college-diversity.html.

10. William Keylor, "The long-forgotten racial attitudes and policies of Woodrow Wilson," *Professor Voices*, March 4, 2013, http://www.bu .edu/professorvoices/2013/03/04/the-long-forgotten-racial-attitudes-and -policies-of-woodrow-wilson/.

11. Mary Hui, "After protests, Princeton debates Woodrow Wilson's legacy," *Washington Post*, November 23, 2015, https://www.washingtonpost.com /news/grade-point/wp/2015/11/23/after-protests-princeton-debates-woodrow -wilsons-legacy/.

12. Eve Fairbanks, "A Paradox of Integration," *New York Times*, October 17, 2014, http://www.nytimes.com/2014/10/19/opinion/sunday/a-paradox-of -integration.html.

13. Katherine W. Phillips quotations from an interview with the author, November 2015.

14. Lauren Brom et al., editors, *CBS Reflects: Gender Equality 2013–2014*, Columbia Business School, http://www8.gsb.columbia.edu/programs/sites /programs/files/files/CBSReflects_GenderEquality_Report_2014.pdf.

Chapter 13 The Media Mirror

1. Gloria Steinem, introduction to *Wonder Woman* by William M. Marston (New York: Holt, Rinehart and Winston, 1972).

2. Dr. Stacy L. Smith et al., *Inequality in 700 Popular Films: Examining Portrayals of Gender, Race, & LGBT Status from 2007 to 2014*, Media, Diversity & Social Change Initiative, USC Annenberg School for Communication and Journalism, http://annenberg.usc.edu/pages/~/media/MDSCI/Inequality%20in%20700%20Popular%20Films%208215%20Final%20for%20Posting.ashx.

3. Ellen Goodman, "The 3 ages of woman," *Baltimore Sun*, October 1, 1996, http://articles.baltimoresun.com/1996-10-01/news/1996275085_1_goldie-hawn-cineplex-husband.

4. Todd VanDerWerff, "Universal made more money than any movie studio ever this year—without a superhero movie," Vox, August 20, 2015, http://www.vox.com/2015/8/20/9183589/straight-outta-compton-box-office-universal.

5. Nell Scovell, "The 'Golden Age for Women in TV' Is Actually a Rerun," *New York Times*, September 12, 2015, http://www.nytimes.com/2015/09/13/opinion/sunday/the-golden-age-for-women-in-tv-is-actually-a-rerun.html.

6. Interview with the author.

7. Spencer Kornhaber, "The Emmys Speech of the Night," *The Atlantic*, September 20, 2015, http://www.theatlantic.com/notes/2015/09/harriet-tubman-at-the-emmys-viola-davis-first-black-woman/406360/.

8. *2015 Hollywood Diversity Report: Flipping the Script*, Ralph J. Bunche Center for African American Studies at UCLA, http://www.bunchecenter.ucla.edu/wp-content/uploads/2015/02/2015-Hollywood-Diversity-Report-2-25-15.pdf.

9. *The Status of Women in the U.S. Media 2015*, Women's Media Center, http://wmc.3cdn.net/83bf6082a319460eb1_hsrm680x2.pdf.

10. Aisha Harris, "Same Old Script," *Slate*, October 18, 2015, http://www.slate.com/articles/arts/culturebox/2015/10/diversity_in_the_tv_writers_room_writers_and_showrunners_of_color_lag_far.html.

11. All Quiroz quotations from interview with the author.

12. Sonali Kohli, "American TV shows might look more diverse, but their writers aren't," *Quartz*, July 24, 2014, http://qz.com/238696/tv-shows-might-look-more-diverse-but-their-writers-arent/.

13. Lacey Rose, "'Empire': Meet the Writers Behind Broadcast's Biggest Hit," *Hollywood Reporter*, September 17, 2015, http://www.hollywoodreporter.com/live-feed/empire-meet-writers-behind-broadcasts-824097.

14. Harris, "Same Old Script."

15. Jason T. Low, "Where is the diversity in publishing? The 2015 Diversity Baseline Survey results," *The Open Book* blog, Lee & Low Books, Janu-

ary 26, 2016, http://blog.leeandlow.com/2016/01/26/where-is-the-diversity-in
-publishing-the-2015-diversity-baseline-survey-results/.

16. Jim Milliot, "The PW Publishing Industry Salary Survey 2015: A
Younger Workforce, Still Predominantly White," *Publishers Weekly*, October
16, 2015, http://www.publishersweekly.com/pw/by-topic/industry-news/pub
lisher-news/article/68405-publishing-industry-salary-survey-2015-a-younger
-workforce-still-predominantly-white.html.

17. Daniel José Older, "Diversity Is Not Enough: Race, Power, Publishing," *BuzzFeed*, April 17, 2014, http://www.buzzfeed.com/danieljoseolder
/diversity-is-not-enough.

18. Ibid.

19. Interview with Karl Weber.

20. Quoted in Lynn Neary, "To Achieve Diversity in Publishing, A Difficult
Dialogue Beats Silence," NPR, August 20, 2014, http://www.npr.org/sections
/codeswitch/2014/08/20/341443632/to-achieve-diversity-in-publishing-a
-difficult-dialogue-beats-silence.

21. Kathryn Zickuhr and Lee Rainie, "A Snapshot of Reading in America
in 2013," Pew Research Center, January 16, 2014, http://www.pewinternet
.org/2014/01/16/a-snapshot-of-reading-in-america-in-2013/.

22. Annie Lowrey, "Why Disruptors Are Always White Guys," *New York*,
September 10, 2014, http://nymag.com/daily/intelligencer/2014/09/why
-disruptors-are-always-white-guys.html.

23. Jennifer Lawrence, "Why Do I Make Less Than My Male Co-Stars?"
Lennyletter, October 13, 2015, http://www.lennyletter.com/work/a147/jennifer
-lawrence-why-do-i-make-less-than-my-male-costars/; Jason Guerrasio, "Bradley
Cooper says he'll start sharing salary information with female costars before movies go into production to help them negotiate," *Business Insider*, October 15, 2015,
http://www.businessinsider.com/bradley-cooper-on-gender-pay-gap-2015-10.

Chapter 14   Transcendence

1. Juliana Schroeder and Jane L. Risen, "Peace Through Friendship," *New
York Times*, August 22, 2014, http://www.nytimes.com/2014/08/24/opinion
/sunday/peace-through-friendship.html.

2. Peter Holley, "The surprising thing that happened when this Islamo-
phobe protested at a mosque," *Washington Post*, October 14, 2015, https://
www.washingtonpost.com/news/acts-of-faith/wp/2015/10/14/the-surprising
-thing-that-happened-when-this-islamophobe-protested-at-a-mosque/; Carol
Kuruvilla, "The Surprising Welcome This Anti-Muslim Protestor Got At A
Mosque," *Huffpost Religion*, October 12, 2015, http://www.huffingtonpost.com
/entry/the-surprising-welcome-this-anti-muslim-protestor-got-at-an-ohio
-mosque_561bc168e4b0082030a3215a.

Index

About the Author

LAUREN LEADER-CHIVÉE is an author, activist, expert, and advisor on diversity and women's issues. She is cofounder and CEO of All In Together, a nonprofit, nonpartisan campaign dedicated to engaging American women in politics and civic action. She advises a wide array of organizations on diversity issues and public policy. She was named one of *Fortune* magazine's 50 Most Influential Women on Twitter.